THE COVERSTITCH
TECHNIQUE MANUAL

Dedication

I'd like to dedicate this book to my mum, Margaret Hincks, because I really couldn't have done this without you. Thank you for all your sewing knowledge, for being my sidekick, idea bouncer and slave to your machines in producing numerous beautifully created samples which are photographed throughout this book. Thank you for answering my many phone calls and sorry that under lockdown, you were unable to go to the shops and had to sacrifice so much of your own wardrobe for this book!

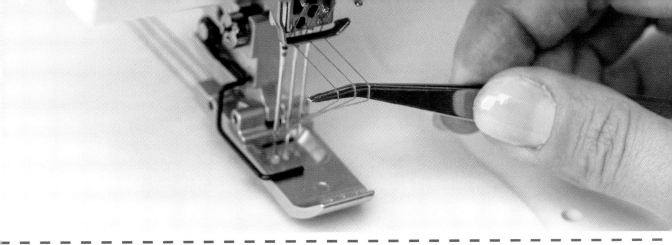

THE COVERSTITCH
TECHNIQUE MANUAL

The complete guide to sewing
with a coverstitch machine

Julia Hincks

SEARCH PRESS

Acknowledgements

I would like to thank the following people and companies firstly for their time and also their generous loans of machines and accessories:

Deborah at Janome for the use of the Janome CoverPro 2000CPX, Janome 1200D and an incredible amount of accessories for these machines for both myself and my mum; Keith at World of Sewing for spending more than two hours of his Saturday talking everything coverstitch-machine related and demonstrating how to use the baby lock BLCS2 and Juki MCS1800 machines; Lawrence at Franklins Group for the loan of the Juki and Britannia machines and accessories and for putting me in touch with Keith; Mike at baby lock for the loan of a huge number of accessories for the BLCS2 and a few bonus gifts;

Stuart, Melanie and Jo at Brother for the loan of the Brother CV3550 and accessories; Laura at SVP for the loan of the Pfaff Coverlock 4.0 and Huskylock S21; Vicki and staff at Minerva for providing fabrics for most of the projects; Josie at Fabric Godmother for providing fabrics for many of the samples in the book and for putting me in touch with Laura; Bryony at Cocobeautico in Portslade for making my hands and nails look amazing; Lyndsey and the team at Search Press for answering my many questions and keeping me going throughout this project.

Huge thanks and all my love to my husband Michael who has listened to me endlessly talk about coverstitch machines. My appreciation of you is far greater than this very small acknowledgement.

First published in 2021

Search Press Limited
Wellwood, North Farm Road,
Tunbridge Wells, Kent TN2 3DR

Text copyright © Julia Hincks 2021

Photographs on page 12 © baby lock
Photographs on pages 94 (bottom left), 143, 144, 146, 149 (bottom), 151, 153 (right), 154–155, 160, 164, 166, 169 (bottom), 170 and 174 by Stacy Grant
All other photographs by Mark Davison at Search Press Studios

Photographs and design copyright © Search Press Ltd. 2021

ISBN: 978-1-78221-856-2
eBook ISBN: 978-1-78126-819-3

Suppliers
If you have difficulty in obtaining any of the materials and equipment mentioned in this book, then please visit the Search Press website for details of suppliers: www.searchpress.com

You are invited to visit the author's websites: www.juliahincks.com and www.houseofmisssew.com

Publishers' note
All the step-by-step photographs in this book feature the author Julia Hincks. No models have been used.

Contents

Introduction

WHY DO YOU NEED A COVERSTITCH MACHINE?

Depending on the types of projects that you sew and the amount of time you invest in sewing, you may or may not need one of these machines… but I bet you want one!

Like many of you who sew, I've made a fair few items of clothing from stretch fabrics and, having tried a number of different techniques for hemming and finishing necklines, cuffs and armholes on my overlocker (serger) and sewing machine, I wanted my homemade items to look like they weren't homemade.

Although there are a number of uses for this type of machine, coverstitch machines are mainly used for hemming stretch fabrics and they do this job so much better than your regular sewing machine. If you've ever tried to sew a hem on jersey or other knitted fabric then you'll know that the results produced on your sewing machine just don't resemble the professional finish you see in shop-bought (ready-to-wear) garments.

A coverstitch machine will most likely be the third type of sewing machine that you buy. After purchasing a regular sewing machine and investing in an overlocker, next you'll be looking for ways to achieve more professional results with hemming and finishing garment openings, especially when working with stretch fabrics – and for this you'll need a coverstitch machine.

If you sew as a hobby, space is often an issue. We don't all have a dedicated sewing room and may be fighting for the use of the kitchen table or squeezed into the corner of a room on a fold-up table. The good news is that some of the domestic coverstitch machines are much more compact than sewing machines and don't take up much space. You can also buy combination machines that work as both an overlocker and a coverstitch machine so you'll just need two machines in your workspace instead of three.

The other good thing to know about coverstitch machines is that they are generally much easier to thread than an overlocker, so if the idea of rethreading your overlocker fills you with dread, don't be worried about having to get your head around threading and using a new machine as this one is much more simple.

If you already have a coverstitch machine, I hope that this book will take you through the basics to improve your confidence with using your machine and also show you new and exciting techniques to try on your next project.

If you're not yet convinced that you need a coverstitch machine, hopefully by the time you've read through this book and seen all the various techniques and finishes that you can try out and achieve you'll be making a trip to your local sewing shop or browsing the internet to research the right model for you.

WHAT'S THE DIFFERENCE BETWEEN AN OVERLOCKER AND A COVERSTITCH MACHINE?

The simplest answer is that one machine will overlock and the other will produce a coverstitch. There are also a few machines that will do both and are called combination machines or coverlockers.

An overlocker works with one or two needles and two loopers: an upper looper and a lower looper. This machine also has a knife that trims the fabric as it is fed into the machine. The needles produce straight stitches on the top of the fabric and the looper threads wrap the edge of the fabric to create a neat finish. A basic overlocker will produce a three- or four-thread overlock stitch which can be used for creating seams or edge-finishing seam allowances.

A coverstitch machine works with one, two or three needles and one looper, and doesn't have a knife. This machine will produce both chain stitch (a straight stitch formed with two threads, one needle and the looper) and a coverstitch (double or triple rows of straight stitch on the top of the fabric using two or three needles and an overlocked look on the reverse formed with the looper). This machine can be used for both seams (using the chain stitch) and hemming techniques (using the coverstitch). It is most commonly used for hemming stretch fabrics since it handles the fabric much better than a regular sewing machine.

This coverstitch machine is your route into new and exciting techniques for professional-quality results.

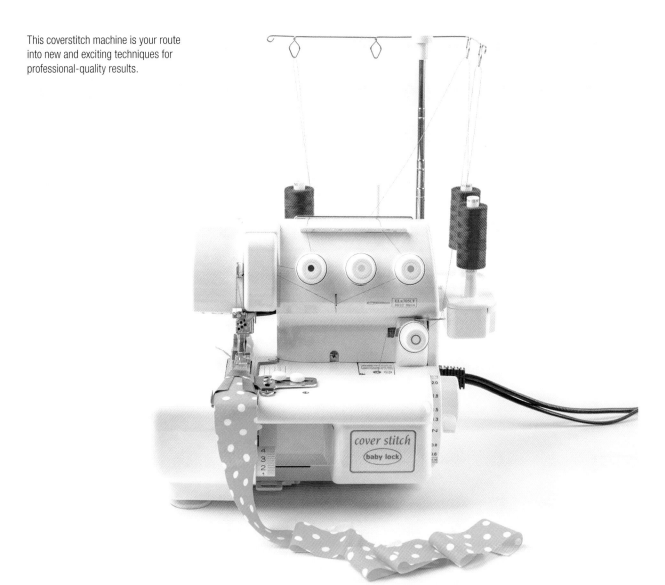

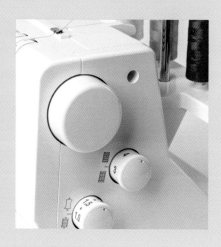

Coverstitch machine basics

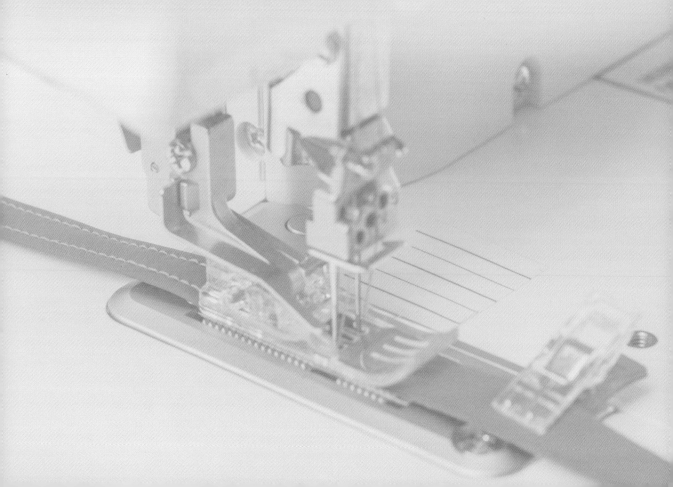

Congratulations, you are now the proud owner of a coverstitch machine! But where to start?

This chapter will introduce you to the basics, so that you can set up your machine and feel confident to start stitching.

We will begin by looking at the various components on your machine along with the accessories and other essential tools that you will need. There are instructions on how to set up your machine, how to adjust the settings to perfect your stitching and how to get your coverstitch machine to work for you.

Anatomy of a coverstitch machine

All coverstitch machines operate in a similar way and have the same basic features. Although models and brands differ greatly in appearance and functionality, it is likely that your machine will have the same components as listed below.

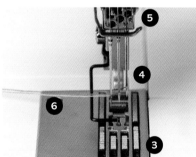

1 Presser foot A standard foot is provided with the machine which can be used for nearly all types of stitching. On the front of the presser foot are three raised bars – these indicate the position of the needles to help with the correct placement of fabric and stitching lines. The presser foot can be removed by pressing the lever at the back of the foot and replaced by lowering the presser-foot lever and snapping it back on. Additional feet can be purchased as accessories and these will be explained in more detail on page 15.

2 Presser-foot lever This raises and lowers the presser foot. The position of the lever may differ between machines but this is generally found behind the presser foot. On most models, when the presser foot is raised the tension on the threads is released. You may be able to raise the presser foot an additional 1–2mm (1/16in) by exerting more pressure on the lever, which helps when removing threads and fabric from the machine and is also useful when working with thicker fabrics.

3 Feed dogs These are the teeth below the presser foot that help move the fabric as you stitch. On a coverstitch machine there are two sets of teeth: shorter teeth at the front to guide the fabric under the foot towards the needle and longer teeth at the back to take the fabric from behind the needle. The two sets of teeth work independently of each other and their speed can be adjusted using the differential-feed dial.

4 Needles This coverstitch machine can hold one, two or three needles depending on the type of stitch required. Some machines may only hold up to two needles. The needles recommended for this machine are ELx705 size 80/12 or 90/14. Each machine manual will recommend a type of needle to use for the best results. More details about needles can be found on pages 18–19.

5 Needle clamp This holds the needles in position. Make sure that needles are pushed up into their highest position in the needle clamp and tightened in place. Your machine will come with a small screwdriver or Allen key (sometimes known as an Allen wrench or hex key) for loosening and tightening the needle clamp. Don't try to adjust the needles so they sit at the same height: the right-hand needle(s) will sit slightly higher in the machine than the left.

6 Needle plate Sometimes referred to as the throat plate, this is usually made of metal and provides a smooth surface for fabric to pass under the foot of the machine. It will have a hole in for the needles and the feed-dog teeth. Ensure the plate is kept clean, free of oil or dirt and does not become damaged from incorrectly positioned needles.

7 Throat space Also known as harp space, this is the space on the sewing bed of the machine, to the right of the needles. The size of the space varies on each machine – machines with a larger space are more suitable for decorative stitching.

8 Thread cutter Positioned on the left side of the machine, this allows for quick cutting of threads. Keep this sharp by removing lint and thread build up.

9 Tension discs Each thread has its own tension disc and this controls how tightly or loosely the thread is held in the machine. The tension discs may be the 'lay-in' type dial, as shown on this model, that sit on the top front of the machine, or your machine may have knobs on the front. For basic stitching set the tension dials to the neutral position. On this model the neutral position for the needle threads is 4 and the looper thread is 3. The tension can be tightened (higher number) or loosened (lower number) according to the threads and fabrics being used. On most machines the tension on the discs can be released by raising the presser foot.

10 Spool pins These are situated at the back of the machine on the spool stand. This machine has four spool pins since it can hold up to four threads but other machines may only have three and some models may have up to eight. Small spools of thread can sit directly on the pins but for larger spools or cones of thread, use a spool mat or spool holder to stop the spool from rattling around as you sew.

11 Thread guides Each thread needs to be directed from the spool to its location on the machine, following a specific pathway through the thread guides. Incorrect threading can cause irregular stitching, tension issues or snapping threads. On most machines the thread guides are

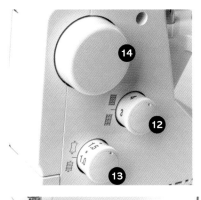

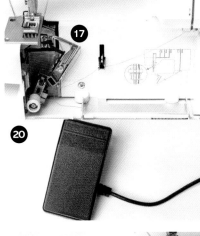

12 Stitch length On this model, the stitch-length dial is on the right-hand side of the machine and allows you to make shorter or longer stitches, just like on a sewing machine. For regular sewing on this machine the stitch length should be set from 3 to 3.5; the numbers on the dial indicate the length of the stitch in millimetres.

13 Differential feed This may be a dial or a lever depending on your machine. The differential feed alters the speed of the front feed-dog teeth and can be used to accentuate or eliminate gathering or stretching on seams and hems. The numbers on the differential feed indicate the ratio of speeds between the front and back teeth. When this is set to the neutral position (1 or N depending on the machine), the front and back feed-dog teeth move at the same speed. If the differential feed is set to a higher number the speed of the front teeth will increase and when set to a lower number the front teeth will move more slowly. The speed of the back teeth does not change.

14 Handwheel The handwheel (or flywheel) can be found on the right side of the machine. Turn this by hand to move the position of the needles and looper, to remove or replace a needle or when threading the machine. Generally, when sewing, always turn the handwheel towards you. When the handwheel is turned away from you this will disengage the looper thread from the needle threads and may cause the stitching to unravel more easily.

15 Presser-foot pressure adjuster Most machine models will have a dial to adjust the pressure that the presser foot has on the fabric. For general sewing on medium-weight fabrics, adjustments are not necessary and fabrics can be sewn without any problems. For heavier fabrics, more pressure may be needed to help the fabric feed evenly and prevent stitches from skipping. For lighter fabrics, less pressure may help to prevent the fabric from stretching as it is stitched.

16 Looper cover Open this to thread or clean the machine. Use your right hand to push the cover to the right and then pull it towards you. You will probably find a colour-coded threading guide inside. Keep the inside of the looper cover clean and free of lint as this can affect the tension on the looper thread. Some models may also have a looper cover positioned on the left side of the machine.

17 Looper On all coverstitch machines you'll find the looper, a large-eyed needle type device, below the needle plate. The looper works in a similar way to the bobbin on a regular sewing machine, carrying the lower thread which wraps with the needle threads to form a stitch. The looper thread will be seen on the underside of the fabric and forms a chain when one needle is used or a zigzag pattern when two or more needles are used. On a combination machine, you'll find three different types of looper: an upper and lower looper which work together to form an overlocking stitch, and a chain looper for use for chain and coverstitching.

18 Stitching guidelines (not pictured) You may find numbered markings on the top of the looper cover. These will usually show both metric and imperial units of measure and can be used as guidelines when you sew to keep your stitching straight. If your machine doesn't have these you can purchase an adjustable seam guide or simply use masking tape to create your own guide.

19 Thread guide bar Also known as a thread tree. It holds the threads and allows them to unravel smoothly from the spools. This bar should be raised up to its highest position and locked in place to keep threads moving smoothly and to prevent any issues with tension.

20 Foot pedal Position this under your sewing table with the taller part of the foot at the back. The harder you press, the faster the machine will go.

21 Free arm Some models offer a free arm to utilize when stitching tubular items. Remove a part on the front of the machine to enable this feature.

22 Dust cover Dust can clog thread guides and affect the stitching regularity of your machine. Use the dust cover when your machine is not in use to keep it clean. If your machine doesn't have a dust cover, make your own or use a piece of fabric instead.

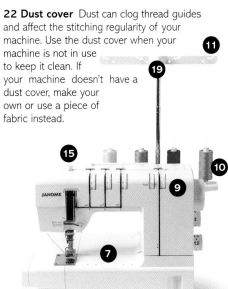

colour coded, making it easier to thread up correctly. Your manual will suggest the order in which to thread the machine e.g. needles first or looper first. In this case the machine should be threaded from left to right, starting with the left needle. Check your manual to see which is the correct order for your machine – threading out of this order may result in snapping threads or skipped stitches.

DIFFERENCES BETWEEN MODELS

The overall appearance of your machine may differ to the one shown on the previous page. Your presser-foot lever may be on the right side of the machine or the position of the control dials for stitch length and differential feed may be in another place on your machine but they will all function in the same way. The front of your machine may also look different – some models have 'lay-in' tension discs that are found on the top of the front of the machine and other models have tension knobs on the front of the machine.

Other differences in the features of domestic coverstitch machines are the range of stitches that can be formed and the number of threads it can hold at one time. Most machines will perform a single chain stitch (using two threads) and a coverstitch (using three threads); other machines may be able to perform a triple coverstitch (using four threads) or top coverstitch using five threads. The range of stitch length, width and differential feed will also vary between brands and models.

ADDITIONAL FEATURES

1 Knee lift Some machines come with an optional knee-lift device for operating the presser-foot lever. This can be attached to the front of the machine so you can keep both hands on the project and operate the presser foot with your right knee.

2 Easy-thread system Some high-end models offer an air-threading system where the thread is pushed around the machine into the correct position by a jet of air. This may be the ideal solution to save you becoming frustrated with threading your machine.

3 Safety no-sew system Some machines have a safety feature that stops the machine from working if the looper cover is open or the presser foot is raised. This means that the machine

won't stitch until the cover is closed and the presser foot is lowered.

4 Built-in storage Some models offer this feature where useful tools and accessories can be accommodated in a storage compartment within the machine, either inside the looper cover or under the spool pins. Other models may provide an accessory box for you to keep your tools in.

5 Tilting needle clamp Some models have a clamp so you can tilt the needles towards you, making it easier to change or reposition the needles.

6 Needle threader It's not always easy to see to thread the eye of the needles and so on certain models you'll find an automatic needle threader that will make the job more straightforward.

7 Stitching speed control It's not always easy to regulate the sewing speed with the foot pedal, so this added feature gives you much more control over the speed that you can stitch.

8 Needle-drop drawer Some machines have a handy needle-drop drawer so if you lose your grip on the needle and it falls into the machine, just open the drawer and it will be there.

9 Automatic tension settings The tension settings on most models need adjusting for different stitches, fabrics and threads. Some models automatically adjust the tension settings to maintain a balanced stitch regardless of stitch, thread or fabric choices. Settings can be further fine-tuned for particular techniques.

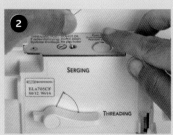

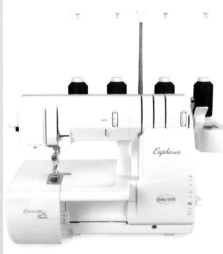

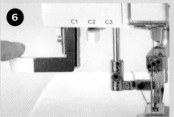

COMBINATION OVERLOCKER AND COVERSTITCH MACHINES

These machines offer both the functions of an overlocker and a coverstitch machine so if you're short on space, this type of machine may be a good option. To change the stitch settings from regular overlocking to coverstitch or chain stitching you will need to move the needles and change the needle plate or looper cover. This can mean additional time is needed to set up the machine for the type of stitching you require.

1 Wider range of stitches Combination machines work both as overlockers and coverstitch machines so you will have a broader range of stitches to choose from. On some models the stitch type can be selected and changed using a dial, lever or electronic screen which will also control the thread tension and provide guidance on what settings to change on the machine for the selected stitch. When the machine is set to overlocking you can create two-, three-, four- or five-thread stitch patterns (some machines will perform up to eight-thread stitch patterns), rolled hems and flatlock stitches. As a coverstitch machine you can produce a two-thread chain stitch, three- or four-thread coverstitch and, on some models, a top coverstitch as well.

2 Interchangeable overlock cover or sewing table When operating the machine as an overlocker, the regular overlock or blade cover is used which covers the loopers and knife area. When the machine is set to perform chain stitch or coverstitch, the sewing table or alternative looper cover will need to be used instead. This cover is flat and allows the fabric to move through the machine to the right of the presser foot like a sewing machine so you can stitch anywhere on the fabric, not just along the edge.

3 Tension-release device On many machines the tension is released when the presser foot is raised but if the machine has automatic tension setting then this may not be the case. Instead the machine will have a tension-release device to effectively cancel any tension on the threads to help with threading the machine and for removing fabric from the machine.

4 Additional spool pins A basic coverstitch machine will hold two, three or four spools. The most elaborate machines may hold up to eight spools and offer a wider range of stitch length, width and type.

5 Top cover spreader On machines that feature the top coverstitch you'll find a top cover spreader device to allow you to convert the machine to produce the top coverstitch. This device may already be fixed to the machine or may come as an additional accessory that will need to be attached before this type of stitch can be created.

6 Knife As this machine will operate as an overlocker, it will have a knife to trim the edge of the fabric. When operating as a coverstitch machine, the knife is disengaged so it does not cut.

7 Cutting width dial Turning this dial will move the blade closer to or further away from the needle, decreasing or increasing the cutting width. The cutting width may need to be reduced in order to attach the alternative looper cover/sewing table correctly.

8 Stitch finger Also known as the chaining finger, this is a metal prong that helps to regulate the width of overlock stitches. As the stitch is formed the threads wrap around the stitch finger and the completed stitch feeds off the end of the stitch finger. The stitch finger is disengaged or removed to form a narrow or rolled hem. On some models it also needs to be disengaged to attach the sewing table correctly and perform a coverstitch or chain stitch.

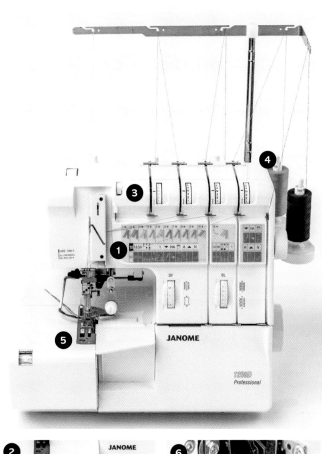

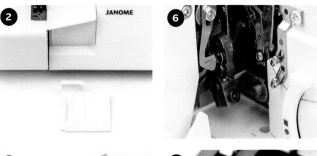

Must-have tools for coverstitch machines

GENERAL TOOLS

1 Screwdrivers Your machine will come with the right sized screwdriver, spanner or Allen key (also known as Allen wrench or hex key) for replacing the needles and general machine maintenance.

2 Tweezers Most machines come with a pair of long-nosed tweezers. Useful for threading the needles, looper and thread guides and handy when cleaning your machine to remove stray threads or lint.

THREADING ACCESSORIES

3 Needle holder Perfect for holding onto machine needles when trying to remove or replace them, this handy device is found on the end of the needle threader (see page 16), on the end of your lint brush or on a compensation plate.

4 Spool holder Use these to hold cones of thread securely while you stitch. For larger cones, turn the spool holder upside down so the widest part is on the top – this will help them to grip the cone and be more effective. Squeeze the spool holder slightly to help it fit inside the cone. Remove these holders when using smaller spools of thread.

5 Spool cap These can be used with regular sewing machine thread or smaller spools of thread to allow the thread to unravel smoothly. As the spool cap is usually wider than the spool, the cap will help to stop the thread from being caught in the nicks on the top of some thread spools and avoid issues with tension or snapping threads.

6 Spool nets These can be used with woolly nylon or for decorative threads such as silks that unravel and slip off the spool easily. Place the net over the spool to allow the thread to unwind evenly without tangling. The net can be folded over if it is longer than the spool to avoid threads being caught on the ends of the net. Spool nets can also be used when storing threads to keep them tangle free.

7 Spool mat Foam mats to use with woolly nylon or decorative threads to prevent the threads from slipping under the spool and becoming tangled around the spool pin. Position the thread spool directly onto the spool mat and then use a spool cap to keep the spool in place and ensure an even thread feed. You can make your own spool mats from foam or wadding (batting).

8 Looper threader Perfect for threading woolly nylon or thicker threads through the looper. It looks similar to a basic needle threader with a small metal loop at one end. Insert the metal loop from back to front through the looper, pass the thread through the metal loop, then pull the loop back through the looper.

CLEANING TOOLS

9 Lint brush Most machines come with a very small brush to keep your machine free from lint and build-up of dust and fluff. However, a make-up brush or standard household paintbrush is a good substitute and if you use one with a larger head this will remove the dust more quickly.

10 Vacuum cleaner (not pictured) This is the quickest way to rid your machine of dust and debris. If you're worried about losing screws or other small parts, put a sock over the end of the vacuum cleaner so you can check what is being collected from the machine. Look out for mini accessory kits for your vacuum cleaner to help you clean in small spaces. Combine the lint brush for hard to reach places and the vacuum suction and you'll have your machine clean in no time.

11 Dental floss This works brilliantly for cleaning the tension discs. Use it as you would to floss your teeth, pulling a small length back and forth through the tension discs to keep these lint and dust free. Upholstery, topstitching or any other thick thread is a good substitute.

12 Lint roller (not pictured) This household device is ideal for removing stubborn threads when unpicking (see page 41) or for general removal of lint from fabrics in the construction phase.

ADDITIONAL EXTRAS

13 Clearance plate This is a brilliant tool for helping you to stitch over bulky seams when hemming or topstitching. The clearance plate (also called a hump jumper or height-compensation tool) can be used to keep the presser foot level with the height of a bulky seam, allowing it to stitch over the lump without causing any irregular stitching. Some clearance tools also come with a handy needle hole to assist with inserting and removing needles. You can make your own clearance plate by folding up bulky fabric such as denim to create the height required for your seam.

14 Awl This pointy tool has a variety of uses: as a marking tool for darts; pleats or buttonholes; to guide small or slippery pieces of fabric under the presser foot; and as a tool for pulling threads from under the presser foot when finishing coverstitching.

15 Loop turner This is a long rod with a latch at one end. Use this for turning narrow loops or straps from the wrong side through to the right side. It can also be used to weave in thread ends or overlocking chains to stop them unravelling.

16 Bias tape maker Make your own folded strips of bias binding with this handy device. Pass your bias-cut strip into the widest end of the bias tape maker and as it is fed through the device it will be folded into shape. As you pull the folded strip out of the narrow end, press the folds in place. A range of size options are available to create binding of differing widths. This tool can also be used in place of the belt-loop attachment.

17 Snap-on thread guide Use this with decorative threads to allow for smooth, tangle free thread feeding from the spool to the machine.

18 Tension-release clips Place these under the tension clips when using heavy threads to keep thread flowing evenly through your machine.

19 Seam sealant Depending on your project, it might be suitable to use a seam sealant, a type of fabric glue, to secure the ends of thread. Once the sealant is dry, cut the threads close to the fabric.

MACHINE ACCESSORIES

20 Thread palette A handy device to blend your threads. This is essentially a thread spool holder for up to four threads. The combined threads can be used in place of a single thread to add decorative stitching to projects (see page 93).

21 Extension table This is a great accessory to use when working on larger projects to increase the workspace on the flatbed of the machine.

22 Adjustable seam guide An additional accessory to use with your machine – this will help you to maintain an even space between rows of decorative stitching and can also be used as a seam- or hem-allowance guide.

23 Elastic gathering attachment This attachment can make sewing elastic onto fabric much easier. The device holds the elastic and stretches it evenly as you attach it to your fabric. You may be able to use a variety of elastic widths with this accessory, or purchase attachments in different sizes. (Pages 109 and 112 have more details.)

24 Tape binder attachment This is the ideal accessory to gain a professional bound finish on woven or knit fabrics. These can be purchased to suit a variety of widths of binding. Perfectly cut fabric strips are fed into the tape binder and the device folds over the edges of the fabric strip to create single- or double-fold binding which is then applied to the raw edge of your work. (See page 131).

25 Belt-loop attachment A handy accessory for creating belt loops. These are available in a range of sizes to allow you to create belt loops in different widths. These work in the same way as a bias tape maker, either folding the fabric so the edges meet in the middle or so they overlap. This device can also be used for making straps, bag handles, drawstrings and decorative tape. (Page 134 has more details.)

26 Hemming guide Many brands of coverstitch machine offer these handy devices which will help to fold the hem and keep stitching aligned correctly as you sew. (Page 80 has more details.)

27 Top-coverstitch accessories For machines that offer the top-coverstitch function you will need to attach a top coverstitch spreader device and a top cover thread guide to your machine to create this type of stitch. These accessories will be provided with the machine. (Page 62 has more details.)

ADDITIONAL FEET

28 Clear presser foot This transparent foot allows you to see your stitching more clearly as you work. This foot may come with your machine or can be purchased for most models as an accessory.

29 Chain-stitching foot For some machines a separate chain-stitching foot is available. This is narrower than the standard presser foot. (Page 58 has more details.)

30 Pintuck and cording foot Only available for a small number of models of machine, this foot has a groove underneath and can be combined with either the pintuck or cording guide to produce a number of decorative effects. (Pages 95 and 106 have more details.)

31 Compensating foot This foot is standard on some machines and is designed to manage bulky or uneven layers. The left and right side of the foot move independently and will raise or lower as necessary to allow you to stitch over different layers of fabric without skipping a stitch.

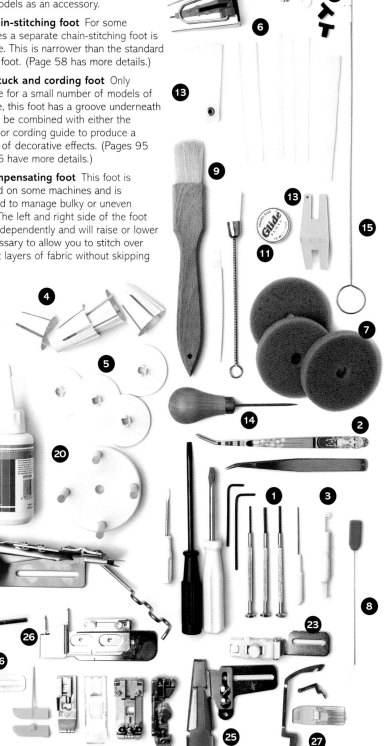

Essential toolkit for sewing

If you've already bought or are considering the purchase of a coverstitch machine then you almost certainly have a variety of general sewing items to hand. The following is a list of the main items you will need for any sewing project.

SCISSORS AND CUTTING TOOLS

1 Fabric scissors These can be purchased for right- and left-handed use and come in a range of weights and sizes. Tie a piece of ribbon or fabric to the handle and keep them only for cutting fabric so the blades stay nice and sharp.

2 Thread snips or small scissors A small pair of scissors are ideal to keep at the side of your machine for trimming threads from fabric or for use when threading up your machine.

3 Paper scissors Don't mix these up with your fabric scissors – every sewer should have a separate pair of paper scissors for cutting paper and anything else other than fabric.

4 Pinking shears These will neaten the fraying edges and give your fabric that zig-zag edge. They won't stop all fabrics from fraying and work best on cottons, cotton blends or other stable fabrics with a tight weave.

5 Duck-bill scissors Also known as appliqué scissors, these are the perfect tool for trimming excess seam or hemming allowances. The angle of the blade and scissor handle allows you to cut flat and close to the fabric surface, without accidentally cutting through the underlayer.

6 Rotary cutter This can be used instead of scissors and is ideal for cutting out long straight pieces such as bias strips or for slippery stretch fabrics. Waved- and scalloped-edge blades can be purchased for decorative use. Protect your table tops and use your rotary cutter with a cutting mat.

7 Quick unpick tool This tool makes removing your stitches quick and easy. It is formed of a long pointy tip and a shorter blunt end with a red ball on the top. Between the tips is a curved blade which is the cutting area.

8 Cutting mat A self-healing cutting mat is essential when using a rotary cutter to protect the surface under the fabric and prolong the life of the blade. Gridlines help you to cut straight.

MEASURING AND MARKING TOOLS

9 Tape measure These are usually 150cm (60in) in length. Choose one with both metric and imperial units. Retractable tape measures will save you time in rolling up the standard ones. They can stretch over time so replace your old one to make sure your measuring is accurate.

10 Sewing gauge This handy little device comes in a variety of forms (shown on page 76) and is the perfect alternative to a tape measure or ruler for accurate measuring of hemming or seam allowances.

11 Tailor's chalk Ideal for temporary markings as the chalk can be brushed away or washed off when you've finished your project. It comes in a variety of forms and colours including pencils, blocks of chalk and chalk wheels. You'll find different types of chalk will work better on different fabrics.

12 Vanishing marker pens These are great to use on lighter coloured fabrics and will (hopefully!) fade or wash out over time. Always test first on a piece of scrap fabric to make sure that they will come off before marking up your project fabric.

13 Masking tape Also known as painter's tape, this is ideal for marking temporary stitching guidelines on your machine and for use as a seam guide. Simply stick it to the sewing bed so that the edge is your hem or seam allowance away from the left-hand needle. It comes in a range of widths and colours and is easy to tear. The tape holds in place and can be easily removed when it is no longer needed, without leaving any residue.

PINS AND NEEDLES

14 Pins There are a huge range of pins available including ones specifically designed for use with stretch fabrics, so choose the right type of pin for your fabric and project needs. Try to keep pins within the seam allowance at the edge of fabric pieces, to avoid damage or visible pin holes showing on your finished work.

15 Pin cushion Magnetic pin cushions and dishes are brilliant for keeping pins together and for picking up dropped pins off the floor.

16 Pattern weights An alternative to pins for holding paper patterns on fabric. Ideal for use with a cutting mat and rotary cutter.

17 Safety pins Use safety pins for threading elastic or cord through casings.

18 Binding clips These are ideal for fabrics that are difficult to pin or those that may be damaged by pins. Clip your fabric pieces together and remove the clips as you sew.

19 Basting tape Instead of pinning and hand tacking before machine stitching, use this double-sided tape to hold your fabric pieces together, then use the sewing machine. This also works brilliantly on zips. Single-faced and water-soluble versions are also available.

20 Water-soluble glue Another alternative to pins – use this to hold fabric pieces before machine stitching in place. The glue is often coloured but dries clear. When washed, the glue will come out of the fabric. You can purchase specific fabric glue, but any washable glue should do the trick.

21 Machine needles Check your manual and use the needles specified for your machine. More details on needles can be found on pages 18–19.

22 Hand sewing needles These are useful when finishing off the thread ends after stitching on your machine or for fixing skipped or broken lines of stitching (see page 40). Keep a selection of sizes that can be used with different thread types. Large-eyed needles or bodkins are perfect for threading narrow elastics through casings or for weaving in overlocker thread tails.

23 Needle threader The traditional version used for threading hand sewing needles consists of a fine wire loop in the shape of a diamond attached to either tinplate or plastic. You will also find other types of needle threader designed to help with threading machine needles. These are demonstrated on page 26.

PRESSING EQUIPMENT

24 Iron and ironing board It is essential that pressing is done while you are constructing an item to embed stitches into fabric and make the stitching lie flatter. Be cautious with heat settings and always test first on scrap fabrics. Keep the soleplate of your iron clean by using paracetamol (acetaminophen) to remove stubborn scorch marks.

25 Sleeve board A smaller ironing board for ironing seams of sleeves and trouser legs. It is also handy when working on small projects.

26 Tailor's ham and seam roll These tools provide you with more accuracy when ironing. The seam roll is a round sausage shape that can be pushed into sleeves or trouser legs so you can press seams more easily. The ham is a rounded cushion which can be used for pressing sleeve heads, curved seams or darts. Both tools are usually packed with sawdust, so as you are ironing, the sawdust draws out the heat and moisture.

27 Tailor's clapper This heavy wooden tool will help to flatten bulky seams. This is great for springy fabrics that struggle to lay flat. Press your seam with an iron using lots of steam and then lay the clapper on top. The wood draws out the moisture and sets the crease.

28 Rubber mallet or small hammer The ideal tool to help flatten seams: simply hammer the section that you want to be flattened until the seams are flat enough to be stitched over (see page 84).

29 Pressing cloth (not pictured) Avoid damaging your fabric or thread when ironing by using a pressing cloth. A small piece of organza works well as this can withstand high temperatures and is transparent.

Needles

It's really important to use the right needles for your machine and for the type of sewing that you are doing in order to achieve the perfect stitch. Understanding the differences between needles can be confusing and it's not always possible to see any physical difference in needles as they are so small. When choosing needles for your machine, always check your manual to see which type is recommended. Don't assume that the needles you use for your sewing machine and overlocker will work just as well on your coverstitch machine – you may need to use a different needle type for each of your machines. Using the wrong needle can cause a series of problems from uneven or skipped stitches to actual damage to the machine parts.

REMOVING OR REPLACING NEEDLES

For information on removing or replacing your needles, see page 49.

NEEDLE ANATOMY

Butt The very top of the needle, this has a slightly rounded end to help with insertion into the machine.

Shank The upper part of the needle that is clamped into the machine. The brand and needle size are usually etched into the shank. On domestic sewing machine needles the back of the shank is flat and this flat part faces the back of the machine when the needle is inserted.

Shoulder The part between the shank and the blade. Some brands display colour coding here to identify the needle type and its size.

Blade The long narrow part of the needle that goes into the fabric. The width of the blade denotes the size of the needle.

Scarf This is the hollow part above the eye of the needle which allows the bobbin hook or looper to grab the needle thread so a stitch can be formed.

Eye The hole through which the thread passes. This varies in size depending on the needle type.

Groove On universal needles this is above the eye of the needle on the front of the needle. As the needle passes through the fabric, the thread sits in the groove so the needle can pass through the fabric easily. Some needle types have two grooves, one on the front and one on the back to enable the formation of specific stitches. The number of grooves, length and size varies depending on the type of needle.

Point and tip The first parts to enter the fabric. The length, shape and size will vary depending on the needle type.

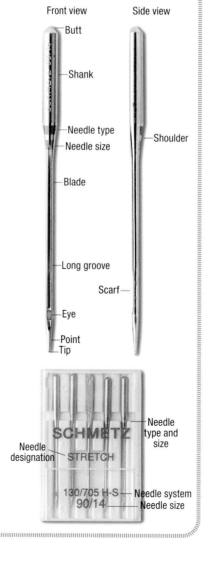

Front view / Side view

Butt
Shank
Needle type
Needle size
Shoulder
Blade
Long groove
Scarf
Eye
Point
Tip

Needle designation
SCHMETZ
STRETCH
Needle type and size
130/705 H-S — Needle system
90/14 — Needle size

Tips

- If you misplace your manual and are not sure which needles to use in your machine, look at the needles currently in the machine and use these.
- Change needles regularly, not just once they break. Some brands suggest changing your needle every 8–10 hours. Needles become blunt over time and will wear out more quickly when using certain fabrics, especially synthetic fibres such as polyester and metallic fabrics.
- When sewing with knitted fabrics try using a needle labelled 'SUK' to avoid skipped stitches.

NEEDLE SYSTEM

Nearly all modern domestic sewing machines will use needles that have a scarf and a shank with a flat back. This needle system is referred to as HAx1, 15x1 or 130/705 H where the H is the German word Hohlkehle which indicates the shape of the scarf.

While some brands of overlockers and coverstitch machines will suggest 130/705 H needles, many brands will recommend using the ELx705 needle system for their machines (see further details right).

NEEDLE SIZES

On a needle packet there are two numbers to indicate the size of the needle – the first is metric and the second imperial. The metric size is sometimes referred to as 'Number Metric' (NM) and denotes the diameter of the needle blade, measured just above the scarf of the needle, in hundredths of a millimetre. A needle that is labelled 90/14 indicates NM 90 or a blade diameter of 0.9mm and imperial needle size of 14. The higher the number, the thicker the needle and the type of fabric that it would be suited to. The sizing goes from 60 for fine light-weight fabrics to 120 for very heavy fabrics but not all sizes are available in all needle types. For coverstitch machines, usually a size 80/12 or 90/14 will be suitable for most fabrics.

NEEDLE TYPES

There are a range of different needle types for a variety of sewing applications. Each type has a slightly altered shape. For coverstitch machines the three needle types to use are universal, jersey (or ball point) and stretch:

- **Universal**: a slightly rounded point also known as a 'light ball point' and is suitable to use with a range of fabrics including both wovens and knits. This comes in sizes from 60/8 to 120/19. Needles with a light ball point may also be labelled as 'SES'.

- **Jersey**: a slightly more rounded tip than the universal needle or a 'medium ball point.' This type of needle is designed specifically for sewing with knits: the tip of the needle does not damage or break the knit fibres but pushes them apart as it travels through the fabric. Needles with a medium ball point may also be labelled as 'SUK'.

- **Stretch**: a medium ball point, a shorter, narrower eye and a deeper scarf. This type of needle is specifically made for sewing highly elasticized synthetic fabrics and elastic materials as the design of the eye and scarf helps to prevent skipped stitches. These may be labelled as 'special' or 'super stretch'.

SPECIALIST COVERSTITCH NEEDLES ELX705

This needle system was first designed to work with Elna machines and has a groove on the front and back of the blade to reduce skipped stitches. The second groove on the back of the needle is necessary to create chain stitches and perform a coverstitch. The needles are also said to be stronger due to a reinforced blade, so they will break less and give a straighter stitch.

Within the ELx705 needle system there are three types of needle currently available in sizes 65/9, 80/12 and 90/14. These are recommended for use in many domestic combination and stand-alone coverstitch machines and often have 'overlock', 'serger' or 'coverstitch' on the packaging:

- **ELx705**: a universal needle for sewing with a good range of fabric types.

- **ELx705CF**: a universal needle with a chrome finish (CF) for sewing with a range of fabric types. The chrome finish makes the needle much more resistant to wear.

- **ELx705CF SUK**: a medium ball point with a chrome finish for sewing with knitted fabrics.

- ELx705 needles are equivalent to the Singer 2022 and Organ SY2922 needle systems.

See page 187 for suitable needle types for specific fabrics.

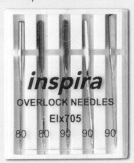

Threads

A wide range of threads can be used on a coverstitch machine. The choice will depend on the type of fabric you are working with, the purpose of your project and the desired finish. The best-quality thread gives the best-quality stitching, so don't be tempted to buy cheap packs of threads as this may create issues with tension, skipped stitches or snapping threads. Choose thread types that are branded, preferably a brand you've heard of. Here I provide a guide to the types of threads that can be used on coverstitch machines.

Tips for colour matching

- You don't have to colour match all the threads: use contrasting colours in the looper or thread in a similar shade.
- Trying to match the thread colour to the fabric? Choose a slightly darker shade – this will blend in, whereas a lighter shade will stand out.
- You don't need to buy three or four cones of each colour: you can use the threads you already have by winding them onto sewing-machine bobbins and placing the bobbins on your machine. If you think you might run out of thread as the bobbin doesn't hold much, attach empty thread reels to empty bobbins. Attach the bobbin to the machine as if to wind this, then direct the thread to the empty spool instead (see right).

ESSENTIAL THREAD TYPES

Coverstitch machines are predominantly used for sewing with knitted or stretch fabrics so you'll need a thread that will move with your fabric. The following types of threads will allow for stretch, strength and durability.

1 General-purpose thread Ideal for your sewing machine, overlocker and coverstitch machine as it comes in a wide range of sizes and colours. Threads may be 100% polyester or polyester covered with cotton. Polyester provides durability, resistance to abrasion and elasticity. Cotton tolerates higher temperatures and makes the thread easier to sew with. General-purpose thread suits any sewing project but take care when pressing – cotton wrapped polyester will provide resistance to higher temperatures but 100% polyester may melt.

2 Overlocker thread This thread is slightly finer than general-purpose thread and enables you to reduce the bulkiness of your seams. It is designed to work well at high speeds and is available on cross-wound cones in a range of colours, including variegated thread.

3 Textured thread Commonly known as 80s bulk thread, woolly nylon or woolly polyester, textured thread looks fuzzy, like yarn, and feels soft to the touch. It fluffs or bulks out once it is sewn so gives great coverage on seams and hems. Its soft and stretchy nature makes it ideal for use in close-fitting garments made from highly elasticized fabrics such as activewear, swimwear and lingerie. It is usually used only in the looper but can also be used as a needle thread. Polyester threads are slightly easier to thread as they are less fuzzy. Polyester will also tolerate a higher heat. Nylon threads are stronger but can discolour and become brittle over time. A longer stitch length and lower looper tension may be necessary when working with textured threads due to their thickness (see page 30).

ALTERNATIVE AND DECORATIVE THREADS

These threads are not recommended for use in every brand and type of coverstitch machine. Due to the thickness and texture of many of these thread types you may need to adjust tensions and stitch length to achieve the desired results.

4 Monofilament thread A transparent, almost invisible thread that is available as polyester or nylon (polyamide). It comes in two colours, clear and smoke, and can be purchased in different weights from very fine up to a fishing-line thickness. This thread is soft and pliable and will lie flat once sewn. The finest thread has more use for a range of projects. Polyester may be the best choice in fibre as although nylon can feel softer, it tends to yellow or become brittle over time and is also less resistant to heat.

5 Silk thread This will add a luxurious sheen to your stitches but it is expensive so consider using it either in the looper or just as needle thread to make it go further. There are alternative fibres that give a similar silky appearance but cost less, such as polyester or rayon threads.

6 Rayon thread This is also known as viscose rayon, artificial silk or art silk and has a sheen which gives it a similar appearance to silk. It is available in a wide range of colours and can be used as a decorative thread. However, this thread type isn't as strong as other threads and may break easily when used in the needles. Thicker rayon threads are best used in the looper only.

7 Topstitching thread Sometimes known as jeans thread or buttonhole twist, this is a polyester thread that is thicker and stronger than general-purpose sewing thread. It has a high lustre and works well for decorative use but due to its thickness it is best used only in the looper.

8 Upholstery thread Also known as 'extra-strong thread' this is thicker than general-purpose thread but finer than topstitching thread. For machines which can't manage the thickness of topstitching thread, this could be an alternative for decorative stitching.

9 Metallic thread These threads come in a range of thicknesses and are excellent for decorative use. They can be made from a variety of different fibres – polyester, rayon or nylon which will affect their strength and heat resistance. They can be thicker than general-purpose threads and so may cause tension issues and problems with the continual flow of thread. Use this thread in the needles if it will fit or only in the looper to add some sparkle and embellishment to seams and hems.

10 Cotton thread Resists heat and can be pressed at high temperatures but doesn't offer any elasticity and can snap easily on seams that are stretched. Thinner cotton thread is ideal for tacking since it can be easily broken and removed. Heavier cotton threads, such as mercerized or perle cotton that would typically be used for crochet, can be used in the looper and are ideal for decorative work. If your machine can produce a top coverstitch, try using cotton crochet thread as the top cover thread to produce a braid-like effect.

11 Elastic thread Fine round elastic cord or shirring elastic can be used in the looper. Rows of stitching can be formed to create a gathered effect, also known as shirring.

12 Glow-in-the-dark thread A novelty type of polyester thread that can be used for decorative work. Try using this in the looper and reverse coverstitch seams on activewear to make them glow in the dark.

13 Water-soluble thread Ideal for use as a tacking thread, particularly when working with zips. Hold the fabric pieces together for machine stitching and then submerge in water and the tacking threads will simply wash away.

Tips

- Cross-wound spools are designed to unravel from the top, so are the best type to use. Parallel-wound spools are designed to unravel from the side so use these with spool caps to ensure an even feed.
- Polyamide is another name for nylon – not polyester – polyamide will melt if ironed too hot.
- Use heavy threads in the looper only.
- Some threads will work better than others for no apparent reason. If you're having issues with stitch quality and you've tried all the machine settings, try switching your thread.
- An even feed of thread from the spool is key to stitching perfection. Consider switching threads that regularly tangle, change the direction the thread is unravelling in (turn the spool upside down), or try using thread nets, spool caps or spool mats to solve any problems.

Setting up the machine

If you've already used an overlocker and are a bit worried about learning how to thread a new machine, don't be. The coverstitch machine is a much easier beast to tame and just like the majority of overlockers it will come pre-threaded so you can just take it out of the box and get stitching. If your machine doesn't come pre-threaded, don't fear – threading the needles on a coverstitch machine is just as easy as any other machine, and there's only one looper to learn how to thread, unless you're operating a combination coverstitch and overlock machine.

The next few pages will give you guidance on how to set up a three- or four-thread coverstitch machine. Refer to your manual also, as not all models are the same.

GETTING STARTED

Make sure you have sufficient space and a sturdy table for your machine. Connect the machine to the power cable and place the foot pedal on the floor. Your machine's manual most likely suggests that you should keep the machine switched off while you are threading. However, the light on the machine is rather useful to help you see what you're doing, so if you do turn on the machine please be careful and keep your foot well away from the foot pedal.

1 Attach the thread guide bar if it isn't already attached and pull this up to its highest position, turning it so that the thread guides are above the spool pins. You may need to continue twisting to lock it into position.

2 Place your spools of thread onto the spool pins. If your machine is colour coded you may wish to use threads in the same colour while you get to grips with your machine.

3 Raise the presser foot – on most models this will release the tension on the tension discs, making it easier to pull the threads through the machine and ensuring that the threads sit correctly between the tension discs.

4 Open the looper cover – inside the looper cover there will most likely be a colour-coded diagram to show you how to thread your machine and where you'll find each of the thread guides (see diagram at the top of page 23).

ORDER OF THREADING

The machine's manual will state which order to thread in, usually starting with the looper, left needle, centre needle and then right needle. For many types of coverstitch machine, the order in which they are threaded doesn't make a difference in the performance of the machine. However, to be sure, do check your manual and thread in the order specified.

Tip for threading

At some point you will need to learn how to thread your machine, but an easy option to start with is to tie the new thread onto the old, as explained on page 31.

Repeat these steps for each of the threads:

1 Take the thread from the spool through the slot guide on the top of the thread guide bar from back to front. For some decorative threads, you may need to also pass the thread through the hole in the thread guide bar to stop it from slipping out of position.

2 Before reaching the tension dial, slide the thread into the clip of the thread guide plate on top of the machine. Some models have holes through which to pass the thread – check your manual.

3 Use both hands to hold onto the thread, holding the end and about 10cm (4in) away from this. Take the thread down through or around the tension dial, tugging gently on either side of the tension dial to make sure the thread sits correctly in tension. You should be able to feel a little resistance on the thread when the presser foot is lowered and/or the tension discs are engaged.

4 Hook the thread around the thread guide below the tension dial.

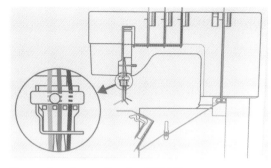

Diagram from Janome CoverPro 2000CPX. Used with permission.

   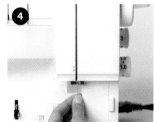

Each of the threading paths will now be explained in more detail.

THREADING THE LOOPER

Follow the colour-coded guides on your machine carefully to make sure that you don't miss out a step. Check your manual to see if you thread the looper first, or last.

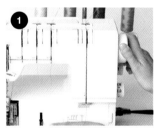  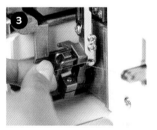 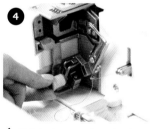

1 Turn the handwheel towards you to align the looper take-up levers.

2 Pass the thread through the looper take-up levers from right to left.

3 Slip the thread behind the looper thread guide on the bottom right of the looper.

4 Pull the looper release knob – this will cause the looper to slant to the right.

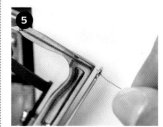  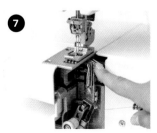

5 Pass the thread through the hole at the top of the right side of the looper. You may find tweezers useful at this point.

6 Bring the thread in front of the looper and pass this through the eye to the left from front to back, pulling at least 10cm (4in) of thread through the looper.

7 Push the looper to the left so it clicks back into its original position.

THREADING THE NEEDLES

Check your manual to see if you should thread the left or right needle first. It is really easy for the needle threads to become tangled so make sure you thread through the guides correctly and keep the threads separated using the prongs below the thread guide plate in the needle clamp area.

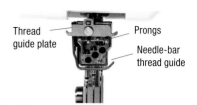

Thread guide plate — Prongs — Needle-bar thread guide

Threading the left needle

1 Take the thread from the right to the left of the machine, taking the thread under the next thread guide and then up, behind and to the left of the take-up lever cover.

2 Pull the thread down and slip it behind the next thread guide.

3 Pass the thread behind the thread guide plate from the left so the thread sits between the first and second prongs.

4 Pass the thread through the needle-bar thread guide plate from the right.

5 Thread the left needle from front to back and position the thread to the left and back. Pull around 5–10cm (2–4in) of thread through the needle.

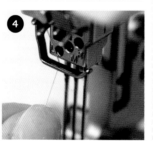

Tips for easy threading

- Your machine may come with a short length of thread attached, tie on the new threads as described on page 31 and you'll be stitching in no time.
- Your machine will be easier to thread if it is clean and lint-free. Dust down your machine before or after each use.
- Depending on your machine, if the looper thread breaks and needs rethreading, you may need to cut the needle threads, rethread the looper, then rethread the needles for optimum performance.
- For ease of threading the needle, lower the presser foot or remove it altogether to give more space for your fingers. Tweezers or a needle threader can also help. (See page 26 for how to use the needle threader.)

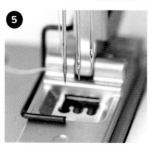

Threading the centre needle

1 Take the thread from the right to the left of the machine, taking the thread under the next two thread guides and then up, behind and to the left of the take-up lever cover.

2 Pull the thread down and slip it behind the next thread guide.

3 Pass the thread behind the thread guide plate from the right so the thread sits between the second and third prongs.

4 Pass the thread through the needle-bar thread guide plate from the right.

5 Thread the centre needle and position the thread to the left and back. Pull around 5–10cm (2–4in) of thread through the needle.

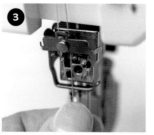

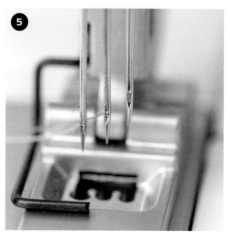

Threading the right needle

1 Take the thread from the right to the left of the machine, taking the thread under the next three thread guides and then up, behind and to the left of the take-up lever cover.

2 Pull the thread down and slip it behind the next thread guide.

3 Pass the thread behind the thread guide plate from the right so the thread sits between the third and fourth prongs.

4 Pass the thread through the needle-bar thread guide plate from the right as before.

5 Thread the right needle and position the thread to the left and back. Pull around 5–10cm (2–4in) of thread through the needle.

6 Close the looper cover if it is still open.

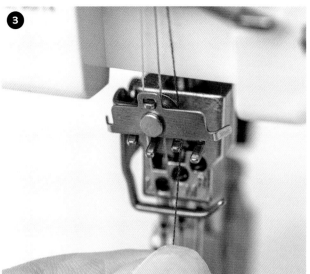

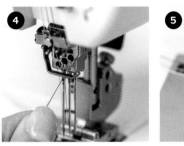

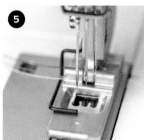

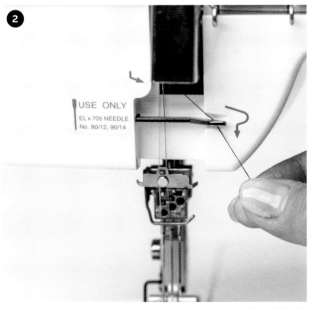

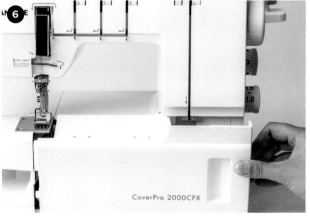

Using a needle threader

This handy device is sometimes designed with two functions — one end helps thread needles and the other end can be used to hold needles when removing or replacing them. (See page 49, 'Removing or replacing needles', for how to replace needles.)

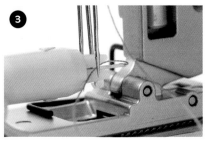

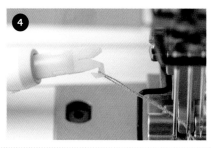

1 Hold the needle threader with the triangle mark facing up. Take the thread and place it horizontally into the slit.

2 Place the needle threader up to the needle, just above the eye.

3 Slide the needle threader down the needle until the metal threader pin enters the needle eye. Keep pushing and the threader pin will take the thread through the eye of the needle.

4 Remove the needle threader from the needle and use the hook on the needle threader, tweezers or fingers to pull the loop of thread out of the back of the needle.

THREADING THE NEEDLES ON DIFFERENT MODELS

Check the thread route guidance in your manual to make sure you haven't missed out a thread guide or threaded it incorrectly — you may need to make an 'S' loop with the threads to ensure the correct tension and a balanced stitch.

For machines with tension dials on the front of the machine, check that the thread sits within the tension discs correctly as you thread up the machine. Pull on either end of the thread in a flossing (back-and-forth) motion. When a slight resistance is felt on the thread it is correctly positioned within the tension discs.

If your machine is a combination coverstitch and overlocker, check the position of the needles. It will have two or three needle positions for coverstitching plus two separate needle positions for overlocking. If you are switching from overlocking to coverstitching you'll need to move the needles into the correct position.

'S' loop on Juki MCS1800.

Brother CV3550 threading tree.

Needle positions on Janome 1200D.

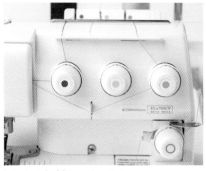

baby lock BLCS2 tension dials.

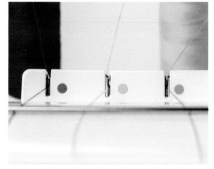

baby lock BLCS2 tension guides.

Threading the looper on baby lock machines

All baby lock machines have an air-threading system that makes threading the looper quick and easy: one push of the threading button or lever and the looper is threaded.

Close-up of the aligned threading tubes.

The threading/serging lever from baby lock Gloria.

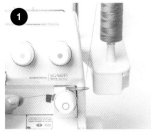
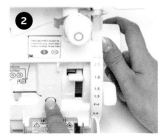

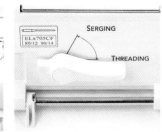

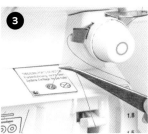
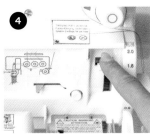

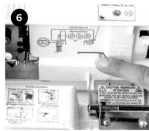

1 Bring the thread from the spool through the thread guides and around the tension dial.

2 Raise the presser foot and open the looper cover. Press the machine lock button and turn the handwheel towards you until the threading tubes are aligned. On some baby lock machines you will need to change the settings from 'serging' to 'threading'.

3 Pull 40cm (16in) of thread through the tension dial and insert 2.5cm (1in) of thread into the threading port.

4 Press the threading button or push down on the threading lever to push the thread into the eye of the looper.

5 Open the left side cover and check the thread appears in the chain looper thread tray. Trim excess thread to around 10cm (4in).

6 Move the lock-button release lever back to the 'stitching' or 'serging' position. This will open the threading tubes ready for sewing.

Threading the looper on Juki machines

Threading a Juki machine is a little unusual as the looper is threaded from the back of the machine round to the left side. The looper should be threaded first, then the needles. Follow the colour-coded pathway and series of threading guides as follows:

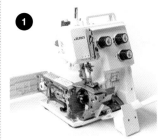

1 Open the looper cover (front) and the cloth plate (left).

2 Raise the presser foot. Take the thread from the spool and pass it through the three thread guides: on the thread guide bar (a); just below the spool (b); just above the tension dial (c).

3 Hold the thread at both ends and take it down and around the tension dial, tugging gently to ensure the thread sits correctly between the tension discs.

4 Take the thread around the next two thread guides above and to the right of the tension dial.

5 Continue threading to the right, into the next thread guide at the front of the mechanism.

6 Take the thread back to the left.

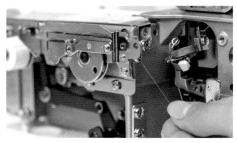

7 Loop the thread around the back of the mechanism.

8 Pull the thread to the right so it sits inside the mechanism.

9 Thread the guide at the far right of the mechanism.

10 Turn the handwheel towards you so the needles are in the lowest position and the looper is positioned as far left as possible.

11 Pass the thread through the guide below the looper.

12 Push the looper auto threader (the small white button) up towards the looper.

13 Pull the button and looper down together so you can see the looper more clearly.

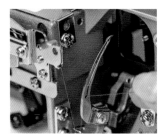

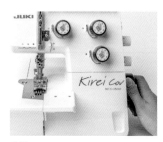

14 Thread the eye in the base of the looper from back to front.

15 Thread the eye in the top of the looper from front to back and pull around 10cm (4in) of thread through the eye. It might be easier to use tweezers.

16 Push the looper up into its original position.

17 Close the looper cover and cloth plate and turn the handwheel towards you so the needles are in their highest position, ready to thread.

THREADING THE LOOPER FOR DIFFERENT MODELS

To prepare to thread the looper you will need to turn the handwheel towards you to give the clearest pathway for threading. Depending on the model, this might mean raising the needles to their highest position, lowest position or aligning markings on the handwheel to optimize the access to the looper.

THREADING FOR TOP COVERSTITCH

Some coverstitch machines have the added function of performing a top coverstitch using two or three needles, a top-cover spreader and the chain looper. This stitch forms a double-sided coverstitch with a grid pattern on the top and bottom side of the fabric.

If you have this function, your machine will come with additional accessories, including a top-cover foot, spreader device and top-cover guide.

Attach the additional accessories according to your manual. Make sure the machine is forming a coverstitch correctly before threading the top-coverstitch guide.

See more details on page 62 for top coverstitch.

Above right: Handwheel markings on the Brother CV3550.

Below: Top coverstitch accessories.

THREADING FOR COMBINATION MACHINES

To switch from overlocking to coverstitch or chain stitching on a combination overlocker and coverstitch machine there may be a number of changes that you need to make which can include the need to:

1 Disengage the cutting knife.

2 Reduce the cutting width.

3 Disengage the stitch finger.

4 Disengage the upper looper.

5 Swap the overlock cover with the sewing table – you may need to disengage the stitch finger and/or reduce the cutting width for the sewing table to fit correctly.

6 Change the position of the needles and change the presser foot.

Check your manual for details specific to your machine.

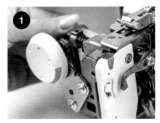
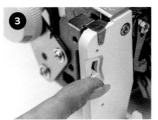
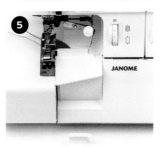

Tips for threading the looper

• Raise the presser foot when threading your machine – on the majority of machines this will release the tension on the tension discs and make it much easier to pull the threads through the machine. Where the tension is not released by raising the presser foot, lower the tension setting to 0 and/or use a flossing motion on the threads to ensure they are properly engaged between the tension discs.

• Many coverstitch and combination machines have a looper-release lever which allows for easier threading. Depending on the model you may need to push, pull, raise or lower the lever for this to work.

• On some combination machines the thread route for the lower looper may differ when setting the machine to create chain stitch or coverstitch. Be sure to check your manual for the correct thread route.

USING AND THREADING DECORATIVE THREADS

For some slippery threads, such as rayon or silk, you may need to use additional thread guides (a) on the thread guide bar or use snap-on thread guides to help keep the thread from becoming tangled. Thread nets (b), spool caps, mats and holders should also be considered. (See 'Must-have tools for coverstitch machines' on pages 14–15.)

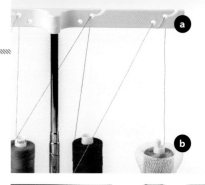
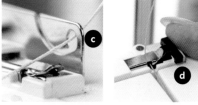

When using bulky threads, you may need to bypass one or more of the thread guides (c) or use a tension-release clip (d) to allow the thread to feed correctly.

If you're using woolly nylon and struggling to thread the eyes of the needles, use a **thread cradle**: take a length of fine thread around 10–15cm (4–6in) in length, fold this in half to form a loop and align the two thread ends. Push the ends of the thread through the eye of the needle. Place the decorative thread into the loop of thread and continue to pull on the fine thread until the decorative thread is pulled through the eye of the needle. It is not always possible to use woolly nylon in the needles of all machines and achieve a consistent stitch, so test this first on scrap fabric.

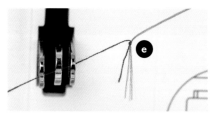

If you're using decorative thread such as woolly nylon and struggling to thread the eye of the looper, try tying some fine polyester thread to the end and thread this through the looper, pulling the knot and your woolly nylon thread through (e). Alternatively, use a looper threader (see page 14) or thread cradle (see above).

If your machine has a jet-air threading system you can use the thread cradle to help with threading decorative threads. Form a thread cradle using around 15cm (6in) of fine thread. Fold this in half to form a loop, align the thread ends and then follow the steps below.

1 Push the ends of the fine thread into the threading port, pushing around 2.5cm (1in) of thread into the port.

2 Press the button to activate the jet of air. The thread cradle should now be visible in the eye of the looper and a tail end to the left of the machine. Place the decorative thread(s) into the loop of the thread cradle, pulling around 20cm (8in) through the loop.

3 Pull on the tail end of the cradle to the left of the machine to bring the decorative thread(s) through the eye of the looper.

CHECKLIST BEFORE STITCHING

- Is the thread guide bar in its highest position?
- Have the threading pathways been followed correctly?
- Are the threads held correctly in the tension discs? (A slight resistance can be felt when pulling on the threads when the presser foot is lowered.)
- Do needle threads sit to the left and back of the presser foot with around 5–10cm (2–4in) of thread tail?
- Is the looper correctly threaded with around 10cm (4in) of thread tail? (This will be on the underside of the machine.)
- Is the looper engaged or has it been pushed back into position after threading?
- Is the machine plugged in and switched on?

CHANGING THE THREADS

There are two ways to change the threads on your coverstitch machine: remove the old threads completely and rethread from scratch, or cut the threads near to the spools and tie on the new threads. The latter method may save you time or you may find it just as quick to rethread the needles from scratch and use the tie-on method just for the looper.

Tying on new threads

1 Cut the old threads just above the spools, leaving plenty of thread to attach the new thread. If you cut this too short you won't have enough room to tie on the new thread.

2 Remove the old spools from the machine and put your new spools in place. Tie each new thread to the old thread using a thumb knot or overhand bend: take both the old and new thread ends together, form a loop and pass the ends through the loop and then pull tight. Trim the tail ends if they are longer than 5cm (2in).

3 Raise the presser foot. This will release the tension on the tension discs on most machines. If it doesn't, turn the tension dials to 0 and/or press the tension-release lever when pulling the threads through the machine in the next steps. Separate the needle threads from the looper thread: turn the handwheel away from you to disengage the looper thread from the needle thread. Hold the tail ends of thread in your left hand and gently pull the needle threads out of the needles. The needle threads should now be free from the needles and the looper thread.

4 Pull the looper thread from the top of the needle plate, pulling the new thread through the machine. If the thread resists you may need to lift the knot over the tension disc. Also, try alternating where you pull the threads – pull from the thread guide below the tension disc with your right hand, then pull from the looper thread on top of the needle plate with your left hand.

5 Pull the needle threads through the machine. You may be able to pull all of them together or do this one at a time. Lift the knot in the thread over the tension disc if it gets stuck. Once the knots reach the eyes of the needles you will need to cut the thread and then rethread the needles. Lower the presser foot when threading the needles so you have more space for your fingers to manoeuvre.

6 Make sure the needle threads aren't tangled and are separated from each other using the prongs above the needle-bar thread guide.

7 Turn the handwheel towards you and complete one rotation. Take a pair of tweezers or other tool and run this under the presser foot, taking the needle threads through to the underside of the presser foot. You should now have all the needle threads and looper thread on top of the needle plate.

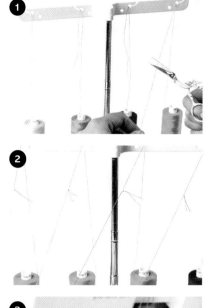

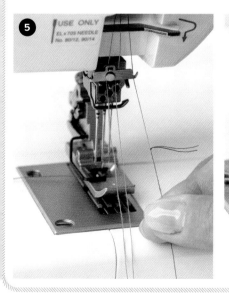

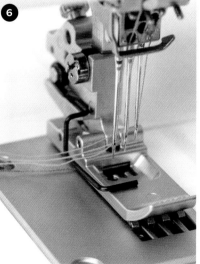

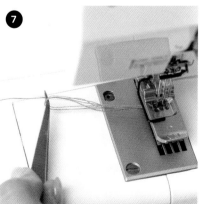

Getting started

You've threaded your machine and you're ready to begin. Start with some scrap fabric and a few test runs to make sure the machine is sewing correctly before stitching onto your project. Some coverstitch machines allow you to 'chain off' (stitch a chain of thread without any fabric under the presser foot), but most machines will only work properly with fabric under the needles. Check your manual to see how your machine operates.

Tips

- Sew at a steady pace – stopping and starting can cause irregularities with the stitches.
- Check your stitch sample. Does the stitch look balanced or do the tensions need adjusting on the threads? Pages 44–47 provide more details.
- Make sure you use the correct needles for your machine and the type of fabric you are working with. Pages 18–19 provide more details.
- Don't pull on the fabric as you stitch as this can create issues with the stitches; let the feed-dog teeth feed the fabric evenly.

TESTING YOUR MACHINE

If you've just threaded up your machine you'll be able to see the needle threads on the top of the machine but not the looper thread. This is okay – the looper thread will wrap around the needle threads and be pulled to the top of the needle plate as you begin to stitch.

Always test your stitches using the same fabric and thickness that you'll use for your project. While getting to grips with your machine and trying out different techniques, use a medium-weight non-stretch fabric such as calico (known as muslin in some countries) to test your stitches. The fabric shown has been folded to form a hem.

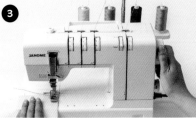

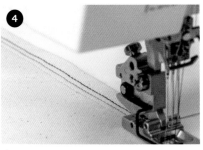

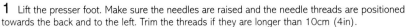

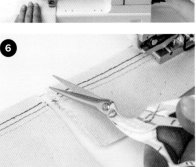

1 Lift the presser foot. Make sure the needles are raised and the needle threads are positioned towards the back and to the left. Trim the threads if they are longer than 10cm (4in).

2 Push your fabric under the presser foot so the end of the fabric is just below the needle tips and the fold is aligned with the right edge of the needle plate. Lower the presser foot. Ensure both needles stitch through a double layer of fabric – you may end up with an unbalanced stitch or tension issues if one needle is only stitching through a single layer.

3 Turn the handwheel towards you to lower the needles into the fabric. Keep turning the handwheel and take the first two stitches. The feed-dog teeth will take the fabric under the presser foot and you should see three rows of parallel stitching on the top of the fabric.

4 If the machine is feeding the fabric and stitching correctly, gently press on the foot pedal and continue stitching. If not, work through the 'Checklist before stitching' on page 30 or see the troubleshooting section on page 182.

5 When you get to the end of your test piece, place another piece of fabric scrap under the presser foot and stitch until your original fabric piece is no longer under the presser foot.

6 Cut the threads between the scrap and the test piece. Check your stitches.

Finishing and securing ends

When you begin to stitch on a coverstitch machine the starting threads will be locked into place by subsequent stitching and won't easily come undone. Like an overlocker, there is no reverse button or lever on this machine to back tack and fasten your thread. Ending your stitching is a very different process to that on a sewing machine or overlocker and when you first start to use your machine you may find it difficult to release the fabric from under the presser foot. When you end your stitching on a coverstitch machine the threads can unravel easily and you'll need to choose a method to secure them. There are a number of different ways to finish off your stitching and these are explained in more detail below.

METHODS OF SECURING THE THREADS

Using a fabric scrap

When stopping and starting your stitching, most machine manuals recommend that you use scraps of fabric and avoid stitching without fabric under the presser foot. A scrap of tear-away or wash-away stabilizer is ideal as it can be easily removed when it is no longer required.

1 When you get to the end of your stitching, place a fabric scrap or piece of stabilizer under the presser foot.

2 Continue stitching until your original fabric piece is no longer under the presser foot and there is about 3–5cm (1⅛–2in) of stitched scrap fabric behind the presser foot.

3 Cut the fabric scrap close to the presser foot.

4 Leave part of the scrap attached to the original fabric and the remaining scrap under the presser foot.

Depending on what stage you are at in the construction of your project, you may need to use a seam sealant to prevent unravelling. Apply the seam sealant to the stitching at the end of your original fabric piece and the beginning of the fabric scrap. Once this is dry, cut away the fabric scrap.

If you are stitching a hem using a coverstitch and will later sew a seam that will stitch over and enclose the coverstitching, leave the fabric scrap attached until the seam is completed.

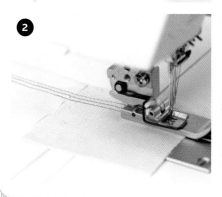

Swipe, snip and lock threads

This method is the quickest and most often used method to secure the threads at the end of your stitching.

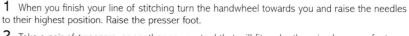

1 When you finish your line of stitching turn the handwheel towards you and raise the needles to their highest position. Raise the presser foot.

2 Take a pair of tweezers, or another narrow tool that will fit under the raised presser foot. Hold the tool behind the presser foot and above the fabric.

3 Draw the tool under the presser foot towards you, bringing the needle threads with it. Pull until this loop of thread is around 5cm (2in) long. If the threads won't pull easily, use the extra lift on the presser foot to further release the tension on the tension discs or press the tension-release lever if your machine has one.

4 Cut the threads around 5cm (2in) from the needles.

5 Hold the stitches in the fabric tightly between your thumb and fingers and pull the fabric to the back and then out to the left side. If the fabric doesn't pull out easily, use the extra lift on the presser foot or press the tension-release lever if your machine has one.

6 Keep pulling: the needle threads will be pulled to the wrong side of the fabric, securing the stitches.

7 Cut the looper thread to separate your fabric from the machine.

8 Trim the threads close to the fabric or for extra security, tie the threads in a knot or weave in the ends using a hand sewing needle or loop turner (see pages 36 and 37).

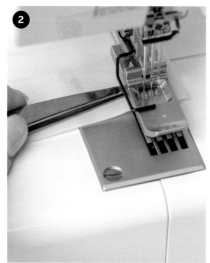

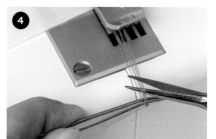

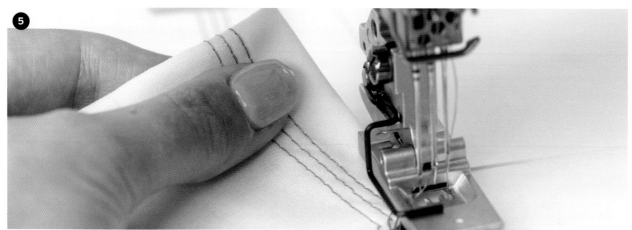

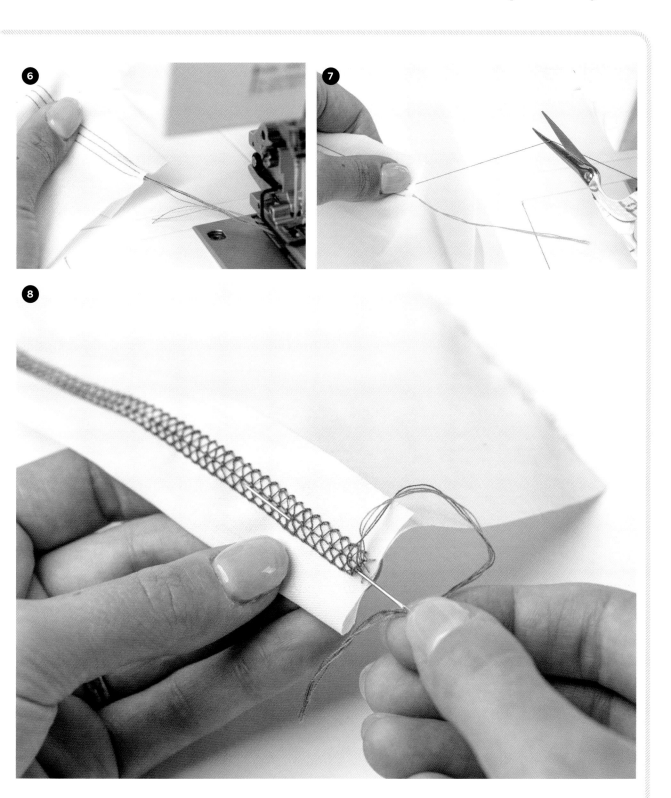

Weaving in the thread ends

This method is good for decorative threads and reverse coverstitching. Once you finish stitching, follow the instructions for the swipe, snip and lock method up to and including step 7.

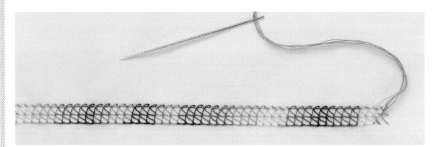

1 Take a hand sewing needle and pass all the threads into the eye.

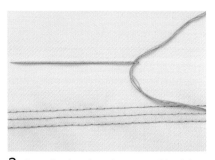

2 Draw the threads to the wrong side of the fabric. Thicker threads can be transferred one at a time.

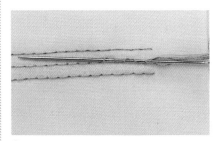

3 Once all the threads are on the wrong side of the fabric, run the needle through the stitches on the underside to secure them. You can also secure the threads by stitching into the fabric as long as it won't show on the right side of your work. Trim the thread ends.

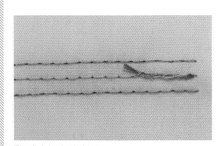

The finished stitching.

Tips for removing fabric from under the presser foot and releasing threads

1 Make sure the presser foot is raised.

2 Check the position of the needles – are they in the highest position? Adjust the position of the handwheel and try again.

3 Try a quick tug of the threads to the back of the machine and then pull to the side.

4 Use the extra lift on the presser foot, if you have this function, to release any tension on the threads within the tension discs when pulling out the fabric.

5 Release the tension on the tension button or lever if your model has one.

6 Turn the handwheel away from you (clockwise) to release the looper threads from the needle threads.

7 Pull slack on the needle threads, just above the needle eye.

8 Check that the threads are feeding evenly from the spools and are not caught on something or tangled.

9 Try setting the tension dials to 0.

10 Open the looper cover and release the looper by pushing or pulling the release knob, as you would when threading. Don't forget to push it back to its original position before you start sewing again.

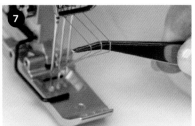

Finishing with a knot

A knot is always a secure finish.

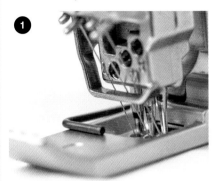

1 When you've finished stitching, turn the handwheel towards you to move the needles to their lowest position. The machine may click when the needles reach the lowest point.

2 Turn the handwheel in the opposite direction, to raise the needles to their highest position. This will release the needle threads from the looper thread.

3 Raise the presser foot to release the thread tensions.

4 Hold the fabric and stitches with your thumb and fingers. Pull the fabric and threads out to the back left of the machine. If the threads don't pull easily, use the extra lift on the presser foot to further release the tension on the tension discs.

5 Cut the threads, leaving at least 10cm (4in) in length.

6 Pull gently on the looper thread to reveal a loop of needle thread. Holding down the looper stitches, pull the needle threads through to the wrong side.

7 Tie all threads together, then cut the thread ends close to the knot.

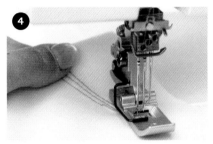

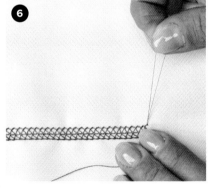
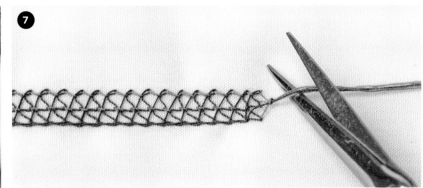

Chaining off

This technique is only possible on specific brands, combination machines or top coverstitch models. If your machine allows for this, once you reach the end of the fabric, continue stitching off the fabric to run off a chain. Let the machine feed the thread, don't pull it. Cut the chain using the thread cutter and tie off the threads or pass the thread chain through the machine stitches using a hand sewing needle, bodkin or loop turner.

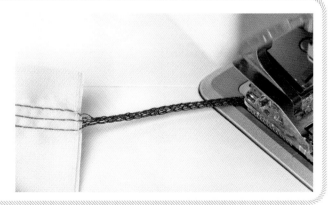

Fixing mistakes

There will come a time, as it always does when sewing, when things go wrong and you need to fix or unpick your stitching. The good news is that unravelling chain or coverstitches is much easier than unpicking regular sewing-machine stitching or overlocked stitches. There are some tips and tricks explained below for mending, removing and replacing faulty or incorrect stitches and you'll also find details in the troubleshooting section on page 182 on how to fix machine issues.

STITCHING ISSUES

If your machine starts to skip stitches or the threads break you'll need to remove the fabric from under the presser foot and then run through the 'Checklist before stitching' (page 30) before troubleshooting any issues and testing your machine again. There are a number of ways to release the fabric and remove it from under the presser foot as explained on pages 33–37.

Try to avoid using the swipe, snip and lock method as this will make it more difficult to remove stitching. Instead, turn the handwheel towards you (anticlockwise) to move the needles to the lowest position, then turn the handwheel clockwise and raise the needles to their highest position. This will release the needle threads from the looper threads and you'll be able to release the fabric easily from the machine.

REMOVING CHAIN STITCHING

This stitch has just one needle and one looper thread and can be unravelled easily, so long as you do this from the right end of the stitching. As this stitch can be removed so easily it can be used as a tacking stitch and taken out when it's no longer needed.

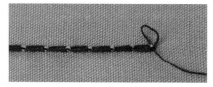

1 Turn your work to the wrong side so the chained side of the stitch is facing you.

2 From the finishing end of the stitching (the last stitch that you sewed), pull on the looper thread – this should start to unravel and come away from the fabric.

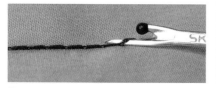

3 If it doesn't pull easily, check you are pulling from the correct end of the stitching. The threads where you started stitching will not pull out easily but the threads at the end of the stitching should. If you're still having trouble, run a quick unpick tool through a couple of stitches and then pull on the looper thread.

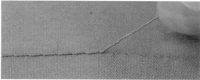

4 Turn the work back over to see the needle thread. Pull on the needle thread to pull this away from the fabric.

Tip

You may find that you need to pull on the needle and looper threads simultaneously for the thread to unravel, particularly when using textured thread.

REMOVING COVERSTITCHING

As with chain stitching, coverstitching can be easily removed if the threads are pulled from the finishing point of stitching. The same techniques can be used for two- or three-needle stitching. If you've secured the thread ends then removing the stitches might take a bit more time.

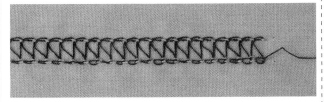

1 Turn your work to the wrong side so the looper side of the stitch is facing you.

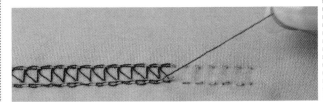

2 From the finishing end of the stitch, pull on the looper thread. If you've secured the threads you'll need to release them. If you've tied the thread ends in a knot, cut the knot. If you've used a seam sealant, carefully cut the stitching away from this. If you've used hand stitching to fix the threads, unpick or cut these.

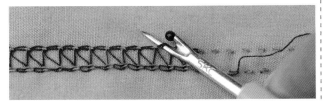

3 If the looper thread doesn't pull easily, check that you are pulling from the correct end of the stitching. If you're still having trouble take a quick unpick tool and cut through a couple of stitches before pulling again on the looper thread. It should begin to unravel.

4 Turn the work back over to see the needle threads. Pull on the needle threads to remove these easily.

REMOVING TOP COVERSTITCHING

This can be removed in the same way as regular coverstitching. Once the looper thread begins to pull away from the fabric the needle threads and top-cover thread will be released and can be easily removed.

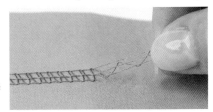

REMOVING A FIVE-THREAD SAFETY STITCH

This type of stitch combines a two-thread chain stitch with a three-thread overlocking stitch. Some machines will also produce a combination of coverstitch and overlock stitches which can be removed in a similar way. To remove the chain or coverstitches, follow the instructions above.

REMOVING OVERLOCKED STITCHES

The secret to removing overlocked stitches is to remove the needle thread first, then the looper threads will easily pull away from the fabric.

For long stitches on a short piece of stitching

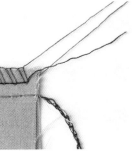 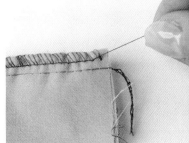

1 Separate the needle thread and the looper threads from the overlocked thread chain.

2 Pull the needle thread out of the fabric. The looper threads will now pull away easily.

For short stitches or longer lengths of stitching

1 Use a quick unpick tool, snips or small scissors to cut the needle thread at intervals along the length of overlocked stitching.

2 Pull out the needle thread in sections. Once this is all removed, the looper threads will pull away from the fabric.

FIXING SKIPPED STITCHES

There are some tips for solving the problem of skipped stitches in the troubleshooting section on page 182, but if the majority of your stitching is perfect apart from one or two skipped stitches, don't undo all your hard work as this can be easily fixed with a hand sewing needle and matching thread. In this example I've used a contrasting thread so you can see the repair.

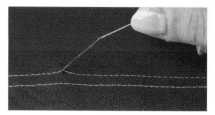

1 Thread a hand sewing needle with matching thread, tie a knot in one end, leave the knot on the wrong side of the work and bring the needle up at the exact point of the skipped stitch. (You should see a tiny hole in the fabric from the machine needle.)

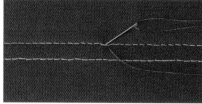

2 Take the needle over the thread and back into the same hole.

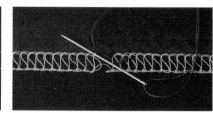

3 A skipped stitch can unravel so to avoid this, take a few stitches through the looper thread on the back of your work.

FIXING A BROKEN SECTION OF STITCHING

You may find that your hemming stitches break after wearing a garment a few times. You can fix this problem by filling in the gap made from the broken stitches with either machine stitching or hand stitching, depending on how big the gap is and how secure you want the stitching to be. When using these techniques, use a thread type and colour to match your original stitching. In these examples, I use a contrasting colour so that you can see the repairs.

Using hand stitching

Sometimes you just don't want to get your machine out and rethread it to the right colour so if the problem is small then you can fix it with hand sewing. This isn't the most secure way to fix broken stitches and doesn't offer any elasticity so don't use this technique if the stitching will be placed in tension when worn as it is likely that the stitching will break again.

1 Pull any machined needle threads through to the wrong side of your work. For extra security, tie these off with a knot if the threads are long enough (or see step 6).

2 Thread a hand sewing needle with thread to match your original stitching and tie a knot in one end of the thread.

3 Leaving the knot on the wrong side of the fabric, bring the needle to the right side three or four stitches away from the gap.

4 Stitch over the machine stitches, keeping the stitch length correct and then continue, sewing across the gap and then over the next three or four machine stitches.

5 Repeat steps 3 and 4 for each line of stitching that needs repairing.

6 Finish off your stitching on the wrong side, taking a few stitches through the looper threads and wrapping the broken threads from step 1 if you were unable to tie these off.

Using machine stitching

1 Pull any machined needle threads through to the wrong side of your work. For extra security, tie these off with a knot if the threads are long enough.

2 Make a test to check that the stitch length is correct to match your project.

3 Position the project fabric under the presser foot, align the needles to the stitching line, three or four stitches before the gap in the stitching. Use a clear foot to make it much easier to see where you're stitching or use the raised marks on the presser foot to indicate the stitching lines.

4 Turn the handwheel to lower the needles and make sure they are correctly positioned.

5 Make two or three stitches into the fabric using the handwheel.

6 Press down on the foot pedal to cover the gap in the stitching and continue to stitch over the next three or four stitches.

7 Finish off your stitching using one of the techniques described on pages 33–37.

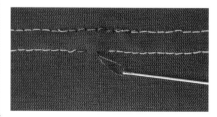

If the old needle holes can be seen in the gap of stitching, use these to keep your stitching aligned.

Using machine stitching will provide more secure stitches and a neater finish.

REMOVING AND REPLACING A SECTION OF STITCHING

If you don't want to remove and rework all the stitching on your project, you can just remove the stitches you're not happy with and replace them. These threads may come away easily or it might take a bit longer to remove them.

Method 1: Unravelling the looper thread

This is the quickest way to remove unwanted thread and makes it easy to clear up stray thread ends. Turn your work so the straight stitches of the needle threads are facing you.

1 Use a quick unpick tool, snips or pair of small scissors to cut through the needle threads at the beginning and the end of the section you wish to replace. Make sure the broken needle threads stay on the top of the fabric.

2 Turn your work to the other side so the looper stitches are facing you. Cut through the threads at the start and end of the faulty section in the same place as you cut the threads on the other side.

3 Starting from the finishing end of the stitches (the place that would have been stitched last when you made your seam or hem), pull on the looper thread – this should unravel easily from the fabric.

4 Turn your work and pull on the needle threads one at a time, pulling these out of the fabric.

5 Replace your stitching using the method described on page 40 for fixing a broken section of stitching by machine.

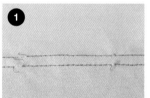
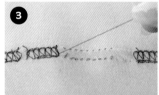
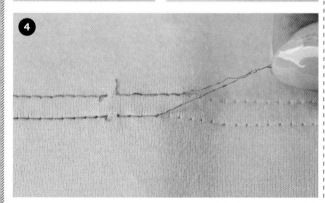

Method 2: Removing the needle threads

Sometimes the threads just won't budge, particularly textured thread such as woolly nylon, so a different approach may have to be used.

1 Follow steps 1–3 of method 1 then cut through the loops all the way along the length of the faulty section. Take care not to cut through your fabric.

2 From the needle-thread side, pull on the needle threads to pull these out of the fabric.

3 Using a lint roller, remove any looper thread from the wrong side and pull the remaining needle threads through to the wrong side of the fabric to make sure threads are locked and won't unravel.

4 Replace your stitching using the method described on page 40 for fixing a broken section of stitching by machine.

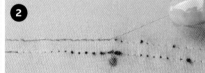

FABRIC NOT CAUGHT WHEN HEMMING

This will happen at some stage when you're using a coverstitch machine. You stitch all the way around your hem with a perfect line of stitching on the right side, only to realize that on the wrong side there's a section that hasn't caught the fabric properly and the hem is coming undone. If it's only a small section and there's nothing wrong with the rest of the stitching, hand stitch it in place. No one will know and it will look perfect from the right side. If it's a bigger problem then you may have to unravel those stitches using the methods described above and sew the hem again.

Adjusting the coverstitch settings

To get the most from your machine you will need to know how to make a number of adjustments to a variety of settings in order to produce the perfect finish. Creating a balanced stitch using a range of different threads and fabric types will take practice. It is really important to test out stitch settings on fabric scraps to make sure these are correct for your chosen fabric and thread before continuing with a project. This will also ensure that you don't have to spend as much time unpicking your work.

ADJUSTABLE SETTINGS

There are generally five settings on all coverstitch machines that can be adjusted to fine-tune your stitching:

1 Thread tensions

2 Stitch length

3 Stitch width

4 Differential feed

5 Foot pressure

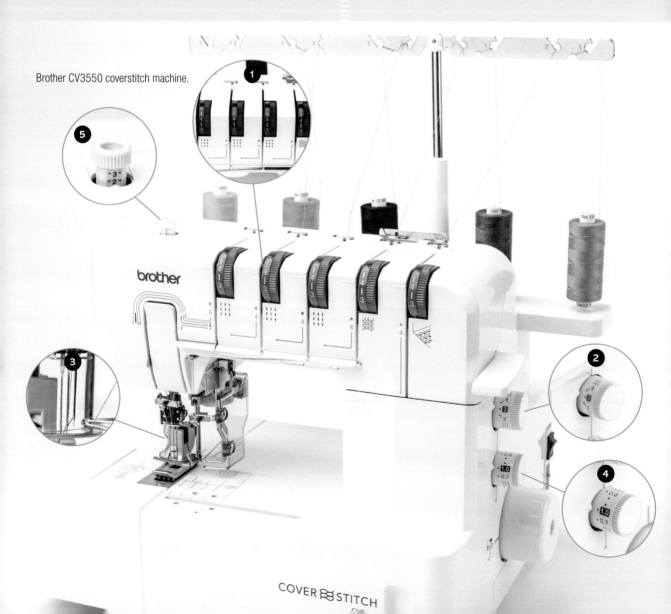

Brother CV3550 coverstitch machine.

COVER ⊗ STITCH

Each of these different settings will be discussed in more detail over the next few pages. There are additional notes on page 186 for suitable stitch length, differential feed and presser-foot pressure for a range of common fabric types.

Note

Multifunction coverstitch and overlocker machines will also have an adjustable cutting width, allowing you to move the upper knife blade away from or towards the needle plate. This feature only needs adjusting when operating the machine as an overlocker to help overcome stitching problems where loops form on the edge of the fabric or where the fabric edge becomes rolled within the stitch. This setting is not discussed further in this book since it is not relevant to coverstitching. If your machine has this function, check your machine manual for how to adjust this setting.

DO THE SETTINGS NEED ADJUSTING?

Before starting any project always test your machine using the same thickness and type of fabric that you will be using. Check your stitching, make any corrections to the machine settings and test again until you are happy with the stitch formation before continuing on to your project fabric. Keep a notebook of which settings work best on different fabrics for your machine. Use the following checklist to recognize issues with your stitching.

Does your stitching:

- look correct for your project, or are the stitches too short?

- appear regularly formed, without any gaps or skipped stitches?

- sit flat, without any ridges forming or tunnelling when creating a coverstitch?

- sit flat without stretching, gathering or causing the fabric to twist out of shape?

- look balanced without any irregular loops forming on either side of the fabric?

- allow the fabric to stretch, or are there too few stitches for the amount of fabric?

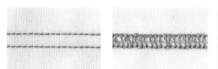

Short stitches: front (left) and back (right).

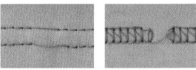

Skipped stitches: front (left) and back (right).

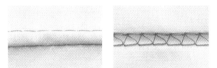

Tunnelling: front (left) and back (right).

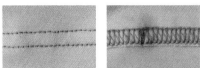

Wavy hem: front (left) and back (right).

Irregular stitching: front (left) and back (right).

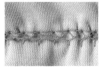

Bunched fabric: front (left) and back (right).

If your stitching looks like any of the images above then you will need to adjust your settings. It may be necessary to make more than one adjustment to solve each of the issues. It is also possible that the issue may be caused by the thread, how the machine is threaded and also the needles that you are using. More details are given on adjusting machine settings over the next few pages but you may also need to consult the troubleshooting section on page 182 if problems persist.

Thread tension

Perfecting the tension settings is essential for creating a well-balanced stitch. Your machine will have adjustable tension dials for each of the threads, either as lay-in style dials on the top front of the machine or protruding dials on the front of the machine. These dials control how tightly or loosely the thread is held and fed through the machine. On some machines the thread tensions are adjusted automatically according to the selected stitch programme but they can be fine-tuned manually using the tension dials. Unfortunately, tension issues can occur as a result of other factors, not just the settings on these dials. The type and quality of thread, how the machine is threaded and the type of fabric being used can all cause tension-setting problems.

SETTING THE TENSION DIALS

Turn the dials to the neutral settings specified in your manual and test on non-stretch medium-weight fabric before trying out other fabrics. Your machine should manage medium-weight fabrics without any puckering or tunnelling so it will be easier to assess whether the tension on the threads is correct.

Neutral settings may be indicated on the dial as N or the number for neutral settings may be in a box or another colour. The tension setting may be different for the looper and needles so don't assume they should all be the same. For example, on the Janome CoverPro 2000CPX, the basic tension setting for the needles is 4 and the looper is 3. To create a balanced stitch for different fabric or thread types you will need to adjust this tension setting. Turn the dial to a higher number to tighten the thread and to a lower number to loosen the thread.

> ### Tips
> - When balancing the stitch, you may need to tighten the needle thread(s) and loosen the looper thread or vice versa. Only change one tension setting at a time so you can see what it does.
> - Light-weight fabrics may require a looser tension setting for the needles and a higher tension setting for the looper to create a balanced stitch and avoid puckering.
> - Heavy-weight fabrics or multiple layers of fabric may require tighter tensions on the needle threads and a looser tension on the looper to achieve a nicely balanced stitch.
> - Heavy or thicker threads may require a looser tension to create a balanced stitch.
> - When creating a coverstitch with two or three needles you may need to set each needle to a different tension to create a balanced stitch depending on the thickness of fabric and the type of thread used.
> - If you need to adjust your tension dials to the highest or lowest settings to create a balanced stitch, there may be something wrong with your machine or the other settings may be incorrect.

Tension dials on the Janome CoverPro 2000CPX.

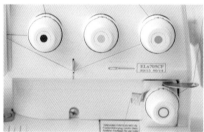

Tension dials on the baby lock BLCS2.

Tension dials on the Juki MCS1800.

Tension dials on the Janome 1200D.

LOOPER TENSION

On some machines the tension dial for the looper thread is inside the looper cover or on the side of the machine. The looper tension dial may use L (low), M (medium) and H (high) rather than a numbered system. For most fabrics and threads the standard setting is M. To loosen the thread set the dial to L and to tighten the thread set the dial to H.

Some combination models have a chain-looper dial with specific settings for chain stitch or coverstitch, so make sure this is set within the correct stitch settings.

Some machines have an additional tension-adjustment lever on the front of the machine or in the looper cover for fine-tuning of the looper tension when working with different fabrics or non-standard threads.

While you get to grips with your machine it may be useful to change the thread colours for each of the needles and looper. In the following examples, the thread colours match the colours of the numbers on the thread dials so it is easier to see the difference in the thread tensions. Not all machines require the same adjustments, so this information is purely guidance to help you achieve the right settings for your machine. Start with the tension-setting checklist below and if you need to alter the tension do this one thread at a time so you can keep track of what you're doing, changing the tension, testing, then changing again if necessary until the desired stitch is formed.

If changing the tension doesn't fix the problem, another setting could be out of place. Read the next few pages about machine settings, the 'Checklist before stitching' on page 30 and the troubleshooting section on page 182 to diagnose the issue.

Janome CoverPro 2000CPX tension-adjustment lever.

Janome 1200D tension dial.

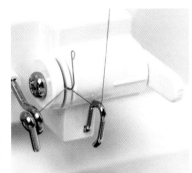

Brother CV3550 tension-adjustment lever inside the looper cover.

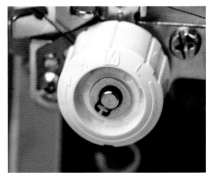

Juki MCS1800 tension dial, showing 'L', 'M' and 'H'.

TENSION-SETTING CHECKLIST

Make sure you've done each of the following before changing the tension settings on your machine – it might be a threading issue or lint build-up that's causing the problem.

• Are you using high-quality threads? If your thread looks fuzzy with lots of short strands sticking out it is most likely poor quality which will cause irregular stitching.

• Are the threads sitting correctly in the tension discs? Hold the thread on either side of the discs and pull in a 'flossing' motion until you can feel some resistance on the thread.

• Are all the threads running through the specified thread guides? Check the threading diagram and/or machine

manual to ensure that the machine is threaded correctly. For thicker threads your manual may suggest bypassing some of the threading guides, while for slippery threads you may need to use extra guides.

• Is your machine clean and lint free? A build-up of fluff in your machine can cause tension issues – use a small brush to clean any dust or lint build-up from between the tension discs. Thick thread such as upholstery or topstitching thread, or even dental floss can also be used to clean between the tension discs.

• Is the thread feeding from the spool correctly? Check that it isn't caught and will feed evenly as the machine is in operation. Use thread mats, nets and/or caps as necessary to help.

ADJUSTING TENSIONS FOR CHAIN STITCH

To create a chain stitch, one needle and the chain looper are used. When the stitch is correctly balanced it will look like the images right, top. Some machines specify which needle position to use to create a chain stitch so check your manual to make sure you are using the correct one.

Needle thread This thread should appear as a straight row of stitching on the right side of the fabric and as a small loop wrapped around the looper thread on the wrong side.

If the thread is too tight it will pucker the fabric and the looper thread may become visible from the top side of the fabric, as shown right, centre.

If the thread is too loose then the stitch on the right side of the fabric will be uneven and loops may form. The needle thread will also form large loops on the wrong side of the fabric, as shown right, bottom.

Looper thread This thread should appear as a chain on the wrong side of the fabric. If the thread is too tight it can pucker the fabric and make the needle stitching appear uneven. If the thread is too loose, larger loops of thread will form on the wrong side.

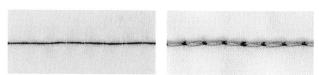
Correctly balanced stitches: front (left) and back (right).

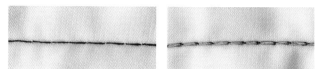
Needle thread too tight: front (left) and back (right).

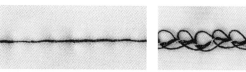
Needle thread too loose: front (left) and back (right).

ADJUSTING TENSIONS FOR COVERSTITCH

To create a coverstitch, two needles and the chain looper are used. When the stitch is correctly balanced it will look like the images right, top, as either a narrow coverstitch or a wide coverstitch, depending on the settings available and which needle positions are used.

Needle thread These threads should appear as straight parallel rows of stitching on the right side of the fabric and as small loops wrapped around the looper thread on the wrong side.

If the threads are too tight it will pucker the fabric and the looper thread may become visible from the top side of the fabric, as shown right, centre.

If the needle threads are too loose then the stitches on the right side of the fabric will be uneven and loops may form. The needle threads will also form larger loops on the wrong side of the fabric, as shown right, bottom.

Looper thread This thread should appear as a row of rectangles with diagonals on the wrong side of the fabric. If the thread is too tight this can pucker the fabric and make the needle stitching appear uneven or cause tunnelling where ridges are formed between the two lines of needle stitches. Tunnelling may also be caused if other settings are incorrect, see the troubleshooting section on page 182. If the thread is too loose, larger loops of thread will form on the wrong side.

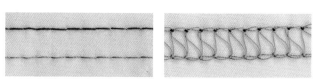
Correctly balanced stitches: front (left) and back (right).

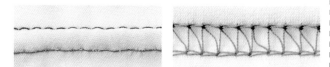
Needle threads too tight: front (left) and back (right).

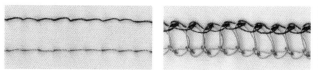
Needle threads too loose: front (left) and back (right).

ADJUSTING TENSIONS FOR TRIPLE COVERSTITCH

To create a triple coverstitch, three needles and the chain looper are used. When the stitch is correctly balanced it will look like the images right, top.

Needle thread These threads should appear as three straight parallel rows of stitching on the right side of the fabric and as small loops wrapped around the looper thread on the wrong side.

   If the threads are too tight it will pucker the fabric and the looper thread may become visible from the top side of the fabric, as shown right, centre.

   If the threads are too loose then the stitches on the right side of the fabric will be uneven and loops may form. The needle threads will also form larger loops on the wrong side of the fabric, as shown right, bottom.

Looper thread This thread should appear as two rows of rectangles with diagonals on the wrong side of the fabric. If the thread is too tight this can pucker the fabric and make the needle stitching appear uneven. If the thread is too loose larger loops of thread will form on the wrong side.

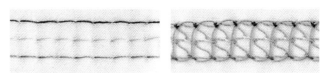

Correctly balanced stitches: front (left) and back (right).

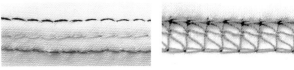

Needle threads too tight: front (left) and back (right).

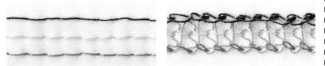

Needle threads too loose: front (left) and back (right).

ADJUSTING TENSIONS FOR TOP COVERSTITCH

To create a top coverstitch, two or three needles, a top cover spreader and the chain looper are used. When the stitch is correctly balanced it will look like the images right, top, as a narrow, wide or triple coverstitch, depending on which needle positions are used. (The image shows triple top coverstitch.)

   Make sure your machine is stitching a balanced coverstitch first, before including the top-cover thread. See the guidance above for any necessary adjustments to the coverstitch.

Top-cover thread This thread should appear as horizontal rows of stitching between the needle threads, crossing the centre needle thread if three needles are used. If the thread is too tight this can pucker the fabric and pull on the needle threads. If the thread is too loose then the thread will appear loopy, extending beyond the needle threads on the right side of the fabric.

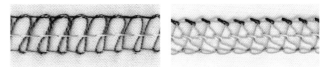

Correctly balanced stitches: front (left) and back (right).

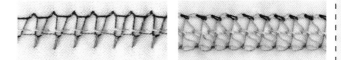

Top-cover thread too tight: front (left) and back (right).

Top-cover thread too loose: front (left) and back (right).

Tip

It is usual for the threads to appear a little loose on the wrong side of the fabric. Coverstitching should be able to stretch, so the slight slackness of thread will allow for this.

Stitch length

Changing the stitch length is very easy to do, just like on a regular sewing machine. On all machines you will find a stitch-length dial but the range of this will depend on the model. Most machines will be able to perform a stitch length of 2–4mm (¹/₁₆–³/₁₆in) and some machines will be able to produce a shorter or longer stitch.

STITCH-LENGTH CONTROL

The position of your stitch-length control may be on the front of the machine, on one of the sides or inside the looper cover. Most dials will be numbered and the number will indicate the length of the stitch in millimetres, meaning that the higher the number, the longer the stitch length.

The majority of machine manuals will recommend a stitch length of 3–4mm (⅛–³/₁₆in). Some stitch-length dials will have a marker on them to indicate the stitch length to choose – this may be for a specific type of stitch, so check your manual and don't be afraid to alter the stitch length to achieve the look you want. The length of stitch that you choose may be determined by your project, the type of fabric or the type of thread you are working with.

Tips for the perfect stitch length

- Use a shorter stitch length for light-weight fabrics and a longer stitch length for heavier fabrics.
- Using a longer stitch length may result in less stretch in your stitches.
- If you are stitching through a number of layers of fabric or using thicker threads, a longer stitch length will probably be required.
- If you are having problems with the fabric feeding through the machine, a longer stitch length can help.
- If you're using a longer stitch length, you may also need to decrease the tension on the threads to avoid any puckering.
- If you're using a shorter stitch length you may need to increase tensions on the threads to avoid irregular or loopy stitching.
- Always test your stitching on a scrap piece of fabric until you have perfected your stitch.

Huskylock S21.

Juki MCS1800.

Brother CV3550.

baby lock BLCS2.

Janome 1200D.

Stitch width

If your machine can create a triple coverstitch using three needles and the chain looper thread, you will be able to set your machine to create two different widths of coverstitch using two of the needles and the looper thread (see page 57). Generally, the width of the stitch is 2.5 or 3mm (⅛in) for the narrow setting and 5 or 6mm (¼in) for the wide setting.

STITCH-WIDTH CONTROL

To alter the stitch width, choose either the left and middle needle or middle and right needle for the narrow setting and choose the left and right needles or all three needles for the widest setting. The narrow setting is best for fine and light-weight fabrics and the wide setting can be used for heavier or more stable fabrics. The setting you choose will depend on the look of the stitch that you want. Do experiment until you achieve the desired result.

REMOVING OR REPLACING NEEDLES

Your machine will come with all the necessary tools to remove and replace needles. There will either be a small screwdriver or an Allen key to loosen and tighten the needle-clamp screws. You may also have a needle holder to hold the needles instead of using your fingers.

Tips

- If you have tunnelling when creating a wide coverstitch and the troubleshooting section on page 182 doesn't help, try using a narrower setting for a flatter result.
- Some manuals recommend using the centre and left needle for the narrow stitch-width setting.
- Always remove needles that you are not using from the machine.
- When replacing needles, always push them up into their highest position before tightening the screw on the needle clamp.
- Each needle will sit at a different height to the one next to it. This is normal – don't try to align them.
- Some multifunction machines have a stitch-width dial or the manual will state that the width of the stitch can be changed by altering the cutting width. This only affects overlock stitches that are created when the cutting blade is engaged and cannot be used as a method to alter the width of coverstitches. The gap between the left and right needles determines the width of the coverstitch.

Using the needle holder to remove needles

1 Lower the presser foot and raise the needles to their highest position by turning the handwheel. Unthread the needle you want to remove.

2 Place the needle holder under the needle that is unthreaded. Slide the needle holder up to the top of the needle.

3 Loosen the needle-clamp screw for the needle you are holding. Loosen the screw just enough to remove the needle but not so much so as to remove the screw.

4 Lower the needle holder and remove the needle.

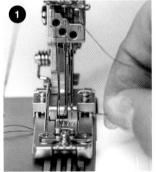
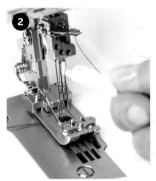
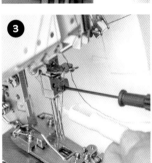
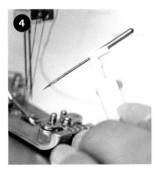

If you're worried about dropping the needle into the machine, place a piece of fabric under the presser foot or take a small piece of fabric and push the needle into it before removing.

Some machines have a needle drop drawer at the bottom of the machine, so if the needle drops when you're trying to remove or replace it, it will be in the drawer.

To replace a needle using the needle holder, follow the instructions above in reverse, making sure that the flat part of the needle is at the back before inserting it into the needle holder. Make sure the needles are pushed up into their highest position before tightening the screw. (See notes on maintenance on page 188.)

Needle drop drawer on baby lock BLCS2.

Scrap fabric placed under the presser foot.

Needle holder on end of brush from baby lock BLCS2 and needle holder on compensation plate.

Differential feed

Underneath the presser foot of a coverstitch machine you'll find two sets of feed-dog teeth: the front teeth feed the fabric into the machine and the back teeth take the fabric from under the presser foot, out of the machine. The differential-feed control alters the speed of the feed-dog teeth and this can be used to alleviate or accentuate waves or puckers in your fabric.

The differential-feed control will generally have a setting from 0.5 to 2, but this may be more or less wide ranging, depending on the brand and model. The numbers indicate a ratio between the speed of the front and the back teeth. There will be a neutral setting where the front and back teeth operate at the same speed, labelled as either N or 1. The speed of the back teeth cannot be altered but the speed of the front teeth can be increased or decreased depending on the effect that you want to achieve. If the control is moved to a lower number the front teeth will move more slowly, feeding fabric into the machine at a slower rate. If the control is moved to a higher number the front teeth will move more quickly, feeding the fabric into the machine at a faster rate. Changes to the differential feed will have the most dramatic results on bias-cut fabrics, light-weight and stretch fabrics.

Different settings will be needed for different fabrics and threads, and will vary between models and brands of machine. You may need to operate the differential-feed control in conjunction with the presser-foot pressure and the stitch length to correct any stitching issues.

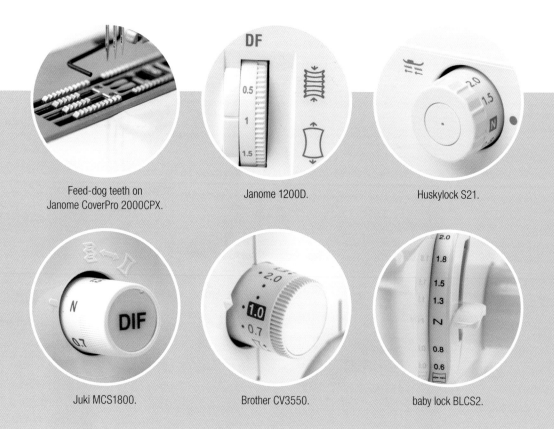

Feed-dog teeth on
Janome CoverPro 2000CPX.

Janome 1200D.

Huskylock S21.

Juki MCS1800.

Brother CV3550.

baby lock BLCS2.

Note

Differential-feed settings for coverstitching will differ to those required for overlocking. Don't assume that you need to increase the differential feed when working with stretch fabrics, as you would do when overlocking. Always test first: a differential-feed setting of N or 1 will create the perfect stitch on many fabric types and it is more likely that a lower differential-feed setting will be required to maximize stretch.

CREATING A BALANCED STITCH

On most non-stretch medium-weight fabric types, you won't need to alter the differential feed at all. Light-weight non-stretch fabrics may pucker and require a lower differential-feed setting to prevent this. For stretch fabrics, a higher differential feed may be required to stop the fabric distorting out of shape and appearing wavy but always start with a neutral setting and test this before making any adjustments.

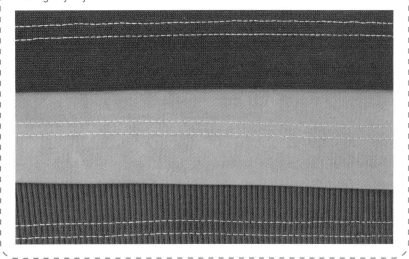

AVOIDING OR CREATING WAVES

If your stitched fabric appears wavy, ruffled or stretched out of shape then the differential feed may be set too low. The fabric is being fed into the machine too slowly, causing it to be stretched as it is stitched.

To solve this problem and flatten the fabric, turn the differential-feed control to a higher number to make the front feed-dog teeth move more quickly. It may also help to reduce the presser-foot pressure and increase the stitch length.

If you want to accentuate the appearance of waves in the fabric to create a decorative effect, lower the differential feed, lower the stitch length and increase the presser-foot pressure. This technique will work best with light-weight, bias-cut or stretch fabrics. Pull the fabric as you feed it into the machine to add more fluting to your stitched fabric.

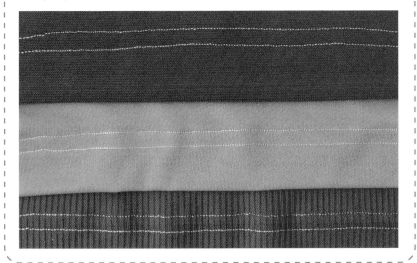

Tips

- Keep the differential feed set to 1 or N when working with easy-to-handle non-stretch fabrics.

- Don't pull the fabric as it enters or leaves the needles as this will cause the fabric to distort and create a wavy effect.

- If your stitching appears wavy, increase the differential feed to a higher number.

- If your stitching appears puckered or gathered, decrease the differential feed to a lower number.

- Using water-soluble or fusible stabilizers can help to prevent hems and seams from distorting as you stitch.

- Lowering the differential feed can help to solve the problem of tunnelling (where a ridge is formed between the needles when sewing a coverstitch) and/or roping (where the hem or binding appears twisted). See additional notes on page 182, 'Troubleshooting'.

AVOIDING OR CREATING GATHERS

If your fabric appears gathered or puckered once it is stitched then the differential feed may be set too high. The fabric is being fed into the machine too quickly causing the fabric to bunch up and the stitches to gather.

To solve this problem, turn the differential feed to a lower number to slow down the front feed-dog teeth. It may also help to increase the presser-foot pressure and reduce the stitch length.

To increase the amount of gathers in your fabric, to create a ruffle, for example, turn the differential feed to the highest setting, reduce the presser-foot pressure and increase the stitch length. The most pronounced gathers will be formed on light-weight fabrics.

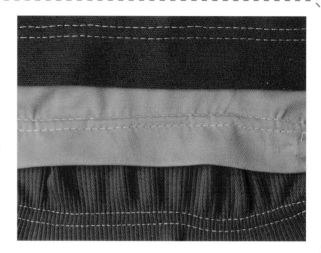

MAXIMIZING ON STRETCH

When you are using a coverstitch machine you must also consider the effect that differential feed has on the amount of stretch that your stitches will have. This is particularly important when considering opening edges of stretch garments at necklines, waistlines, armholes and leg holes. If there are more stitches per centimetre, the stitched fabric will be able to stretch more.

Using a high differential feed for stretch fabrics may mean that the stitching line and fabric appears flat but it will have less stretch. When the differential-feed dial is set above 1, the front teeth will speed up and move the fabric more quickly through the machine. This will force more fabric into each stitch giving less stitches per centimetre and not leaving much room for the fabric to stretch. Conversely, using a low differential feed might create a wavy finish in some cases, but it will allow for more stretch. If the speed of the front feed-dog teeth is lowered then this holds the fabric back, feeding it more slowly into the machine and pushing less fabric into each stitch, giving more stitches per centimetre and allowing the fabric to stretch more.

AVOIDING TWISTED HEMS

When sewing two layers of fabric, either as a single folded piece of fabric or as two separate pieces, the bottom layer of fabric may move more quickly through the machine than the top layer. This is because the feed-dog teeth have more grip on the bottom layer of fabric and the top layer of fabric is held back by the presser foot. If you are stitching a hem on a folded piece of fabric, this conflicting movement of layers can cause the hem to appear twisted, an effect known as 'roping'. To avoid this, lower the differential feed to slow down the bottom layer of fabric. A lower presser-foot pressure can also help to allow the top layer of fabric to feed through the machine more easily.

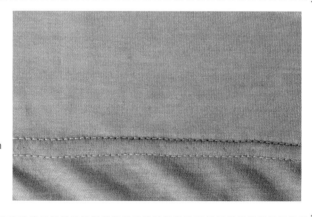

Presser-foot pressure

The foot-pressure control will most likely be found on the top left of your machine, above the presser foot. For the majority of medium-weight fabrics this setting won't need to be changed but, if necessary, pressure can be altered to help your machine to feed heavy- or light-weight fabrics more evenly and easily through the machine.

PRESSER-FOOT PRESSURE DIAL

The presser-foot pressure dial may be numbered, labelled as L, M, H or simply as +/–. Pressure can be increased by turning the dial to a higher number (H or +) and decreased by turning the dial to a lower number (L or –).

The presser-foot pressure will be set at the factory to work with medium-weight fabrics and may need to be adjusted for heavier fabrics or bulky hems (turning the dial to a higher pressure) or for light-weight fabrics (turning the dial to a lower pressure).

This dial can also be used in conjunction with the differential-feed control to alleviate or accentuate waves in the fabric. If your fabric appears puckered or gathered, turn the presser-foot pressure to a higher number; if your fabric appears wavy and stretched out of shape turn the pressure to a lower number.

Tips for using presser-foot pressure

- Increasing the presser-foot pressure can help to stop skipped stitches.
- Increasing the presser-foot pressure may also help to stop tunnelling, where a ridge forms between the needle threads when sewing a coverstitch.
- Decreasing the presser-foot pressure can help to stop roping, where the hem or binding appears twisted.

- For machines without a numbered dial it can be difficult to know where the neutral setting is or where it was you started from before making any adjustments. To help with this, measure the height of the presser-foot pressure dial, measuring from the top of the machine to the top of the dial and keep a note of the measurement that works best for you for the different types of fabrics that you work with. The factory setting for the Janome CoverPro 2000CPX (pictured above) to be used for medium-weight fabrics is a presser-foot pressure dial height of 1cm (⅜in) or where the first ridge on the dial is in line with the machine casing.
- Use a coin to turn this dial to increase or decrease presser-foot pressure.

Juki MCS1800.

Britannia CS4000.

Huskylock S21.

Brother CV3550.

baby lock BLCS2.

Janome 1200D.

Stitches

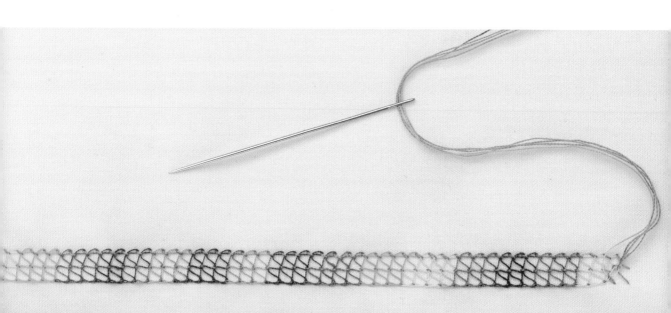

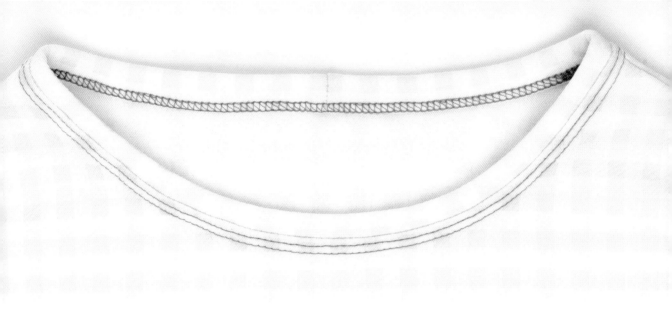

You've threaded up your machine, you know what all the dials and levers do and so it's time to explore the stitch settings. The reason you've bought this machine is because it can sew coverstitch and chain stitch, right? But can it do anything else? The basic models will create coverstitch using just two needles but on most models, you will be able to vary the width of your coverstitch and also sew with three needles. There may even be an adapter to allow you to create top coverstitch. If your machine is a multifunction overlocker and coverstitch machine you'll be able to sew a combination of chain stitch and overlock stitches. Over the next few pages you will find out what each stitch looks like, ideas for what you can use it for and how to set up your machine for the best results.

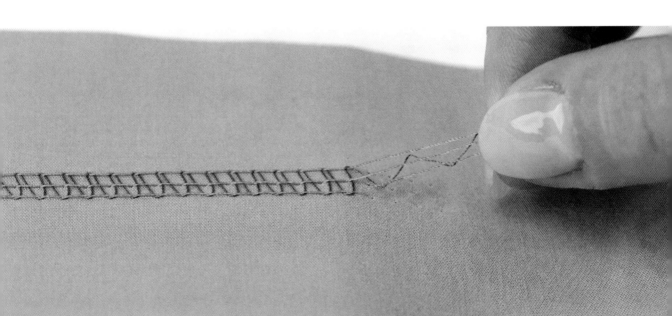

Overview of stitches

The variety of stitches that are available to you will depend on the brand and model of your machine. The most basic coverstitch machines will sew with up to three threads, combining one or two needles and a looper, whereas the most advanced machine will sew with up to eight threads, combining a triple coverstitch with a four-thread overlocking stitch. This section covers the stitches that are available on the majority of machines and explains them in more detail over the next few pages.

CHAIN STITCH

A simple, durable and flexible stitch that uses one needle and the looper. This stitch can be created on all types of coverstitch machine.

It can be used for machine-tacking seams, sewing seams that have a little stretch, attaching binding and elastics, topstitching hems and decorative stitching. It can easily unravel if not fastened correctly at the end which may be an advantage when tacking seams but a disadvantage if the stitch is to be permanent.

For permanent stitching, you must tie off the ends by using, for example, the swipe, snip and lock technique on page 34.

FIVE-THREAD SAFETY STITCH

This stitch is a combination of chain stitch and an overlocked stitch. The chain stitch uses one needle and the chain looper, while the overlocked stitch uses one needle and the upper and lower loopers. This stitch can only be created on a combination machine. Depending on the model of machine, a variety of stitch widths can be created.

This stitch is extremely durable and can be used to sew and finish seams on any fabric but is best used on medium- to heavy-weight woven fabrics and seams that will come under some tension.

COVERSTITCH

Narrow coverstitch

This stitch uses two needles and the looper. This narrow version can only be created on machines that use up to three needles.

It can be used for hemming for both woven and knitted fabrics and is particularly good for fine knitted fabrics such as single jersey. It is also used for attaching elastics or bindings, for decorative topstitching on seams, to create pintucks and to make faux ribbing.

Wide coverstitch

This stitch uses the looper and two needles set at their widest positions. All machines will produce a coverstitch of at least 5mm (¼in).

It can be used for hemming for both woven and medium- to heavy-weight knitted fabrics such as double knits and sweatshirt fleece. It is also used for creating belt loops, attaching elastics or bindings, for decorative topstitching on seams, lapped seam construction, to create pintucks and to make faux ribbing.

Triple coverstitch

This stitch uses three needles and the looper. It can only be produced on a three-needle machine.

It can be used for hemming a range of fabrics, topstitching seams, attaching elastic or binding, creating a mock flatlock stitch and for decorative stitching.

TOP COVERSTITCH

Narrow top coverstitch

This stitch uses two needles, the top-cover spreader and the looper. It can only be produced on specific top-coverstitch machines.

It can be used for hemming a range of fabrics, creating a mock flatlock stitch and decorative topstitching.

Wide top coverstitch

This stitch uses two needles set to their widest positions, the top-cover spreader and the looper. It can only be produced on specific top-coverstitch machines.

It can be used for hemming on both woven and medium- to heavy-weight knitted fabrics such as double knits and sweatshirt fleece. It can also be used for creating a mock flatlock stitch, for belt loops and for decorative topstitching.

Triple top coverstitch

This stitch uses three needles, the top-cover spreader and the looper. It can only be produced on specific top-coverstitch machines.

It can be used for hemming on a range of fabrics, creating a mock flatlock stitch, belt loops and decorative top-stitching.

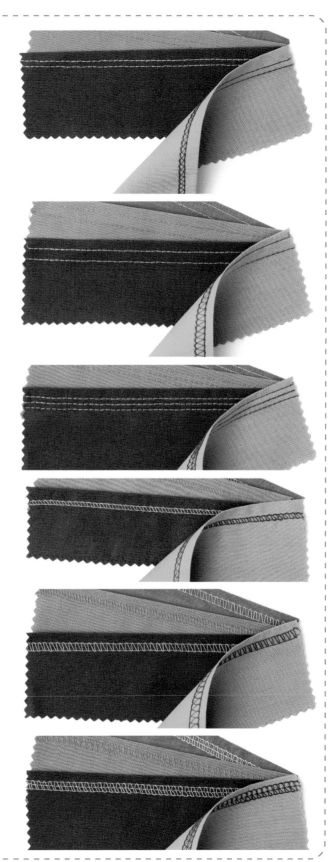

CHAIN STITCH

This two-thread stitch has a range of different uses from sewing seams to decorative stitching. The stitch is formed with one needle and the looper. On the right side it looks like a straight stitch and on the reverse side the looper thread forms a chain which can be used decoratively (see opposite).

Using the chain stitch

There are a variety of uses for chain stitch which are often overlooked. For a start, you can use it in place of a regular sewing machine to create **seams** and **hems**. The bonus of using chain stitch is that this will give a little stretch, so not only can it be used to make seams on woven fabrics but you can create seams on stretch fabrics that will actually stretch. The stretch properties of the stitch mean it's also great for attaching knit bindings and elastics around openings.

Chain stitch is perfect for **tacking** fabrics together as it can be easily unravelled if the stitching is no longer needed. If you want the stitch to be permanent, tie off the threads at the end of the stitch line to avoid it coming undone (see page 34).

Topstitching using chain stitch works brilliantly on a range of fabrics as the two sets of feed-dog teeth make it much easier for medium- and heavy-weight fabrics to pass through the machine. Chain stitch can also be used in a decorative way to create gathers and ruffles or to embellish and create patterns on your fabric using either side of the stitch. All of these techniques will be discussed in more detail throughout this book, and see 'Ideas to try' opposite.

Special feet

You may be able to purchase a specific foot for chain stitching that helps to produce the perfect stitch or you may find a clear-view presser foot will enable straighter and more accurate stitching lines.

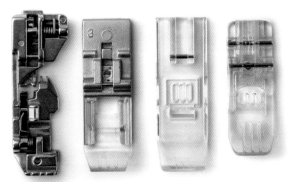

From left to right: Chain stitch foot for Juki machines; clear view coverstitch foot for Janome Coverpro models; clear foot for Britannia coverstitch machines; clear foot for baby lock machines.

Tips

- If you're using the seam guidelines on your machine, they may give the distance from the right needle so check which of the needle positions gives the correct measurement.

- You can create your own stitching guidelines using masking or painter's tape.

- If your chain stitch doesn't look right, follow the checklist on page 30. The most common error is incorrect threading.

- Keep your eyes on the stitching guidelines and not the needle, to keep your stitching straight.

Setting up your machine for chain stitch

To create chain stitch on a stand-alone coverstitch machine just select one of the needle positions and remove any other needles that are not in use to avoid any issues with stitching. (See page 49, on how to remove and replace the needles.) Your manual may specify which needle position to use for the chain stitch or you may be able to choose any position with perfect results. Check your manual for other specific machine settings, for example, you may need to use a shorter stitch length or lower tension settings for a chain stitch.

1 Remove any needles that will not be in use.

2 Pull out any of the threads that won't be used or, to save time on rethreading later, just pull these out as far as the tension discs so they won't get in the way.

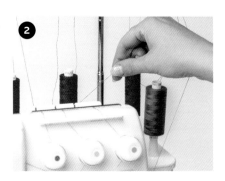

Ideas to try: chain stitch

Many of these techniques are demonstrated later in the book.

A Create decorative pintucks by stitching narrow folds of fabric in parallel and perpendicular rows.

B Topstitch bindings – chain stitch looks like a regular machine stitch from the right side but will stretch.

C Use the thread chains for button loops – chain without fabric if your machine allows for this or stitch onto water-soluble fabric.

D Use thread chains to form a fringe on a scarf, shawl or blanket.

E Use chain stitch for detailed stitching on appliqué projects such as bags and cushions.

F Use a long machine stitch and high differential feed to create a gathered or ruffle effect.

G Use elastic in the looper to produce a shirring effect, shown here on the neckline of a child's top.

H French seams can be easily created using chain stitch. This type of seam is particularly useful for sheer fabrics or linings.

I Sew from the wrong side to use the chain side of the stitch as a decorative quilting technique.

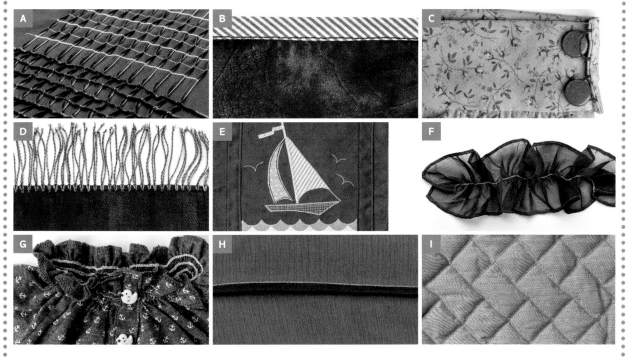

3 Place the fabric under the presser foot so the needles are above the fabric and lower the presser foot.

4 Take the first stitch with the handwheel and then put your foot on the pedal and stitch. Finish your stitch using one of the techniques on pages 33–37 (finishing and securing ends).

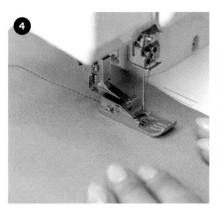

If your machine is a combination overlocker and coverstitch machine, check your manual on how to set up the machine. You'll probably need to move the needle to one of the chaining or coverstitch positions and also use the chaining looper instead of the overlocker's lower looper. Check the order of threading and follow the guidance for your model. See 'Threading for combination machines' on page 29.

COVERSTITCH

This stitch will create a professional-looking hem that will move and stretch with your fabric, transforming the way you sew with knitted fabrics. You can use this stitch on any type of fabric to form parallel lines of stitches on the right side with a zigzag or overlock style pattern on the wrong side of the fabric. The stitch is made with two or three needles and the chain looper. If your machine can hold up to three needles you'll be able to produce a coverstitch of differing widths, depending on the position of the needles.

Using the coverstitch

As this stitch will stretch it is commonly used to **finish hems** on stretch fabrics and for **attaching elastics or bindings** to openings, but the coverstitch also has a number of creative uses beyond these. You can use this stitch for **lapped seam construction** where two fabrics are overlapped and then stitched in place, ideal for bulky fabrics or those that don't fray. The stitch can be used for **topstitching**, showing either side of the stitch on the right side of the fabric. The coverstitch also has a wide range of decorative uses such as creating pintucks, adjusting the thread tensions to draw in the stitches and produce a raised effect. A similar **trapunto effect** can be created by stitching over cord or inserting cord into the loops on the wrong side of the stitch. You can even use the coverstitch to create **faux ribbing**, producing a ribbed fabric for necklines and cuffs to perfectly match your garment fabric (see page 106). In addition to all of these techniques you can also utilize the stitch to create **belt loops**, replicating those found in ready-to-wear clothing. All of these techniques will be discussed and shown in more detail throughout this book.

Special feet

The foot that comes with your machine is designed to be used when sewing coverstitch. It has markings on the front to show the needle positions which will help you guide your fabric. For a better view and even more accurate stitching lines, try a clear-view foot or centre-guide foot.

Tips

- If you're having difficulties in perfecting the setting of a narrow coverstitch, try using the left and centre needle positions.

- If you're using the stitching guidelines on your machine, be sure to check which needle these markings are measuring from.

- If your stitch doesn't look right follow the 'Checklist before stitching' on page 30. The most common error is incorrect threading.

Centre-guide foot for Janome models.

Standard foot for Juki MCS1800.

Setting up your machine for coverstitch

On a stand-alone coverstitch machine, select the two or three needle positions that you require and remove any other needle that is not in use to avoid any issues with stitching. (See page 49 on how to remove and replace the needles.) Your manual may specify a particular stitch length, tension settings or which needle position to use to produce a narrow coverstitch or you may be able to choose any position with perfect results.

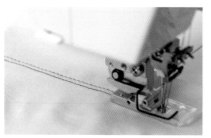
Narrow coverstitch using the left and centre needle positions. On this machine the stitch width will be 3mm (⅛in).

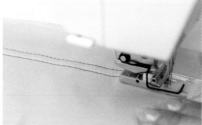
Wide coverstitch using the left and right needle positions. On this machine the stitch width will be 6mm (¼in).

Triple coverstitch using the left, centre and right needle positions. On this machine the stitch width will be 6mm (¼in).

If your machine is a combination overlocker and coverstitch machine then check your manual on how to set up the machine. You'll probably need to move the needles to the chaining or coverstitch positions and use the chaining looper instead of the overlocker's lower looper. Check the order of threading and follow the guidance for your model. See 'Threading for combination machines' on page 29.

Ideas to try: coverstitch

A Triple coverstitch used to create a faux flat-fell seam, by topstitching the seam on a sports top.

B Coverstitch used to topstitch the armhole seam of a child's top.

C Reverse coverstitch used for an appliqué effect, using variegated thread in the looper (see page 92).

D Create a raised or trapunto effect by using the coverstitch and two layers of fabric, filling the channel with cording or stuffing.

E Faux ribbing made by creating pintucks on light-weight knitted fabric to form the lower band of a sweatshirt (see page 106).

F Reverse coverstitch and rayon threads used as a simple embellishment technique on a top.

TOP COVERSTITCH

This type of stitch is only available on a few domestic coverstitch machines. The stitch formed resembles a double-sided coverstitch with parallel lines of stitches on the right side of the fabric and an overlock style pattern on both the top and the underside. The stitch is made with two or three needles, a top-cover spreader and the chain looper. If your machine can create a top coverstitch it will most likely hold up to three needles so you'll be able to produce a top coverstitch of differing widths, depending on the position of the needles.

Using the top coverstitch

This stitch can be used for **hemming** and **topstitching**, just like the regular coverstitch, but you'll have a more decorative effect with a grid pattern on both sides of the fabric. This type of stitch will allow you to experiment with a range of threads, in particular, thicker decorative threads, due to the path that the top looping thread takes as it runs from the spool to the fabric.

Special feet and attachments

If your machine can perform a top coverstitch it will have come with the necessary accessories and special feet. This may include the top-cover foot (if required), spreader device and top-cover guide.

> ### Tip
>
> If your machine doesn't perform a top coverstitch but you want a similar effect, try using reverse coverstitch. Simply stitch from the wrong side of the fabric and you'll see the zigzag pattern of stitching on the right side. See 'Ideas to try: Coverstitch' on page 61, 'Using reverse coverstitch to create a mock flatlock seam' on page 73 and 'Flat construction with reverse coverstitch' on page 75.

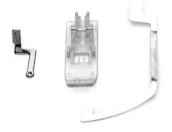

Janome 1200D accessories from left to right: top-cover guide, top-cover foot and top-cover spreader.

Brother CV3550 accessories from left to right: top-cover thread guide and top-cover spreader.

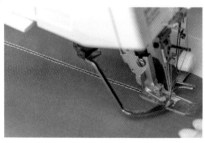

Narrow top coverstitch using the left and centre needle positions. On this machine the stitch width will be 2.5mm (⅛in).

Wide top coverstitch using the left and right needle positions. On this machine the stitch width will be 5mm (¼in).

Triple top coverstitch using the left, centre and right needle positions. On this machine the stitch width will be 5mm (¼in).

Setting up the Janome 1200D for top coverstitch

Follow the instructions on page 60 to set your machine to coverstitch. Attach the additional accessories for top coverstitch as shown below.

1 Attach the blue top-cover foot and keep the presser foot lowered.

2 Place the top-cover spreader in the slot in the spreader holder to the left of the machine and tighten with an Allen key.

3 Loosen the screws that hold the two needles for overlocking and insert the round top-cover guide. Tighten using only the right-hand screw.

4 Open the front cover and pull down the triangle top-cover guide so it sits below the round top cover guide.

5 Thread the looper and the required number of needles. Close the looper cover. Make sure the machine is stitching a coverstitch correctly before threading the top-cover guides and spreader device.

6 To thread the top-cover guides, use the green tension disc and follow the pathway shown in the photo. On this machine there are three different holes on the lower right side of the take-up lever cover. Choose the hole according to the type of thread you are using: upper for decorative stretch threads such as woolly nylon, middle for standard threads and lower for decorative non-stretch threads.

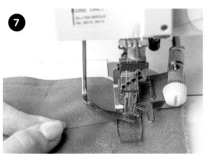

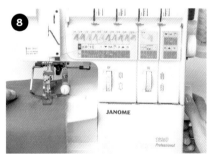

7 Make a test stitch – turn the handwheel towards you to check the spreader device is moving correctly and bring the needles up. Lift up the presser foot and place some fabric underneath. Bring the top-cover thread in front of the needles into the hook on the spreader device as shown.

8 To make the first few stitches, turn the handwheel and hold the thread in the hook. Place your foot on the foot pedal and sew at a low to medium speed.

Tips for Janome 1200D

- Follow the instructions carefully to set up the top-cover spreader and thread guide. If the looper cover is closed and the threading guide moved into position, the top of the sewing or cover table may be scratched.
- Make sure the smaller blue top-coverstitch foot is used on this model as the attachments won't fit with the larger standard presser foot.

Setting up the Brother CV3550 for top coverstitch

This machine should come set up with the top-cover spreader and top-cover guide attached. If not, these accessories can be attached as follows:

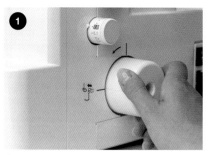

1 Raise the presser foot. Turn the handwheel towards you so the line on the handwheel is in line with the left marker by the handwheel. This will partly lower the needles.

2 Squeeze the grip on the top-cover spreader to open the attachment and from the right side of the machine, clamp this onto the top-cover drive shaft and release your grip.

3 Insert the top-cover thread guide into the slot in the top-cover thread-guide mount. Make sure this is securely pushed into place and can't be easily removed.

4 Thread the looper and the required number of needles. Make sure the machine is stitching a coverstitch correctly before threading the top-cover guides and spreader device.

5 Use the second spool pin from the right and the purple threading route to thread the top-cover thread guide, taking the thread from the spool to the tension disc and through the thread guides as shown in the photo.

6 Turn the handwheel towards you to move the tip of the top-cover spreader to the left.

7 Take the thread from the hook and pull it to the left, take it around the tip of the top cover spreader and under the presser foot from left to right. Lower the presser foot to hold the thread in position.

8 Turn the handwheel towards you slowly to check the top-cover spreader is forming stitches correctly.

9 Put some fabric under the presser foot. Trim the thread next to the presser foot, otherwise it may get tangled as you stitch.

10 Put your foot on the foot pedal and sew at a low to medium speed to form the top coverstitch.

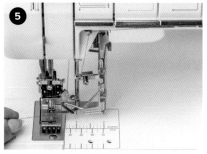

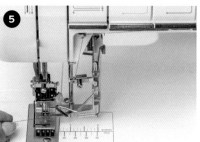

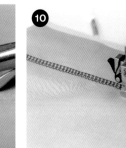

Ideas to try: top coverstitch

A Triple top coverstitch and contrasting thread used for hemming woven fabric.

B Variegated woolly nylon used for topstitching around a neckline.

C Decorative stitching on the ruffle of a pillowcase combining two-needle narrow and three-needle techniques.

D Polyester topstitching thread used to accentuate panel lines on a top.

E Decorative threads used to stitch over ribbon to use for embellishments on a variety of projects.

F Top coverstitch used to create a mock flatlock seam on activewear.

G Variegated overlocker thread and belt-loop attachment used to create belt loops with decorative topstitching.

H Wrap dress neckline and front edge hemmed using metallic threads.

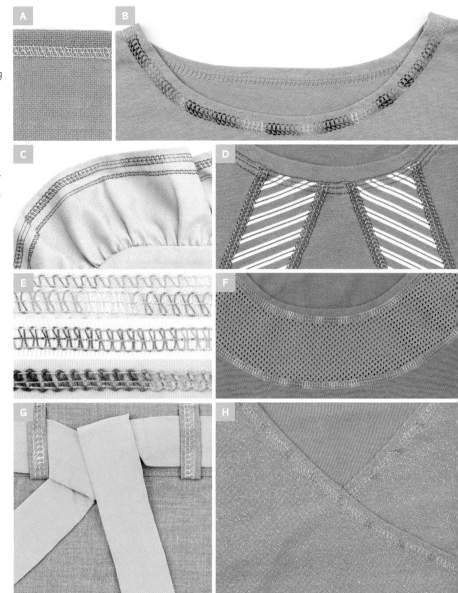

Techniques

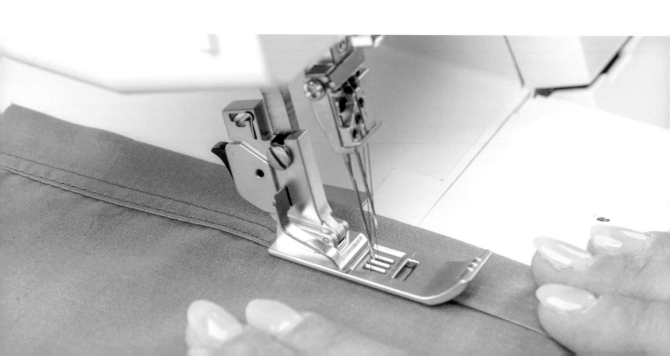

You've got your coverstitch machine threaded up, experimented with the different stitches and so now it's time to try out a few techniques. You may have purchased your machine for the sole purpose of hemming stretch fabrics but there's so much more that it can do, from sewing seams and decorative stitching to attaching bindings and making belt loops. There's a whole range of accessories you can purchase to make some of these jobs easier but there are also a few quick fixes to try first, before you invest in these gadgets. Over the next few pages you'll find out about a variety of techniques and see a range of ideas that can be achieved. You may also need to use a sewing machine and/or overlocker alongside your coverstitch machine for some of these techniques.

Seams

You may be surprised at how many types of seam you can stitch on your coverstitch machine. Chain stitch will be your best friend here. Due to the way the stitch is formed and its elastic properties, chain stitch can be used on knitted fabrics to form a seam which will move and stretch with the fabric. It's also the perfect stitch to use for tacking (basting) seams as it can be easily removed. For a more durable seam finish, combine a chain-stitched or overlocked seam with coverstitch topstitching to give additional strength and a decorative effect.

USING CHAIN STITCH FOR SEAM CONSTRUCTION

You may prefer the strength and security of a straight stitch on your sewing machine but depending on the project, a coverstitch machine may handle the fabric more easily and without fuss. The nature of the chain stitch means it will have a little stretch, so it could be a better choice for knitted fabrics.

However, relying only on chain stitch for seam construction may be problematic and result in weak or unravelling seams so consider topstitching seams with chain stitch or coverstitch to strengthen them and add a decorative touch.

TACKING SEAMS WITH CHAIN STITCH

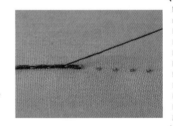

Chain stitch is a great option for holding two pieces of fabric temporarily as part of your project construction process, as the threads can be removed really easily when they are no longer needed. The threads can be locked in position at the end of the seam using the swipe, snip and lock technique described on page 34 or you can leave them unlocked, making it much easier to undo and remove threads when they are no longer needed (see page 38). Use the standard foot, chain-stitch foot or clear foot for working chain stitch.

CREATING A FRENCH SEAM

This seam technique encloses the raw edges of fabric and creates a strong, neat finish for a range of fabric types. This can be achieved by using the chain stitch setting on your machine as follows (the instructions are given for a total seam allowance of 1.5cm (⅝in):

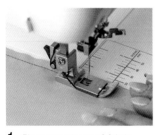

1 Place two pieces of fabric wrong sides together and stitch using chain stitch and a 1cm (⅜in) seam allowance.

2 Press the seam to one side and trim the seam allowance to 3mm (⅛in).

3 Place the fabric right sides together, rolling it between your fingers to make sure that the first seam line is right on the edge. Pin in place.

4 Stitch using chain stitch and a 5mm (¼in) seam allowance. Press seam allowance to one side.

USING THE STITCHING GUIDELINES

On many coverstitch machines you'll find stitching guidelines on the machine casing, looper cover or needle plate. They may be marked with metric and imperial measurements or just a series of parallel lines. These guidelines are really useful to help keep your stitching straight but if you're relying on the measurements, do check which needle, if any, they correspond to and are measured from to ensure the correct seam or hem allowance.

    If you don't have any markings or stitching guidelines you can make your own using pencil markings, masking tape or even a pad of sticky notes.

Tip
Keep your eyes on the guidelines of the presser foot and on the throat space instead of watching the needles to keep your stitching straight.

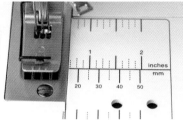

Brother CV3550 with stitching guidelines.

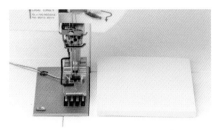

Janome CoverPro 2000CPX with pad of sticky notes.

KEEPING YOUR STITCHING STRAIGHT

There is an assortment of attachments available to help you to align the fabric and keep your stitching straight (see page 80, 'Hemming guides'). These are attached to the machine casing or to the shank of the presser foot and can be adjusted to the necessary width of your seam or hem. Another option is to invest in a **centre-guide foot**.

    This foot helps you to line up your stitching and has an adjustable guide in the centre. It is ideal to use for coverstitching that straddles a seam line. Align the guide with the centre of the foot and place the guide in line with your seam to keep your stitches straight and equidistant from the seam line.

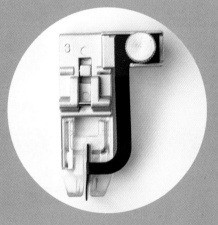

Janome CoverPro centre-guide foot.

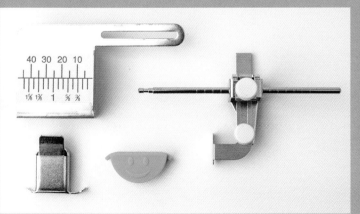

Clockwise from top left: baby lock fabric guide, Janome CoverPro adjustable seam guide, magnetic cloth guides.

USING COVERSTITCH FOR SEAM CONSTRUCTION

A coverstitch setting is usually used for topstitching seams which have already been sewn on a sewing machine or overlocker. However, a quick seam finish can be achieved by using coverstitch and a lapped seam technique. This method works well for a range of different fabric types and can reduce bulk where fabrics are overlapped and sewn through two layers of fabric instead of being stitched, pressed and then topstitched through three layers. To further reduce the bulk, an abutted seam technique can be used where the raw edges are aligned and the seam created by stitching through only one layer of fabric. These two techniques are best used on seams that won't come under stress.

LAPPED SEAM CONSTRUCTION

This is ideal for bulky fabrics which don't fray such as suede, scuba and boiled wool. Instead of making a seam in the usual way, overlap the raw edges of fabric and topstitch in place. To make the process even easier you can use wash-away double-sided tape or water-soluble glue to hold fabrics in place before stitching.

1 Apply a 6mm (¼in) strip of water-soluble double-sided tape along the raw edge where the seam will go, on the right side of your fabric (a). If you don't have any water-soluble double-sided tape, use a washable fabric pen to mark a line 6mm (¼in) from the raw edge of the fabric where the seam will go, on the right side of the fabric (b).

2 Take your second piece of fabric and lay this with right side facing up, so the raw edge overlaps the first piece by 6mm (¼in) and the wrong side attaches to the double-sided tape, or just overlaps the marked line.

3 Coverstitch the seam in place, aligning the needles so the overlapped section of fabric is stitched and all needles are stitching through the same layers of fabric. Stitch from the right side so that the straight stitches are formed on the front.

Alternatively, use the reverse coverstitch technique and sew from the wrong side so the more decorative zigzag stitches show on the right side. For another alternative, the top coverstitch can be used.

ABUTTED SEAM CONSTRUCTION

Sometimes described as a type of flatlock seam, this seam is formed where two fabric edges are aligned or butted up to one another and stitched in place using a wide stitch. This technique works well on fabrics that don't easily fray and reduces the bulk by only sewing through a single layer of fabric. An underlay can be used between the two fabric pieces for added strength or the seam can be formed without one. The two fabric pieces can be fed into the machine and abutted as you stitch but for ease of construction, use a wash-away tape to hold the fabric in place while stitching or try a tear-away or wash-away stabilizer.

1 Apply 8mm (⅜in) wide wash-away tape to the raw edge of the wrong side of a piece of fabric, so the tape is centred and overhangs the edge.

2 Take the second piece of fabric and align the raw edges, attaching the fabric to the overhanging tape.

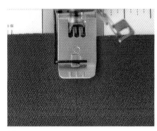

3 Place the fabric under the needles and align the centre needle marker on the presser foot to the raw abutted edges of fabric.

4 Coverstitch in place using a wide stitch setting and a shorter stitch length (set to 2 or 2mm/¹⁄₁₆in).

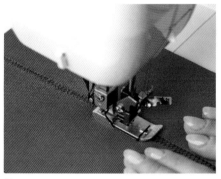

5 Turn the fabric over and stitch again, following the lines of the previous stitching.

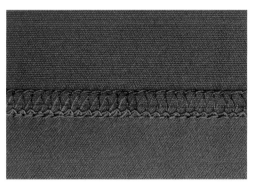

Finished seam.

An alternative finish can be created by using triple coverstitch or the top coverstitch setting.

Top coverstitch.

COMBINING STITCHES

For the strongest seam finish, combine machine straight-stitched, chain-stitched or overlocked seams with topstitching using chain stitch, coverstitch, reverse coverstitch or top coverstitch.

CREATING A WELT SEAM

This type of seam finish may also be referred to as a mock flat-fell seam as the finished seam looks like a flat-fell seam but isn't constructed as such. The welt seam is sewn with right sides together, the seam allowances pressed to one side and then topstitched from the right side. As the seam is stitched more than once, the resulting seam is sturdy so it's an ideal choice for garments that need additionally-reinforced stitching such as those in childrenswear or activewear. It is also commonly seen on the armhole and shoulder seams of sweatshirts.

1 Place fabrics right sides together, pin in place, then stitch using chain stitch or straight sewing-machine stitch and a 1.5cm (⅝in) seam allowance.

2 Trim one seam allowance to 6mm (¼in) to reduce bulkiness and then press the wider seam allowance over the narrower one. Pin in place from the right side. Alternatively, an overlocker can be used to create the seam, and the seam allowance pressed and pinned to one side.

3 From the right side, coverstitch the seam allowance in place through all layers, using the wide setting and aligning one needle approx. 2mm (¹⁄₁₆in) from the seam line.

4 For additional stitch lines, use triple coverstitch to show three parallel lines of topstitching.

5 For a different effect, use coverstitch or triple coverstitch to straddle the seam line.

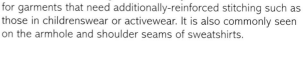

Coverstitch from right side.

Coverstitch with overlocking from wrong side.

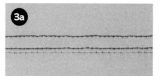

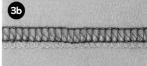

Triple coverstitch from right side.

Triple coverstitch with overlocking from wrong side.

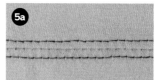

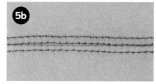

Coverstitch.

Triple coverstitch.

CREATING A MOCK FLATLOCK SEAM

This technique is ideal for activewear: the seam can be constructed on the outside of the garment, then topstitched using coverstitch from the right side. As the bulk of the seam is on the outside of the garment, this gives you a smoother finish next to your skin and has the look of a flatlock seam with the strength and stretch of an overlocked stitch. Use a woolly nylon or polyester thread in the looper for a soft and stretchy finish.

1 Place the fabric layers wrong sides together and stitch in place using your chosen seam allowance and a four-thread overlock stitch.

2 Press the seam allowance to one side.

3 Coverstitch or triple coverstitch from the right side of the fabric. Keep one needle in line with the finished overlocked edge and stitch over the previous stitches.

Tips

- If your needles are each going through a different number of fabric layers, you may need to adjust the needle thread tensions to perfect your stitch. If the stitching looks loose or unbalanced from the wrong side, increase tension on the needle threads that penetrate fewer layers.

- If you're topstitching a seam 'in the round', where the stitching forms a complete circle, follow the tips on 'hemming in the round' on page 79 to start and finish the stitching.

USING REVERSE COVERSTITCH TO CREATE A MOCK FLATLOCK SEAM

In these methods, the seam is formed on the inside of the garment and topstitching is sewn from the wrong side so the finished seam shows the underside of the coverstitch on the right side. If you have a top-coverstitch setting on your machine use this in step 3 from the right or wrong side for a double-sided finish.

Method 1: Finish seam allowance together

This technique works well on most fabrics, but may be too bulky for some projects.

1 Place fabric right sides together and stitch in place using your chosen seam allowance and a three- or four-thread overlock stitch.

2 Press the seam allowance to one side. Coverstitch or triple coverstitch from the wrong side of the fabric, keeping one needle in line with the finished edge. Stitch over the overlocked stitches.

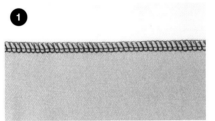

Method 2: Separating seam allowances for a flatter finish

This technique works well on activewear fabrics that don't fray and is ideal for curved seams on leggings.

1 Place fabric right sides together and create the seam with your chosen seam allowance using chain stitch or a stretch stitch on a sewing machine.

2 Press seam allowances open. If you're working on curved seams you may need to reduce the bulk of the seam allowance so that the seam lies flat. On outward curves, cut notches into the fabric edge to remove excess fabric. On inward curves, cut snips that will allow the seam to spread out when turned out the other way.

3 Use triple coverstitch from the wrong side of the fabric, keeping the centre needle over the seam line and straddling the seam allowances. (A regular coverstitch can be used instead, centring the stitch neatly over the seam.)

4 Trim any excess seam allowance from either side of the stitching. Duck-bill scissors are excellent for this.

Hems

A coverstitch machine will produce professional-looking hems on a range of fabrics and it is particularly brilliant at hemming stretch fabrics. The most common stitch used for hemming is a two-needle, three-thread coverstitch and this is what you will see on the majority of ready-to-wear knit garments. The choice of hem finish on your own projects is entirely up to you and there are some tips and tricks to mastering the settings on your machine to perfect your stitching. Experiment a little and try a single-needle chain stitch hem, a more secure two-needle or three-needle coverstitch, or a decorative five-thread top coverstitch if your machine has this option. Information on hemming corners and curves is provided on pages 89–90.

FLAT CONSTRUCTION WITH CHAIN STITCH

Although chain stitch can be unravelled easily and is not always seen as the strongest stitch to use, this technique is commonly found on the hems of ready-to-wear jeans. Here I've used topstitching thread to replicate the look of shop-bought jeans. It may not be possible to use topstitching thread in the needles and looper of all types of coverstitch machine but a similar effect can be achieved. This method demonstrates the use of a double-fold hem where raw edges are enclosed but you could use a single fold and edge finish the raw edge with an overlocker.

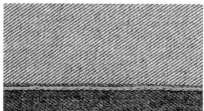

1 Press up the hem to the wrong side of the fabric. Use a sewing gauge to make sure that the measurement is correct and even all the way around the hem line.

2 Open out the fold and turn the raw edge in to meet the fold.

3 Turn the fabric up along the original fold line to create a double-fold hem and press firmly in place.

4 Place the hem under the presser foot with the wrong side facing you. Line up the needle close to the inner folded edge. Make a note of which stitching guideline you need to follow or use masking tape (mine is bright green) to mark where the outer folded edge of the hem lies on the machine casing.

5 Turn your hem over so the right side is facing you, line up the outer folded edge with the correct stitching guideline or masking tape, lower the presser foot and stitch to the end of the fabric. Continue stitching onto a scrap piece of fabric (see page 33) or use a method of your choice as shown on pages 34–37 to end the stitches.

The wrong side.

FLAT CONSTRUCTION WITH COVERSTITCH

Coverstitch is the most commonly seen hemming stitch on ready-to-wear clothing, particularly on knitted fabrics. Depending on the functionality of your machine, you can choose a narrow or wide coverstitch setting or opt for a triple coverstitch with three needles. To avoid stitching over bulky seams, construct the hem as a flat piece and then stitch the seams afterwards.

The right side.

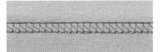
The wrong side.

1 Press up the hem to the wrong side of the fabric. Use pins on the right side to hold the hem if necessary. Use a sewing gauge for precision.

2 Place the hem under the needles of the machine with the wrong side facing you. Line up the left needle close to the raw edge, so it will stitch through both layers of fabric.

3 Make a note of which stitching guideline you need to follow or use masking tape to mark where the folded edge of the hem lies on the machine casing. I have used a bright green masking tape for contrast.

4 Turn your hem over, line up the folded edge with the correct stitching guideline or masking tape, lower the presser foot and stitch to the end of the fabric. Continue stitching onto a scrap piece of fabric (see page 33) or use a method of your choice as shown on pages 34–37 to end your stitches. The scrap fabric can be left attached until the side seam is stitched and secured.

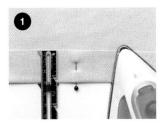

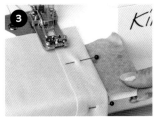
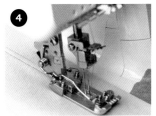

FLAT CONSTRUCTION WITH REVERSE COVERSTITCH

To reverse coverstitch, work from the wrong side of the fabric so the zigzag finish shows on the right side. For most fabrics you'll need to edge finish the raw edge of the hem before coverstitching it in place, unless you have the top coverstitch function on your machine and can simultaneously achieve a zigzag finish on both the top and bottom layers of the fabric.

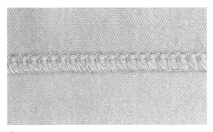

1 Press up the hem to the wrong side of the fabric and edge finish with an overlocker.

2 Place the hem under the needles of the machine with the wrong side facing you. Line up the left needle close to the raw edge, so it will stitch through both layers of fabric. Lower the presser foot.

3 Stitch the hem, keeping a straight line by using masking tape to mark where the folded edge of the hem lies on the machine casing or by following the stitching guidelines provided.

4 Stitch to the end and use a method of your choice to finish off the stitches as shown on pages 33–37.

SEWING GAUGES

There are a variety of devices, beyond the regular tape measure or ruler, available to help you measure your hem precisely and evenly. Some are designed to be placed inside the hem while pressing to maintain an even measurement whereas other plastic versions should be kept away from the heat and used for folding, measuring and pinning only. Some tools provide additional uses including working as point turners and button spacers.

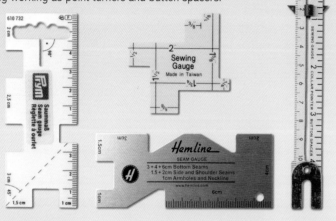

HOW DEEP SHOULD THE HEM BE?

This is entirely your choice but you may want to consider:

- How much hem allowance is specified for your project?

- How much hem allowance can be used to ensure the correct fit or length of your garment?

- What is the finished look you wish to achieve?

- What is the type of project? For straight edges on skirts and trousers, use a wide hem allowance of 3–5cm (1⅛–2in) but for flared and full garments such as circle skirts use a hem depth of around 1–2cm (⅜–¾in) to avoid puckering the fabric as it is stitched. See page 90 for dealing with curved hems.

- What is the type of fabric? Heavier, thicker fabrics require a deeper hem in order to hang correctly.

Tips for pressing a hem

An evenly measured and pressed hem takes time to produce, but there are ways to make it quicker and easier.

Use a sewing gauge or make your own from cardboard.

Machine tack a line of stitching to mark the hem line, use this as your pressing guide.

For fabrics which struggle to hold creases, use pins or seam clips to hold the fabric in place before stitching.

Measure and pin the hem to the ironing board and then press with the iron.

Tips for stitching the hem

- Make sure all the needles are all going through the same number of fabric layers – if not, lower the tension on the needle(s) that are penetrating fewer layers and/or increase the tension on those penetrating more layers.
- Use masking tape or marked guidelines to keep stitching straight.
- Use a clear foot for a better view of your stitching.
- Use a seam or hem guide to keep stitching straight.

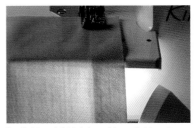

Tack the hem in place with a long machine stitch or chain stitch from the wrong side in a contrasting colour – use this as a guideline to stitch from the right side, aligning the centre needle with this line. Remove the tacking stitches at the end. Use water-soluble thread for tacking and simply wash it out when it's no longer needed.

Draw a line onto the right side of the fabric using a disappearing pen to mark the line that the left/inner needle needs to follow.

For light-weight fabrics, shine a light under the fabric to show w––here the raw edge is aligned.

HEMMING FABRICS THAT ROLL AT THE EDGE

Light-weight knit fabrics, such as single jersey, tend to roll at the raw edge of the fabric. This can be difficult to manage when hemming as the edge needs to stay flat in order to be stitched. There are a few ways to overcome this issue. See pages 80–83 for more information on stabilizing fabrics.

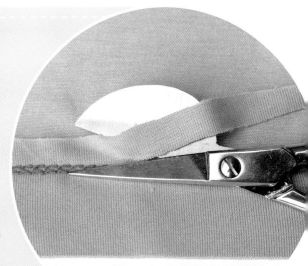

- Use hand or machine tacking to hold the hem in place.
- Use a spray starch to stiffen the fabric and stop it from rolling.
- Use a fusible webbing tape to fix the hem.
- Use a double-sided water-soluble tape to hold the hem in place.
- Use a larger hem allowance of 5cm (2in) or more but stitch the hem 3cm (1⅛in) from the folded edge. Trim off any excess hem allowance once stitching is complete. Duck-bill scissors are perfect for this.

MANAGING HEMS THAT CURL AFTER STITCHING

Sometimes fabric wants to curl no matter what you do and even after you've hemmed, it still wants to roll up. To avoid this happening, try:

- using a fusible webbing tape;

- using a deeper hem of 2.5cm (1in) or more;

- making sure both needles are stitching through two layers of fabric.

See the Troubleshooting section on roping on page 185 and 'Avoiding twisted hems' on page 52.

OVERLOCKING A SEAM AFTER HEMMING FLAT

If a final seam needs to be sewn after the hem has been stitched using one of the flat construction methods, place right sides together and stitch from the hem edge. When overlocking, the hem edges may become misaligned due to the pull of the feed-dog teeth or because of the bulk at the hemmed edge. Secure the hemmed ends first with hand stitching, regular machine stitching or follow these tips for a better result. This technique can also be used for stitching a seam after binding a neckline or armhole opening and works best where there is no seam allowance to be trimmed off with the knife, so trim the edge first, if necessary.

1 Lower the needles and raise the presser foot. Push the hem ends into the overlocker so they touch the needles and are flush with the inside edge of the blade.

2 Lower the presser foot and use the handwheel to take the first couple of stitches to secure the hem ends correctly. For bulky hems, a height-compensation tool can be used behind and in front of the presser foot to maintain an even feed.

3 Complete the seam by operating the foot pedal. Use a bodkin or yarn needle to bury the thread ends from the hem edge into the stitching then trim neatly.

4 Press the overlocked seam to one side and stitch from the right side with a regular sewing machine or use hand stitches on the inside to hold the seam allowance flat.

HEMMING IN THE ROUND

For many projects, hemming will be the final stage of the construction process and will be done 'in the round' where side seams have already been sewn and stitching forms a complete circle. Follow the steps below to overlap your stitching perfectly at the start and finish, and tie off the thread ends securely.

Stitching from the right side of the fabric

This technique will work for any of the stitch types, overlapping the starting stitches and using the swipe, snip and lock method to finish.

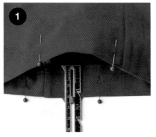
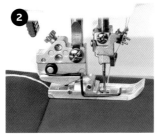

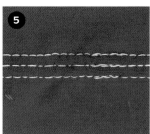

1 Press up the hem to the wrong side of the fabric. Use pins on the right side or hand tacking stitches to hold the hem if necessary.

2 Place the hem under the presser foot so the left needle will be stitching through both layers of fabric (see 'Tips for stitching the hem' on page 77). Start stitching just after a seam so you're not sewing through extra thicknesses to begin with. If this is a garment, start stitching on the back piece. Here you can see the pile of sticky notes I am using as a guide.

3 Stitch all the way around the hem, until you're about 3cm (1⅛in) from the starting point.

4 Cut the thread ends from the starting stitches on both sides of the fabric so these don't become tangled in your new stitching.

5 Continue stitching, using the markings on the front of the foot as a guideline to the needle positions and overlap the starting point by four or five stitches. Finish off by using the swipe, snip and lock method as described on page 34.

Stitching from the wrong side of the fabric (reverse coverstitch)

A similar method to the one above can be followed for hemming in the round using reverse coverstitch.

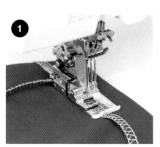

1 Prepare the hem as explained above and edge finish the raw edge. Begin stitching from the wrong side of the fabric just after the seam so that stitching is flat.

2 Once you get to the end and have overlapped your stitches, swipe, snip and lock the threads but don't trim them (page 34).

3 The thread ends will now be locked and appear on the right side of the fabric. Put thread ends onto a needle and bring them through to the wrong side of the fabric. Fasten off by taking a few stitches and then snipping the threads.

HEMMING GUIDES

These may be provided in the pack of accessories with your machine, or can be purchased as additional attachments. There are three types of hemming guides available:

1 The most basic versions will provide a ridge to align with your fabric edge to keep stitching straight. These can be easily adjusted to suit a range of widths. They may be sold as a seam guide, cloth guide or fabric guide. You can create your own easily by using a toy block and attaching this to the machine with adhesive putty or you can simply stick a stack of sticky notes to your machine (see page 79).

2 Some brands offer hemming accessories set to specific widths. Simply feed the fabric into the guide without pressing first and the fabric will be folded by the specified amount. These work best on long lengths of woven fabric where there are no bulky seams to contend with. For the best results on light-weight fabrics the hem may need to be pressed with the iron first.

3 The third type of hemming guide can be adjusted to suit a range of hemming widths. This device can be used on different fabric types of varying thicknesses so long as fabrics are able to move through the guide smoothly. The hem can be sewn without any initial pressing but for the best and most consistent results it is advisable to measure and press the fabric first.

This type of hemming guide can take a bit of practice to set up and use. If you find you can't get along with it, don't give up and put it to one side – try adapting it to use as a basic hemming or cloth guide.

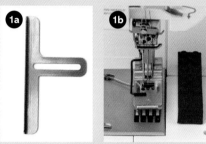

Straight-edge hem guide by Britannia.

Toy block.

Top: baby lock plain hemmer; bottom: baby lock single downturn feller.

Janome Coverpro hemming guide.

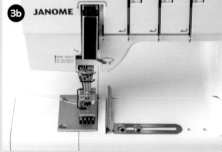

Janome Coverpro hemming guide adapted to be used as a basic hemming guide.

Tips for hemming in the round

- Begin stitching after a seam so you start on a flat surface.
- If you're sewing a garment, start the stitching on the back panel so the finishing stitches are less obvious.
- Utilize the free arm on your machine if you have one and the item fits.
- If there is no free arm or the item is too small, stitch from the inside of the sleeve: turn the sleeve inside out for regular coverstitch hems – see image (a) – or right side out for reverse coverstitching.

- Stitch slowly, making sure you're not bunching or catching fabric underneath.
- When making hems on sleeves, do this first before attaching the sleeve to the garment.
- Use the markings on the top of the presser foot to align the needles and overlap stitching perfectly. See image (b).

Stabilizing fabrics

As part of the construction process, it may be necessary to stabilize seams or certain parts of your project in order to give strength, durability or to retain shape. Shoulder seams, waistlines and curved seams of garments such as armholes may require stabilizing so that these do not distort due to the weight of fabric pulling on them or through general wear and tear. This is particularly necessary on items made from knitted fabrics which can stretch out of shape over time.

Reinforcement is also required on areas where pockets will be applied or for fastenings such as buttonholes, buttons and zips. Stabilizers may be needed, too, for hemming or decorative stitching, particularly on light-weight or knitted fabrics to help the fabric move smoothly through the machine.

There are a number of methods for stabilizing seams or fabric, depending on the project and type of fabric.

STAYSTITCHING

When constructing garments, staystitching is often used for necklines, waistlines and armholes to stop these areas from stretching out of shape as the garment is put together. For some woven fabrics, stitching may be enough to stop any distortion but for slippery fabrics and knit fabrics, particularly those used for activewear, additional strength may be required using one of the methods below.

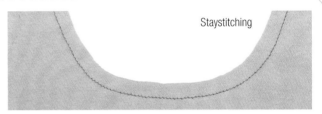
Staystitching

TOPSTITCHING

Using an extra line of stitching can provide strength and stability without the need to apply anything else. French, fell, welt and mock flatlock seams all work on this premise and provide durability through additional stitching. (See pages 68–73.)

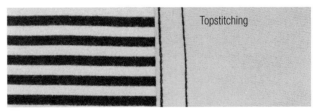
Topstitching

NON-STRETCH TAPE

Cotton tape, twill tape, fusible woven tape or ribbon can be used to stabilize straight edges, openings or seams where stretch is not required. This might be for pockets, zip openings, the back section of a neckline or seams where additional stretch could cause the garment to distort and stretch out of shape.

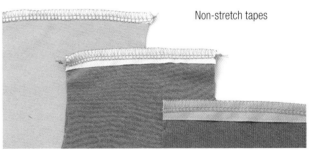
Non-stretch tapes

STRETCH TAPE

Where a little give is required, use clear elastic, fusible seam tape, bias tape or knit stay tape. This can be used to stabilize necklines before hemming or for shoulder seams where some stretch needs to be retained. When applying these types of tape, don't stretch them as you sew but match them exactly to the length of the fabric edge.

FABRIC STRIPS (not shown)

Use the same fabric you're working with and cut narrow strips to apply to the areas that need stabilizing. Fabric strips can be applied in the same way as stretch or non-stretch tape. Choose a woven fabric cut on the straight grain for straight edges or non-stretch seams. Strips of selvedge are ideal for this purpose and it's a great way to use up fabric scraps. For curved edges or seams that need a little stretch, use a low-stretch knit fabric cut in the direction of least stretch or use a woven fabric cut on the bias.

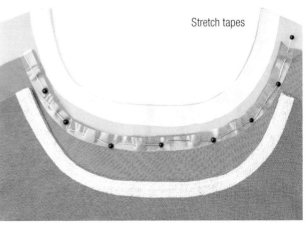
Stretch tapes

INTERFACING

Interfacing is applied to fabric and stays in permanently to add strength or for structure such as in collars and cuffs. It may be fusible or sew-in, woven or non-woven, stretch or non-stretch and comes in a variety of weights. Create your own fusible tape by cutting strips of iron-on interfacing to stabilize areas where pockets or zips will be applied, behind buttonholes and buttons, for reinforcement around V-neck openings or for plackets.

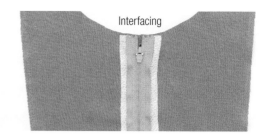
Interfacing

FUSIBLE WEBBING

This is a light-weight double-sided fusible interfacing which can be used for appliqué and hemming purposes. It can be purchased on a narrow roll as fusible webbing tape or as a larger sheet with paper backing. The tape is best for hemming because strips can be cut and placed inside your hem; the larger paper-backed type is more suitable for appliqué. Just like regular interfacing, fusible webbing will add stiffness to your fabric and also affect any stretch in your fabric so this might not be the best choice for all projects.

Fusible webbing tape

STABILIZER

Stabilizers provide temporary support for fabrics and are removed after sewing. They are most commonly used for machine-embroidery purposes and come in a range of forms: water-soluble, tear-away, cut-away or heat-away. When working with light-weight fabrics you may experience tunnelling or issues with the fabric feeding through the machine. If you've tried adjusting the machine setting as described in the Troubleshooting section on page 182, and are still having issues, try using a stabilizer or tissue paper between the fabric and the feed-dog teeth to help the fabric move more smoothly through the machine. Depending on the type used, the stabilizer can be torn away, cut away or washed away after sewing. When experimenting with decorative stitching, stabilizers are a great way to keep stitching uniform in size and the fabric moving evenly through the machine.

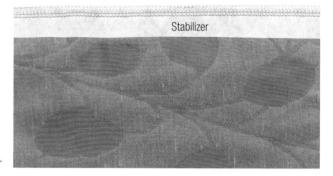
Stabilizer

WATER-SOLUBLE DOUBLE-SIDED TAPE

This is a really useful stabilizer for placing zips or holding hems before stitching, particularly on stretch fabrics to avoid fabrics distorting as you sew. Once you've finished sewing, wash away the tape and any stretch in the fabric will be retained. This tape is also useful for creating lapped or abutted seams (see pages 68–73) or for decorative techniques such as faggoting (see 'Lace effects' page 97).

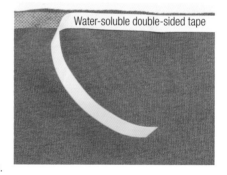
Water-soluble double-sided tape

SPRAY STARCH

Some fabrics are difficult to handle and may roll at the raw edge. Using spray starch allows fabric to be more easily manipulated and able to move smoothly through the machine. Try it on the hems and necklines of light-weight fabrics or for bindings that curl. Starch can be removed by washing once projects are complete.

Spray starch

STABILIZING SEAMS ON CLOTHING

When choosing a method or product for stabilizing seams on clothing, consider:

- How much stretch needs to be retained in the garment – do you need a method that will restrict the stretch, or one which will allow for some movement?

- Will your stabilizer add bulk to the seam? Match your stabilizing product to the weight of fabric you are using.

- Consider which direction the seam will be pressed in and try to position the stabilizer so it will not have direct contact with skin to give greater comfort to the wearer. For example, when stabilizing shoulder seams, apply the stabilizer to the wrong side of the back pieces, stitch in place as the seam is sewn and then press the seam towards the back, covering the stabilizer.

STABILIZING CURVED OPENINGS

Using fusible stay tape

It is easy to stretch fabric pieces out of shape as soon as you have cut out your pattern pieces, especially on light-weight drapey fabrics. Use a fusible stay tape on necklines, armholes, and other openings to avoid distortion as follows:

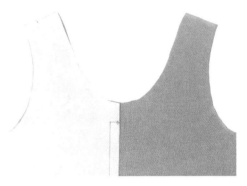

1 Check the fabric piece against your paper pattern before applying the tape. If you fuse the tape onto an edge that's already stretched out of shape there's no going back. Manipulate your fabric until it fits the curve of the paper pattern exactly.

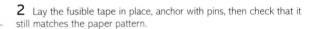

2 Lay the fusible tape in place, anchor with pins, then check that it still matches the paper pattern.

3 Fuse the tape in place, removing the pins as you go. You may wish to use a pressing cloth to protect the iron and tape.

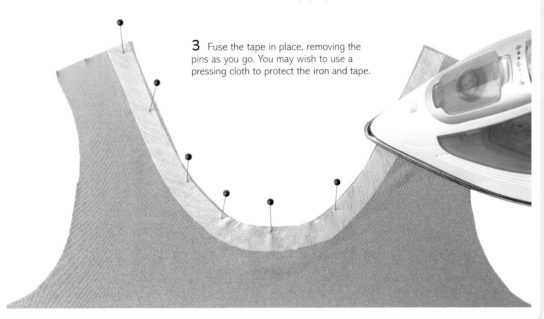

Managing bulky seams and hems

Some machines will stitch more smoothly than others and when it comes to stitching over bulky seam lines you may encounter issues such as skipped stitches or changes in stitch length. On most machines the feed-dog teeth are shorter in the centre of the needle plate, since there is a hole here for the needle. Often the bulk of the seam is moving through the centre of the needle plate and since there is less grip in this part of the machine, the result can be poor stitch quality or irregular feeding of the fabric. Using a narrow coverstitch setting can help, but there are a number of ways to overcome these problems including techniques to reduce the thickness of fabric layers or methods to help your machine sew over bumps without affecting the stitch quality.

SNIPPING THE SEAM ALLOWANCE

Cutting into the seam allowance helps reduce bulk when hemming seams. It can also help reduce bulk when binding seams, as shown on page 124.

1 Measure from the raw edge up to the hem line and mark this on the seam.

2 Snip into the seam allowance through the looper threads but not into the needle thread.

3 Press the snipped part of the seam in the opposite direction to reduce bulk when the hem is folded.

USING A SEAM CLAPPER

Once you've snipped and prepared your seam for hemming, use the seam clapper to further reduce bulk. Use plenty of steam in the iron, then apply the clapper and hold in place – the wood draws out the steam and keeps the heat in the fabric, resulting in a flatter seam.

USING A MALLET OR HAMMER

You may wish to cover the fabric to protect it before hammering. Simply hammer the seams which are bulky to flatten them out prior to hemming.

CHANGING MACHINE SETTINGS JUST BEFORE THE BULK

Some machines can handle changes in fabric thickness better than others. If your machine is struggling to sew evenly over bulky areas, try the following changes to your machine settings just before you reach the bulky section and then change back to regular settings once you're back on a flat surface:

1 Lengthen the stitch length to speed up the movement over the bulk.

2 Increase the differential feed so the fabric moves more quickly into the machine.

3 Reduce the presser-foot pressure so the bulk can pass under the presser foot more easily.

4 Increase the tension on the threads slightly to help manage the extra thicknesses.

CHANGING STITCHING SPEED

In some circumstances, stitching more quickly over bulky areas can keep the machine operating smoothly but on other occasions when you reach a bump in the fabric you may need to use the handwheel with one hand and help the fabric through the machine with the other. Try not to stop and start too often as this may well cause irregular stitching.

USING A HEIGHT-COMPENSATION TOOL

When you sew over bulky areas the presser foot is unable to stay flat which can cause stitching issues.

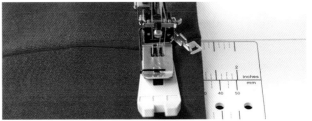

1 As you approach a bulky area of stitching, place the height-compensation tool under the back of the presser foot so that it remains level with the feed-dog teeth, instead of sitting at an angle.

If you don't have a height-compensation tool you can make your own by folding scrap pieces of fabric to the height required – heavy-weight woven fabrics such as denim are ideal.

2 Continue stitching as normal until you're in the middle of the bulky section. Move the height-compensation tool from behind the presser foot and place it under the front of the presser foot. Continue stitching onto the flatter area and remove the height-compensation tool once the bulky section has been cleared.

Stitching corners and curves

Now you've mastered stitching in a straight line it's time to try out the techniques to manoeuvre around corners or curves. Whether you're stitching hems, experimenting with decorative techniques or applying pockets here are a few tips and tricks to perfect your stitching. Using a clear foot will help too.

STITCHING IN CIRCLES

It is possible to sew a perfect circle and you don't need to follow a line on your fabric in order to do it. This technique is ideal for decorative work on medium to heavy fabrics (see examples on the 'Hove skirt', page 160 and the 'Cambridge table runner', page 170). For lighter fabrics, use a tear-away or fusible wash-away stabilizer. Use one, two or three needles and stitch from the right or wrong side of your work, depending on the desired finish.

1 Take a drawing pin/thumb tack and some masking tape. Attach the flat side of the drawing pin to the top of the cover, to the left of the presser foot. The further away the pin is from the needles, the larger the circle will be.

2 Place your fabric under the presser foot and push the pin through the fabric to mark the centre of your circle. Use a stitch length of 2.5 or less and keep the fabric taut as you stitch around the circle. You may find a lower differential feed helps you to control the fabric as it will move more slowly into the machine.

3 Follow the instructions in steps 3–5 for hemming in the round on page 79 to complete your circle.

> **Tip**
> Scratch the fabric around the pin hole to realign the fibres and close up the hole.

CHAIN-STITCH CORNERS

This is almost as easy as cornering on your regular sewing machine but does require the needle to be in the right position before pivoting to avoid additional loops on the wrong side of the stitch. Use matching thread colours in the needle and looper to give a more satisfying appearance and avoid any obvious stitching errors.

1 Work a line of stitches, then use the handwheel to take your last stitch, turning it towards you so the needle goes all the way into the turning point and back out until the eye of the needle is out of the fabric, but the tip is still in.

2 Raise the presser foot and pivot the fabric. Lower the presser foot and continue stitching.

CORNERING WITH COVERSTITCH

Use the same techniques for both two- and three-needle coverstitching. Using matching thread colours in the needle and looper will give a more satisfying appearance and avoid any obvious stitching errors on the looper side of the stitch. I've used different colours so you can see more clearly what happens to each of the threads. There are four methods to choose from, depending on the finish you wish to achieve. Experiment with each of these until you get the right results. Always turn the handwheel towards you to avoid the looper thread unravelling.

Method 1: Overlapping corners

1 Make a line of stitching and use the handwheel to take your last stitch, turning it towards you so the needles go into the turning point, down to their lowest position and then back up to their highest position. Keep rotating the handwheel and lower the needles slightly so the threads show a little slack.

2 Raise the presser foot. You may need to pull a little more slack on the needle threads from just above the needle bar. I use a screwdriver.

3 Pivot the fabric 90° anticlockwise, positioning the needles above the back line of stitches so the *right-hand needle* enters the place it just came out of. You may need to pull the fabric to the back before pivoting to disengage threads from the prongs on the needle plate. If there's too much slack on the threads pull them back towards the thread spools. (To turn the fabric 90° clockwise, position the needles above the back line of stitches so the *left-hand needle* enters the place it just came out of.)

4 Lower the presser foot, using the handwheel to check the needles are going to enter the fabric in exactly the right place. Make sure the threads are sitting inside their corresponding grooves in the presser foot and not twisted, adjust your position if necessary, and then continue stitching.

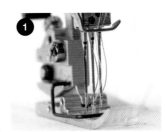

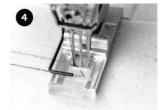

Method 2: Diagonal outer stitching

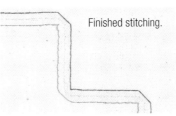

Finished stitching.

1 Follow the instructions above for overlapping corners until the fabric is pivoted. Position the needles above the end of the front line of stitches so the left-hand needle enters the place it just came out of. (To turn the fabric 90° clockwise, position the needles above the end of the front line of stitches so the right-hand needle enters the place it just came out of.)

2 Lower the presser foot, use the handwheel to check the needles are going to enter the fabric in exactly the right place and the threads aren't caught. Adjust your position if necessary, then continue stitching.

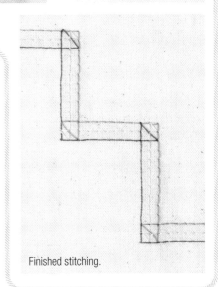

Finished stitching.

Method 3: Perfect corners

This technique requires the most work as it uses hand stitching to fix the stitches in the correct positions at the corners.

1 Follow the instructions for method 2 on page 87.

2 On the right side of the fabric you'll notice diagonal stitches on the outer stitch lines of the corners. These need to be secured in the correct position with a hand stitch.

3 Thread a hand sewing needle, tie with a knot, then take the needle through the looper thread to secure.

4 Bring the hand sewing needle through to the right side of the fabric at the corner points and catch the diagonal threads in place.

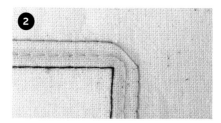

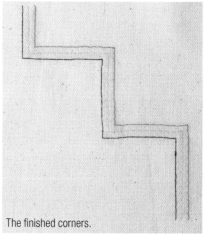

The finished corners.

Method 4: Curved stitching

Try this method using 45° turns for a less curved finish or smaller turns and a smaller stitch length for a more curved effect. On most machines, the needle positions are progressively lower than each other from right to left with the right needle sitting highest on the machine. The instructions that follow will work for these such machines. For machines where the opposite is true, i.e. the left needle sits highest in the machine, the instructions will need to be transposed.

1 Make a line of stitching and use the handwheel to take your last stitch, turning it towards you so the needles go into the turning point and down to their lowest position.

2 Keep turning the handwheel to raise the needles, but leave the tip of the left-hand needle in the fabric.

3 Raise the presser foot and pivot the fabric 30° anticlockwise.

4 Lower the presser foot and turn the handwheel towards you to make one stitch, and then raise the needles again, leaving just the tip of the left-hand needle in the fabric. Repeat steps 3 and 4.

5 Raise the presser foot and pivot the fabric 30° to complete the 90° turn.

6 Lower the presser foot and continue stitching. To turn the fabric clockwise, raise all three needles out of the fabric and pivot, keeping the right-hand needle above the same hole it just came out of, until the curved corner is complete.

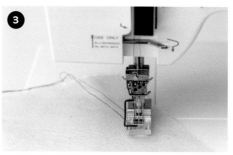

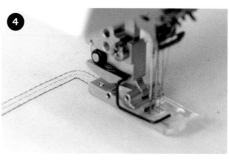

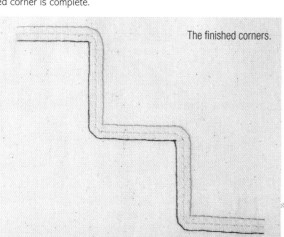

The finished corners.

Tips for turning corners

- If your start and end point will be in the same place, always start midway along an edge, not at the corner as it will be easier to blend your stitches when you finish.
- Mark the stitching line with chalk or an air-erasable pen so you can see clearly where the turning points are.
- Use a clear foot for a better view of your stitching.
- Always turn the handwheel towards you. Turning the handwheel away from you will release the looper thread from the needles and can make the stitches unravel.

HEMMING CORNERS

The easy method for cornering

If you need to turn a hem on more than one edge of your project, for example on the Buenavista beach wrap project on page 150, it is much easier to hem one side at a time, running the stitching off the edge of the fabric and then starting again, rather than trying to stitch one continuous line.

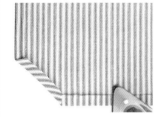 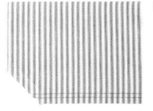 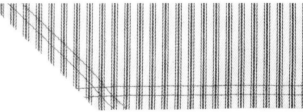

1 Press up the hem by the desired amount around all sides.

2 Make the hem on one edge, stitch to the end of the fabric and fasten off the threads.

3 Fold up the hem on the next side. Tuck the thread ends under the raw edge. Make the hem and run the stitching to the edge of the fabric. Fasten off the stitches. Continue until all the edges are hemmed.

Continuous corner stitching

If you want a challenge, it is possible to turn a corner on your hem using the techniques on pages 87–88 but it's a good idea to press and hand tack the folded edges before machine stitching. If you use water-soluble thread for tacking you can just wash the threads away, rather than spending time trying to pull them out.

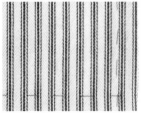 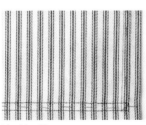 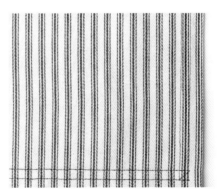

Finished hem with tacking stitches removed.

Hand-tacked hem.

Machined hem.

HEMMING A CURVED EDGE

Curved hems can be tricky to press and stitch successfully. The deeper the hem, the more excess fabric you'll have at the curved edge and the harder it becomes to ease this extra fabric into a neatly stitched flat hem. Roping is also more likely to occur on curved hems (see 'Troubleshooting' on page 182). Use a narrow hem, no more than 1.5cm (⅝in), and try one of the following two methods:

Method 1: Ease stitching on a sewing machine

1 Use a long machine stitch to stitch along the hem line around the curved section. There's no need to back tack – this stitch line will be removed once the hem is sewn.

2 Stitch another line of long machine stitches within the hem allowance, between your stitch line and the raw edge. Don't back tack. Leave long tail ends.

3 Pull on the tail ends of the outer line of stitching, pulling gently enough that the hem-line stitching lays flat.

4 Use the hem-line stitching from step 1 as a guide and press under the hem allowance.

5 Pin and hand tack the hem in place before coverstitching.

6 Use coverstitch, reverse coverstitch or top coverstitch to secure your hem.

7 Remove the hand and machine tacking stitches.

Method 2: Ease stitching on a coverstitch machine

1 Set your coverstitch machine to two-needle narrow coverstitching or three-needle coverstitching. Turn the stitch length to the longest setting and increase the differential feed to 1.3–1.5 for the curved section.

2 Stitch around the curved edge, keeping the left needle on the hem line.

3 Use the left needle line as a guide and press under the hem allowance.

4 Follow steps 5–7 for method 1 to complete the hem.

The amount that the fabric will ease or gather depends on the make and model of the machine and the type of fabric. Adjust the differential feed to achieve the right amount of gathering: a higher number will create the most gathers. Light-weight fabrics will work best using this method and heavier fabrics may not gather at all.

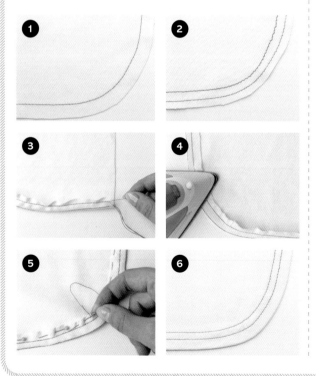

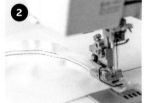

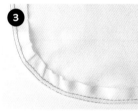

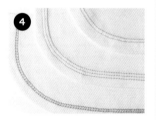

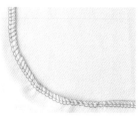

You can also achieve the same effect by using an overlocker with the stitch length set to the longest setting and the differential feed set above 1.

ATTACHING POCKETS

Use the curve and corner techniques to apply pockets to a variety of projects and create a perfectly topstitched finish. For another pocket technique, see the hip pocket used on the skirt on pages 164–165.

Square-cornered pockets

Try the overlapping corner method (page 87) and three-thread coverstitch to attach the pocket and create a decorative effect.

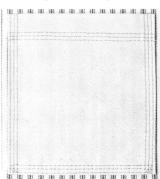

Finished square-cornered pocket.

1 Prepare and position the pocket on the project. Pin or hand tack in place.

2 Start at the right-hand top corner and stitch along the edge, keeping stitching straight. Use a height-compensation tool to start stitching if necessary.

3 Turn the first corner using 'Method 1: Overlapping corners' on page 87)

4 Continue to stitch the pocket in place until the top-left corner of the pocket is reached. Use the swipe, snip and lock method to finish off (page 34) and then use a hand sewing needle to bring the thread to the wrong side and secure the stitches at the start and end points.

Using reverse coverstitch

It can be tricky to use a continuous stitch approach for square-cornered pockets and achieve a flawless finish. Instead, follow these steps for a stop-and-start method.

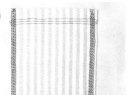

1 Prepare the pocket and pin or hand tack in place.

2 From the right side use a water-soluble thread or contrast thread to stitch around the outside edge of the pocket.

3 From the wrong side, begin stitching from one of the top corners and stitch from the top to the bottom, using the hand-tacking stitches as a guide to the edge of the pocket. Use a height-compensation tool if necessary for the beginning and end stitches. Use the swipe, snip and lock method to finish the threads (page 34) and then bring the threads back to the wrong side of the fabric with a hand sewing needle.

4 Continue stitching each side of the pocket until this is complete. Use a hand sewing needle to fasten off threads on the wrong side of the fabric and remove any hand tacking.

Decorative topstitching or embellishment can be applied to the pocket before stitching it to the project.

Curved pockets

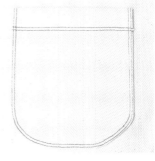

Use one of the methods given opposite to prepare the pocket and turn under the raw edge. Hand tack or pin the pocket in place and then stitch with a continuous stitch from top corner to opposite top corner.

Decorative threads and stitch techniques

You can add texture or embellishment to your projects using a number of decorative techniques on your coverstitch machine. Although it's not always possible to use decorative threads in the needles, you can usually use them in the looper and create interesting effects with regular, reverse or top coverstitching, depending on the functionality of your machine. Experiment with pintucks and quilting techniques using chain stitch and metallic threads, try out creative appliqué using reverse two-needle coverstitching and variegated thread, and on machines with the top-coverstitch feature use a heavier thread such as crochet cotton in the top-cover spreader to create a braid-like decorative feature.

EMBROIDERY AND EMBELLISHMENT TECHNIQUES

Fabrics can be embellished just with stitching, combining the full range of stitches available on your machine, by applying tape and ribbon and stitching through these (see 'Taping foot or guide' below) or by using appliqué techniques. Experiment with contrasting rayon thread, a 'thread palette', and regular and reverse coverstitching to add decoration to an entire project or just a small area such as a patch pocket, cuff or yoke. Simple embroidery techniques can be achieved by weaving yarn or ribbon through the stitching of a hem or line of topstitching.

Tip

For a full range of the different types of threads that can be used with your machine see pages 20–21; for tips on threading decorative threads through your machine see page 30; for notes on threading accessories see page 14.

Appliqué

This is a technique of layering fabrics to build up a picture or design. Fabric shapes are applied to a base layer of fabric, fused, pinned or tacked in place and then edge stitched. Edge stitching is commonly done with satin stitch by hand or on a sewing machine. To create a decorative effect using a coverstitch machine, stitch from the wrong side of the fabric to show the chain or grid pattern of stitches on the right side of the fabric. Contrasting or variegated thread is perfect. For best results, use simple shapes to make it easier to stitch around the outline. (See 'Ideas to try' opposite.)

1 Apply the fabric shape to the background layer of fabric, then use hand or machine tacking stitches to 'draw' around the outline of the shape and transfer the line to the wrong side of the fabric. Water-soluble thread is a great choice as it is easily removed afterwards by washing away, instead of unpicking.

2 Stitch from the wrong side of the fabric. If using one needle, position this in the centre and keep the right needle mark in line with the stitching from step 1 which marks out the raw edge of the fabric shape. If using two or more needles, keep the outer needle in line with the tacking stitches from step 1, so the raw edge of the fabric shape will be covered.

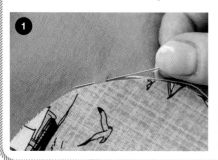

Taping foot or guide

When applying ribbon, tapes, braids or lace, a taping foot or guide is really useful to keep everything positioned correctly, to enable perfect stitching. Depending on the machine you are using and the available accessories, tapes measuring up to 6cm (2⅜in) wide can be applied using these devices. Some standard feet also have slots that can be used for applying ribbon or alternatively, the elastic attachments can be used as a guide as long as no resistance is applied to the tape (see page 109 for elastic gathering attachments).

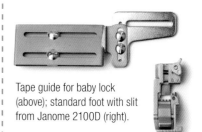

Tape guide for baby lock (above); standard foot with slit from Janome 2100D (right).

Thread palette

This handy device can be used with your sewing machine, overlocker and coverstitch machine. The thread palette will hold up to four different threads which are fed through the same part of the machine to create a blended thread effect. Depending on the thickness of the resulting thread, this can be used in the needles or looper with the heaviest threads used only in the looper.

1 Set the thread palette on the looper spool pin and place your chosen threads onto each of the thread palette pins.

2 Use the 'Tying on new threads' method shown on page 31 (unless you have an air-threading system) to bring these threads through your machine to the eye of the looper. Tie on each of the thread-palette threads and pull through the machine one at a time so the knots are kept small in order for this method to work.

For air-threading systems, use a thread cradle as shown on page 30, 'Using and threading decorative threads') to bring all of the decorative threads through your machine in one go.

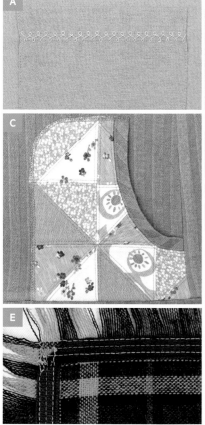

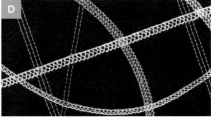

Ideas to try: embroidery and embellishment techniques

A Use a blunt needle to weave fine crochet cotton yarn through triple coverstitching on the top of a pocket.

B Use variegated perle cotton for crochet in the top-cover spreader to create a braid-like effect on the sleeve seam of a sweatshirt.

C Create a feature pocket on a sweatshirt, using scraps of fabric. Topstitch seams with regular and reverse triple coverstitch.

D Make decorative stitching for panels on a garment using the thread palette, coverstitch and reverse coverstitch in random patterns and an assortment of threads.

E Create a fringe on a blanket by applying ribbon using the taping foot and triple coverstitch to secure fabric threads 5cm (2in) from the edge of the fabric, then fraying the remaining edge.

F Use chain and coverstitch to create appliqué designs.

TEXTURED TECHNIQUES

Raised effects can be created using a number of different methods including making ruffles and pintucks or using quilting techniques and faggoting. Some of these techniques require a stabilizer to add strength and enable a consistent stitch to be formed on different fabrics.

Gathers and ruffles

This technique works best on light-weight fabrics. Gather strips of fabric along each of the raw edges to form ruched sections, or down the centre to create ruffles. Ruffles can be used to decorate necklines, cuffs and front edges of garments (see 'Ideas to try' on page 97 and elasticated ruffles on page 112).

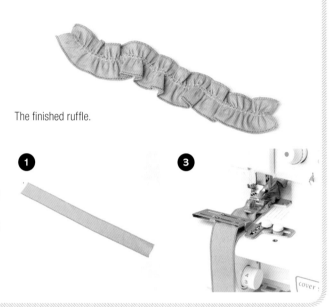

The finished ruffle.

1 Cut strips of fabric 4cm (1½in) wide and long enough for your project. Finish the long edges of the strips using a method of your choice – the overlocked rolled hem is perfect.

2 Turn the differential feed up to the highest number (usually 2) and increase the stitch length to the longest setting. Use a single needle and chain stitch or choose more needles, depending on the effect you want.

3 Feed the fabric through the machine as usual, aligning the needle(s) with the centre of the strip. In this example a taping guide is used to keep the fabric in line but the centre line could alternatively be marked with chalk or disappearing pen.

Another method for adding gathers to a garment is to use narrow or wide coverstitch to create a channel. Feed narrow ribbon or elastic through the channel and bunch up the fabric. This method is shown on the quick and easy drawstring gift bag on page 144.

Ruching can add interest in the panels of any project.

Textured strips

Add a little texture by cutting bias-cut strips of woven fabric and apply them using a stitch of your choice to a fabric base. After laundering, the raw edges of the strips become slightly frayed and fuzzy, giving an interesting texture for garments, accessories and homeware.

Pintucks

The simplest way to create these on any machine is with chain stitch, as explained here, but pintucks can also be formed using coverstitch and intentional tunnelling (see 'Making your own ribbing' on page 106).

1 Mark lines onto the right side of your fabric at regular intervals, at least 1.5cm (⅝in) apart, where you want the folds of the pintucks to be.

2 Fold along each line with wrong sides of the fabric together and stitch 6mm (¼in) from the fold. Use the needle-position markings on the front of the presser foot to keep stitching in line. You may wish to pin or press each of the pintucks before stitching, depending on the fabric being used and the finish required. For a permanent crease, press in place. For a more relaxed look or for fabrics which don't take heat, don't press.

Tips for stitching pintucks

• For light-weight stretch fabrics or other difficult-to-handle fabrics that move around too much, use strips of fusible wash-away stabilizer or double-sided wash-away tape applied to the wrong side of the fabric with one edge aligned to the pintuck line. Fold the line of the pintuck using the stabilizer as a guide for a crisper and more even result.

• For decorative pintucks, after creating a row of pintucks, turn your fabric 90° and stitch across the fabric, pressing the pintucks to one side, then stitch back the other way to press the pintucks in the opposite direction. (See 'Ideas to try: chain stitch' on page 59 or 'Ideas to try: textured techniques' on page 97.)

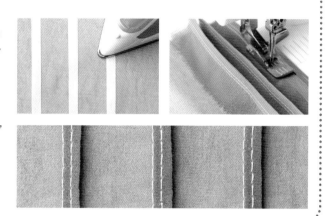

Using the pintuck and cording foot

This foot and cording guide are only available for a small number of brands and models of machine so if you're not able to source this you could use the methods for cording without the pintuck foot shown on page 96.

1 Insert the centre and right needles (or as directed for your machine) to create a narrow coverstitch. Attach the pintuck foot to the machine. Open the left side cover of the machine and place the cording guide on the needle plate. Close the left side cover to hold the guide in position.

2 Insert cord through the cording guide and take this through the groove under the pintuck presser foot and out the back of the machine. Leave enough cord extending from the foot so you can pull on this as you begin stitching.

3 Mark the position of the first pintuck on your fabric with a chalk line or other fabric marker and align the marked line to one of the needle positions. Pull on the cord behind the presser foot and take the first two stitches with the handwheel to make sure that the stitch is formed correctly and the cord is feeding evenly.

4 Continue to stitch the corded pintucks, following the lines of your design or working parallel pintucks by aligning the edge of the presser foot with the previously stitched tuck.

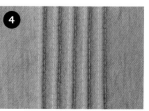

Cording without the pintuck foot

You can create corded pintucks without the cording foot either by creating a series of lines of coverstitching and filling these with cord, or by forming channels by stitching through two layers of fabric using chain stitch or coverstitch and then filling the channels between the lines of stitching with cord or stuffing to create the raised effect. (See 'Ideas to try' opposite.)

1 Create pintucks using the method described for 'Making ribbing without a pintuck foot' on page 106 or make lines of narrow or wide coverstitch using your regular machine settings.

2 Once the lines of coverstitching have been made, from the wrong side of the work use a blunt large-eyed needle or loop turner to pass cord or yarn through the grid of stitching from one end of the pintuck to the other. For narrow coverstitching use a cord of up to 3mm (⅛in) in diameter and for wide coverstitching use a cord of up to 6mm (¼in) in diameter. In this example, I've used four strands of aran (heavy worsted or 10-ply) weight yarn.

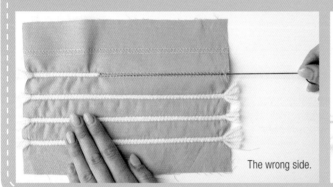
The wrong side.

The right side.

Quilting techniques

Simple quilting projects can be embellished using reverse chain or coverstitch to create an interesting effect on the top side of your work. Using decorative threads will add detail to your work and you may wish to use the thread palette (see page 93) to add a variety of colour and thread types. See examples of quilting and decorative stitches on the Cambridge table runner project on page 170.

1 Mark the lines of your quilting design onto the underside or backing layer of your project. Use a template if you wish to create a repeating design, as shown.

2 Take a layer of wadding/batting and the top layer of fabric and create a sandwich with the wadding in the centre. Pin the layers together, pinning from the centre outwards. If you wish, tack the layers together by hand using cotton or water-soluble thread. This will help stop puckering or distortion in the fabric as you quilt and means you can remove the pins so they don't get in the way later.

3 Stitch from the wrong side of your project, following the marked lines to create your design. You may want to start from the centre and work outwards to avoid the layers puckering.

Wash your project to remove traces of the disappearing pen and water-soluble thread. Alternatively, spray your project with water and use a toothbrush to gently remove the unwanted elements.

Lace effects (faggoting)

Stitching on wash-away stabilizer can be the perfect way to create a lace effect but due to the size of the presser foot, the purpose and design of a coverstitch machine, it is not possible to create the more intricate detail that can be achieved with machine embroidery on a sewing machine. However, a technique known as faggoting can be performed on a coverstitch machine where two pieces of fabric, lace or ribbon are attached, leaving a narrow gap in the centre.

The finished effect.

Tip

A wider gap between strips can be created by overlapping rows of stitching.

1 Set your machine for wide coverstitch using the left and right needles. Use a regular thread in a colour to match your project for the needles and use a heavier thread such as metallic, upholstery or topstitching thread in a matching or contrasting colour for the looper. Stitch length can be adjusted as necessary and longer stitches can be used to create a more open effect.

2 Cut a piece of wash-away stabilizer slightly larger than the size required for your project.

3 Use wash-away double-sided tape or water-soluble thread to apply lengths of ribbon to the stabilizer, keeping a gap of 3mm (⅛in) where stitch width is 5mm (scant ¼in) wide or 4mm (³⁄₁₆in) where the stitch width is 6mm (¼in) wide between each strip.

4 For best results, use reverse coverstitch and work from the wrong side of the stabilizer. If you need to protect the surface of the ribbon from the feed-dog teeth, place another piece of stabilizer between the feed-dog teeth and the ribbon.

5 Stitch the ribbon to the stabilizer, aligning the needles so they catch the edge of the ribbon.

6 Hand wash your work to remove the stabilizer and double-sided tape to reveal a decorative lace effect. When drying, use pins to hold the work in its original shape and stretch out the threads.

Ideas to try: textured techniques

A Use chain stitch to create a ruffle and apply it to the front of a child's dress using coverstitch. Pull out the initial chain stitch after application.

B Create pintucks using chain stitch to add texture to the sleeves of a top.

C Form decorative pintucks by folding along the line of the tuck and stitching in place with a narrow coverstitch. Place small buttons at intervals to hold the pintucks open in different directions.

D Form decorative pintucks by folding along the line of the tuck and stitching in place with triple coverstitch using a contrasting variegated cotton thread in the looper. Rotate the fabric 90° and stitch across in opposite directions to reveal the decorative thread and provide additional texture.

E Make a trapunto quilting effect by using a wide coverstitch and threading cord through the channels after stitching.

F Use faggoting to join strips of satin ribbon to create a lace effect on the yoke of a blouse (see above). Two strands of thread are used in the looper.

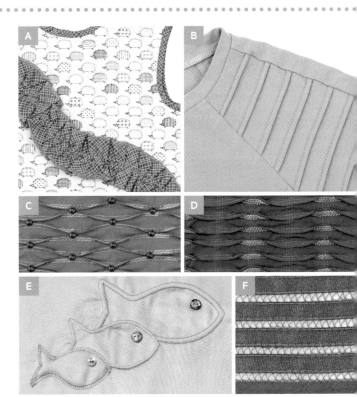

Finishing necklines, cuffs and other raw edges

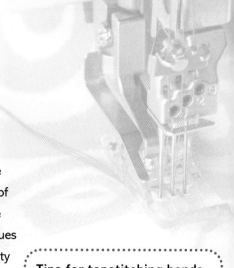

You can easily replicate neckline, armhole and other edge finishes of ready-to-wear garments by using a coverstitch machine. Create a simple turned and stitched hem with one, two or three needles depending on the type of look required, or use your machine to add topstitching to a band of fabric after this has been attached to give a decorative finish and keep the seam allowance in place on the wrong side of the garment. Other techniques that can be used include the mock-band hem shown on page 105, a variety of methods using elastic covered on pages 108–121, and methods for binding edges shown on pages 122–133. Cuff finishing techniques may be applied before sleeves are inserted, before stitching sleeve seams or as a final construction stage, depending on the type of garment being made. Working in the round will give a neater finish but can be difficult for small openings, where a flat construction method can be used instead.

Tips for topstitching bands
- Lower the differential feed to 0.8–1 to allow the neckline to stretch.
- Use a stitch length of 2.5–3.
- Use the edge of the foot or the guidelines on the foot to keep your stitching straight.

TURNED AND STITCHED HEM

The easiest way to finish an opening on a garment is to turn under the raw edge and stitch. This technique works particularly well for curved openings such as armholes and necklines in stretch fabrics. Finish necklines before attaching sleeves or sewing side seams as it is easier to do while the garment is flat. For light-weight stretchy knits or heavy fabrics, apply a stabilizer to the neckline or armhole before hemming as shown on page 83 'Stabilizing curved openings', then use one of the methods for 'Hemming in the round' on page 79 to finish the opening edge.

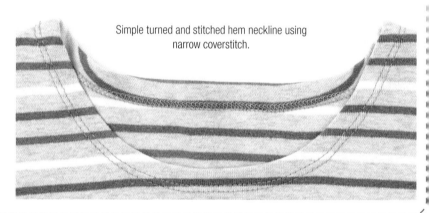

Simple turned and stitched hem neckline using narrow coverstitch.

SELF-FABRIC OR RIBBING BANDS

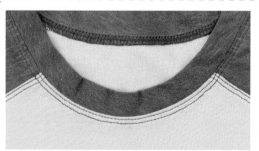

Self-fabric round neck band with two-needle narrow coverstitch to hold the seam allowance in place and give a decorative stitch line.

A self-fabric or ribbing band is a great way to finish opening edges of knit garments. Once the band has been applied it can be topstitched using coverstitch to keep the seam allowance in place on the wrong side of the garment.

Achieving a well-fitting neckband can be difficult and may take a little practice. Cutting the band to the correct size and stretching it just the right amount in the right places will help to create the best results. The desired finish is a band that doesn't gape because it is too big nor gather the neckline of the garment because it is too small.

ATTACHING A SELF-FABRIC OR RIBBING BAND

Follow these steps to apply a band to a neckline, or use it to apply cuffs, armhole bands, and bottom bands to tops and sweatshirts. Align the band seam with a garment seam or centre this at the back as shown in the example below.

1 With the right sides of the fabric together, join the short edges of the band together using either a chain stitch or overlocking stitch. Press the seam open or snip the centre.

2 Press the seam allowances in opposite directions. Fold the band with wrong sides together, align the raw edges and press in place. Tack the raw edges together if necessary.

3 Mark the centre and quarter points on the band with pins.

4 With right sides together, align the raw edges and pin the seam line of the band to the centre back. Match the centre point of the band to the centre front of the neckline and the quarter marks to the shoulder seams. (For raglan sleeves, match the quarter marks

to the shoulder points.) Stretch the band to fit as necessary and pin in place. Press shoulder seams towards the back.

5 Use machine tacking or chain stitch to attach the band. Check the fit of the band and adjust if necessary. Overlock the band to the neckline and press to finish.

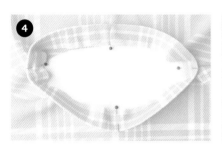

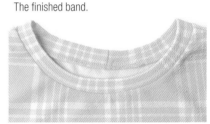

The finished band.

TOPSTITCHING THE BAND

The band can be topstitched in place using one, two or three needles, aligning the needles so that the seam allowance will be held in place, or so that the seam line is straddled. Stitching can be done from the right or wrong side, depending on the required finish. The steps show how to topstitch a neckband, but the same method can be used for any garment band.

Set your machine to one-, two- or three-needle stitching. Begin stitching on the back part of the neckband, just after the shoulder seam.

1 Line up the seam line of the neckband to a position on the foot or use the edge of the foot as a guide so the needle(s) will consistently enter the fabric the correct distance away from the neckband seam.

2 Stitch all round the neckline until you are 3cm (1⅛in) from the starting stitches. Trim thread ends from the starting stitches on both sides of the fabric.

3 Complete your stitching, overlapping the starting stitching by four or five stitches.

4 Finish off using the swipe, snip and lock method shown on page 34.

The finished band.

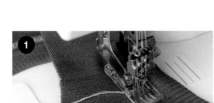

HOW BIG SHOULD THE BAND BE?

For cuffs, armholes and bottom bands of tops, a self-fabric band can be cut to the measurement of the part of the garment where it will be attached. When using ribbing, cut the fabric 10–25% shorter than the garment measurement: how much shorter will depend on the stretchiness of the ribbing you're using and the desired finish. For a closer fit around the wrist or waist, and a flat finish where the band joins the garment, shape the band as a V at the side seams or sleeve seam, using the garment measurement for the widest part and the measurement desired for a closer fit for the smaller part as shown below. For very curved or shaped armholes, follow guidance for round necklines.

When applying a band to a neckline, the type of neckline and the fabric you're working with will determine the measurement of the neckband. Knitted fabrics will behave differently to each other so you'll need to experiment with the length of neckband to achieve the desired finish. Always cut the band on the fabric in the direction of greatest stretch.

Self-fabric bands and ribbing have a different amount of stretch and recovery so there are separate rules to follow for each. Be aware that the more the band is stretched to fit, the more it will reduce in width, so add a little extra to the width measurement for ribbing bands and don't forget to add the seam allowance to your finished neckband measurements.

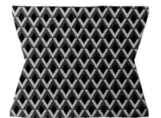
Shaped cuff.

Folded cuff.

Attached cuff.

MEASURING FOR A NECKBAND

1 Fold the garment at the centre front and centre back and align the shoulder seams. Measure along the seam line from centre back to centre front, keeping the tape measure on its side to accurately measure the curve. Double this measurement to give the total neckline measurement.

2 Multiply the measurement of the neckline by 0.85 to make the neckband 15% smaller. (Or multiply by a different number to achieve the correct percentage reduction in length for the fabric you are using.)

3 Cut your neckband piece the measurement you just calculated plus two seam allowances and a width of double the required finished measurement plus two seam allowances, e.g. using a width of 5cm (2in) will give a finished neckband of 1.5cm (⅝in) and two seam allowances of 1cm (⅜in).

Tips for applying a neckband
- Stretch the neckband to fit, but don't stretch the neckline.
- Use chain stitch or long machine stitch to attach the band and then assess how well it fits – it's much easier to remove this type of stitching than an overlocked stitch.
- If you're working with a scooped or very low neckline you will need to adjust the placement of the quarter markings on your band since matching these to the shoulder seams will mean that the band won't stretch around the scooped edge without puckering – see 'Deep necklines', opposite.
- If the band you attach is too big, for a quick finish and to avoid having to remove and adjust the band, fold the band to the inside of the garment and coverstitch in place as shown below.

Oversized band.

Band folded inside.

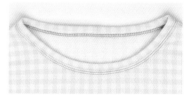
Band stitched in place.

ROUND NECKLINES

For crew, boat and rounded necklines that aren't very deep, the band will be stretched to fit to enable the band to sit flat against the body. When cutting a self-fabric band, the width of the finished neckband should be 1.25–1.5cm (½in–⅝in) and the band cut 15–25% shorter than the neckline. When using ribbing, as this stretches more, cut the band 25–35% shorter than the neckline with a width of up to 5cm (2in).

HIGH NECKLINES

For polo or turtleneck finishes where the band will stand up, cut the neckband the same measurement as the neckline and select a width of your choice for both self-fabric and ribbing bands.

DEEP NECKLINES

For V-neck, scooped and U-shaped necklines, assuming the shaping is in the front of the garment, the back section of the band will require the most stretch and the front edge very little to none at all for straight V-neck shapes. For self-fabric bands, cut the band the measurement of the front section plus 75% of the back neckline measurement. When using ribbing, cut the band 25% shorter than the neckline but only stretch slightly around the front edge and stretch more at the shoulder and in the back neckline.

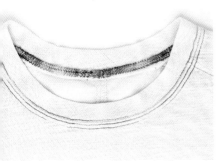

FINISHING A V-NECK

To achieve a professional-looking finish on your V-neck, cutting the neckband the right size, attaching the band correctly and starting your topstitching in the right place are key. See 'Deep necklines' above for how big the neckband should be for the type of fabric that you are working with and follow the directions below on how to attach and topstitch the band.

Attaching the band

There are three techniques that can be used to attach a V-neck band: 1) a perfectly mitred corner; 2) the alternative mitred corner; and 3) the overlapping V. These techniques work for both self-fabric bands and ribbing. The instructions assume that the V section is in the front of the garment.

Method 1: Perfectly mitred corner

This method works best if you already have a pattern, the size of the neckband has been tried and tested and there are notches provided to help you to match the band to the neckline.

1 Staystitch the front neckline 2.5cm (1in) either side of the V, stitching along the seam line. Snip into the seam allowance at the V, up to the staystitching.

2 Cut out the band using the pattern piece, cutting with greatest stretch along the length of the band. Stitch the short edges using a regular sewing machine or chain stitch and snip to the centre of the V.

3 Press seam allowances open, fold the neckband with wrong sides together and press. Tack raw edges together within the seam allowance if necessary. Fold the band in half to mark the centre-back point.

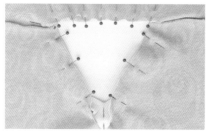

Finished V-neck.

4 On the neckband, measure from the edge of the V up to the seamline and match this point to the staystitching at the V on the neckline.

5 Pin the centre back of the band to the centre back of the neckline. Stretch the band to fit and pin in place, with pins on the inside. If the front edges are straight and you're using a self-fabric band, stretch the band only around the back neckline. If you're using ribbing, stretch mostly around the back neckline and a little along the front edges.

6 Working from the wrong side of the garment, tack the band in place using a long machine stitch or chain stitch.

7 Adjust the amount of stretch along each edge to give the flattest finish and then overlock in place.

Method 2: Alternative mitred corner

The length of the band can be easily adjusted using this technique so it's ideal when you're unsure how long to cut the band for a perfectly flat finish.

1 Staystitch and snip the neckline as described in method 1 (page 101).

2 Refer to page 100, 'How big should the band be?' to cut a neckband the length required.

3 Follow step 3 of method 1 (page 101).

4 Measure the back neckband, then calculate 75% of this. Mark 75% of the back neckline measurement onto the neckband with the mid point of this at the centre-back marker. E.g. if the back neck measurement is 12cm (4¾in), 75% of this is 9cm (3½in), so measure 4.5cm (1¾in) either side of the centre-back point and mark with pins or chalk.

5 With right sides together and raw edges aligned, match the centre-back point on the neckband to the centre-back mark on the neckline. Align the shoulder seams to the markings you've just made on the neckband either side of the centre-back point. Stretch the back neckline to fit and pin in place, with the pins on the inside of the garment.

6 If using a self-fabric band, for V-necklines where the front edges are straight, pin the neckband in place up to the V, without stretching the neckline or band. For V-necklines that are slightly curved, stretch the front section of the band slightly and pin in place up to the V. If using ribbing, stretch slightly around the front for all types of V-neck.

7 From the wrong side of the neckline, start and end stitching at the V and stitch the band in place with a long machine stitch or chain stitch.

8 Check the fit of the band and alter if necessary.

9 Place the ends of the band together at the V and mitre the corner by stitching straight, through the layers of the neck band, in line with the centre front of the garment. You may find it easier to grip the fabric and stitch more evenly by placing tear-away stabilizer under the presser foot.

10 Trim off any excess from the length of band and overlock the neckband in place.

CB

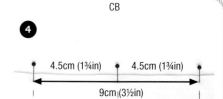

4.5cm (1¾in)   4.5cm (1¾in)

9cm (3½in)

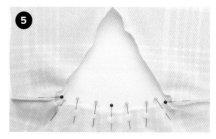

Method 3: Overlapping V

1 Follow steps 1–3 of method 2.

2 Overlap the edges of the band to form a V. Use tacking stitches or chain stitch to hold in place.

3 Follow steps 4–7 of method 1. For tips on how to stretch the neckband into place see steps 4–6 of method 2.

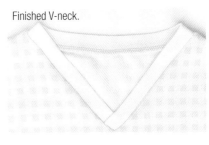

Finished V-neck.

Topstitching the V-neckline

The trick to perfect topstitching on the neckline is knowing where to start stitching. For V-necks that are slightly rounded along the front edges, begin stitching from the back neckline, close to the shoulder seam. Follow the guidance on page 87 for 'Cornering with coverstitch' and follow 'Method 4 – Curved stitching' (page 88). This method also works for topstitching U-shaped necklines. For V-necks where the front edge is straight, start and end the topstitching at the V as follows:

1 Set your machine for one-, two- or three-needle stitching.

2 Turn the V upside down and begin stitching at the V.

3 Line up the seam line of the neckband to a position on the foot or use the edge of the foot as a guide so the needle(s) will enter the fabric the correct distance away from the neckband seam.

4 Stitch all the way round the neckline until you are 3cm (1⅛in) from the starting stitches at the V. Trim the thread ends from the starting stitches on both sides of the fabric.

5 Continue stitching and use the handwheel to make the final stitches, overlapping the first stitches to make a perfect V.

6 Finish off using the swipe, snip and lock method described on page 34.

FACINGS

One way to achieve a clean finish around the neckline, armhole or hemline of a garment is to apply a facing – a piece of fabric that finishes the raw edge and is turned to the underside of the garment. A facing will match exactly the shape of the part of the garment it will be applied to. Stitch the facing right sides together with the garment edge, trim and snip seam allowances and then, if required, understitch and press the facing to the wrong side of the garment. Understitching (stitching through the seam allowance and the facing) should keep the facing in place on the inside of the garment but you can add additional topstitching with the coverstitch machine to secure and add a decorative feature (see 'Ideas to try: necklines' on page 104 and also notes on 'Using binding as a facing' on page 127).

Ideas to try: necklines

A Decorative double band topstitched with two-needle coverstitch straddling the seamline.

B V-neck finished with ribbing and two-needle narrow coverstitch.

C Decorative application of twill tape to finish and stabilize back neckline and shoulder seams of a round-neck T-shirt (see 'Non-stretch tape' on page 81).

D Neckline of button-shoulder top finished with a facing and stitched in place using two-needle coverstitch.

E Neckline finished with matching ribbing and two-needle reverse coverstitch in contrasting thread.

F Turtleneck sweatshirt with two-needle narrow coverstitch topstitching.

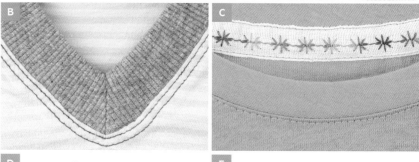

MOCK-BAND HEM

A quick and easy finish for the bottom of tops, dresses, skirts, and cuffs is the mock-band hem – so called since it looks like you've sewn on a band of fabric but you've just turned the edge under and overlocked. This method is completed in the round using a hemming depth of at least 3cm (1⅛in) to keep the hem from turning back up to the right side. For heavier fabrics, a hem of 4cm (1½in) or more is best. Once sewn, the mock-band seam allowance can be topstitched to hold it in place. Using reverse coverstitch to topstitch the seam works well here since the raw edge is already overlocked, although you can use any of the other stitch types instead.

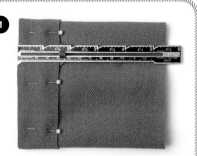

1 Turn up the hem to the wrong side of the fabric and pin or press in place.

2 Turn the folded hem back towards the right side of the fabric and keep the raw edge level with the new fold. Pin in place.

3 Overlock the fold and raw edge together: cut off any fraying ends but avoid cutting into the fold by keeping your eye on the overlocker knife as you stitch.

4 Turn the garment right side out and press the seam allowance away from the hem.

5 To keep the seam allowance flat, this can be stitched in place. For a reverse coverstitch effect, sew from the inside of the garment using two or three needles. Line the right needle up with the seam line and keep this in line all the way round. (See 'Hemming in the round' and 'Stitching from the wrong side of the fabric (reverse coverstitch)' on page 79 and also 'Topstitching the band' on page 99).

Tips for hemming and topstitching narrow cuffs

• Sew on the inside of the tube: work from the wrong side of the garment for reverse coverstitch; turn the sleeve inside out and stitch on the right side of the garment for regular coverstitch. See page 79 – 'Hemming in the round'.

• Use a smaller hem depth of 1.5–2cm (⅝–¾in).

• Sew the hem as a flat piece, instead of working in the round, then stitch the sleeve seam. Use hand or machine stitches to keep the seam allowance flattened inside the cuff. See techniques on page 78, 'Overlocking a seam after hemming flat'.

Cuff hemmed as a flat piece.

MAKING YOUR OWN RIBBING

There is a wide variety of ribbing fabrics available to the home sewer including prefinished ribbed bands and ribbing that can be bought by the metre but if you can't find the exact colour match that you're after you can make your own ribbing using a light- to medium-weight stretch fabric. The easy way to create a ribbing effect is to use a pintuck foot for your machine as follows:

1 Insert the centre and right needles (or as directed for your machine) to create a narrow coverstitch. Attach the pintuck foot to your machine. Open the left side cover of the machine, place the thin end of the pintucking guide under the groove in the pintuck foot and position the guide on the needle plate. Close the left side cover to hold the guide in position.

2 Mark the position of the first pintuck with a chalk line or other fabric marker and align the marked line with the centre of the groove.

3 Take the first two stitches with the handwheel and then continue along the fabric.

4 For the next and consecutive lines of pintucks, align the edge of the presser foot with the previous pintuck.

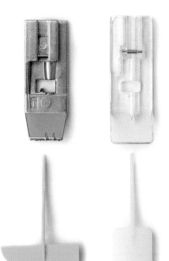

baby lock BLCS2 pintuck foot and pintucking guide (left); Janome 1200D pintuck foot K with pintucking guide (right).

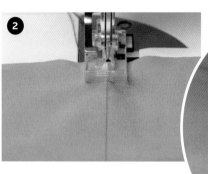

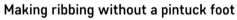

Making ribbing without a pintuck foot

If you don't have a pintuck foot you can still create pintucks using a narrow or wide coverstitch setting. Usually, when using a coverstitch machine, the aim is to avoid tunnelling. In this case, you want to try to accentuate it as much as possible. Try the following, testing out the effects of each before trying the next adjustment to make the pintucks more prominent:

- Stitch length of 3–3.5.

- Tighten the looper tension.

- Decrease the presser-foot pressure.

- Use woolly nylon or woolly polyester in the looper.

- Tighten the needle tension.

- Decrease the differential feed for light-weight fabrics or if the fabric starts bunching.

Tip

Ribbing made using the pintuck method will not have the same stretch and recovery as purpose-made ribbing. The amount of stretch will depend on the fabric used and the number of pintucks. The more pintucks there are, the less it will stretch.

Ideas to try: cuffs

A Mock-band hem technique used for a cuff on a short sleeve, with reverse coverstitching to hold the seam in place.

B Ribbing fabric used for cuffs with triple coverstitching straddling the seam line.

C Faux ribbing made using coverstitched pintucks and used for cuffs.

D Cuffs with thumbholes made in assorted contrasting fabrics with triple coverstitched topstitching.

E Ribbing fabric used for cuff with green piping detail and triple coverstitching to straddle the seam line.

F Shirring used at the wrist to create a gathered and fluted cuff effect (see 'Shirring elastic' on page 109).

G Silicone gripper elastic used on the cuffs of cycling shorts (see 'Using elastic' on page 108).

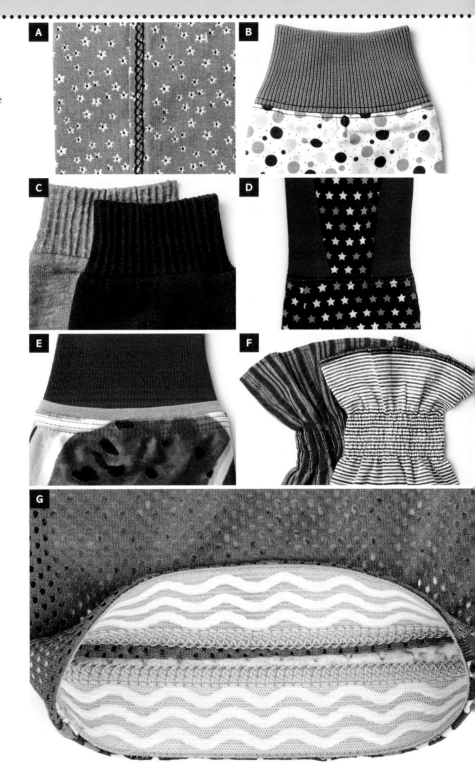

Using elastic

The coverstitch machine can be used to apply a range of elastics, using methods from ready-to-wear clothing to achieve a professional finish. Check your own swimwear, lingerie or sportswear and you'll find a whole range of elastic types which are most likely attached to the fabrics using coverstitch techniques. You may already have tried to apply elastics using your regular sewing machine and zigzag stitch, or perhaps used the overlocker to stitch and edge finish the elastic in one go but with the coverstitch machine, you can take your skills further and replicate the appearance of factory-made garments in your own home.

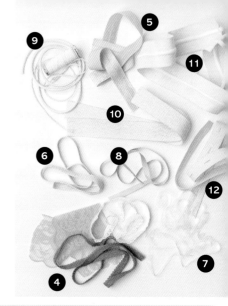

TYPES OF ELASTIC

There are generally three types of elastic: knitted, braided and woven, a variety of types within each of these, and clear elastic. Most elastics are made from polyester, nylon or cotton and rubber (or stretchable synthetic), except for clear elastic which is made from polyurethane.

1 Knitted elastic is soft to the touch and can be stretched without reducing in width. It may roll a little at the edges but is ideal for construction which requires it to be sewn through since it doesn't reduce in elasticity or become damaged from piercing. It is suitable for use with light- to medium-weight fabrics.

2 Woven elastic is a firm elastic that maintains its width when stretched. It is suitable for use with medium- to heavy-weight fabrics, for both casings and applications that require it to be sewn.

3 Braided elastic can be identified by the parallel ridges along the length of the elastic. It is ideal for use in casings as it can become weakened by being sewn or pinned. It can roll at the edges and when stretched the elastic will narrow in width.

SPECIALITY ELASTICS

4 Lingerie elastic There are a variety of types of lingerie elastic, including stretch lace, but the most common type is formed of a band of knitted elastic with a decorative, picot or scalloped edge. Some types have a soft or plush side, designed to lie against the skin. Lingerie elastic is usually used to edge the leg and waist holes of knickers, and the lower band or upper cup edging of a bra.

5 Fold-over elastic This knitted elastic comes in a range of colours and has a line which runs down the centre of the elastic so it can fold in half. Often referred to as FOE, it has similar uses to bias binding but it stretches so it's the ideal finish for anything made in stretch fabric. FOE can be used for creating headbands and hair ties but is more commonly used for edging lingerie and finishing other garment openings such as necklines, armholes, and cuffs. FOE may have a shiny side or fuzzy side so you can decide which side to show on your project.

6 Swimwear elastic This is a type of braided elastic that will narrow as it is stretched. Usually made from cotton and rubber it is resistant to salt and chlorinated water, suntan lotion and a certain amount of heat.

7 Clear elastic This is a light-weight transparent elastic that can be used as a stabilizer for shoulder seams, necklines, pockets and other garment openings or to create gathers in knit garments. Some, but not all types of clear elastic are resistant to swimming conditions and can be used for finishing the openings of swimwear and

lingerie. This elastic can vary in amount of stretch and recovery and also narrows as it is stretched.

8 Rubber or tech elastic Resistant to salt and chlorinated water, this elastic is used in the construction of swimwear and some sportswear for garment openings and straps. This is thinner than cotton swimwear elastic so less bulky to use. It may be coated with talc or silicone to help it grip to the fabric as it is sewn and not stick to your presser foot.

9 Cord elastic This type of elastic comes in a range of thickness. Wider cord can be used within casings of coats, jackets and tops or for button loops. The thinnest type of cord elastic is known as shirring elastic and is used to gather fabrics on cuffs, necklines and waistlines, or for decorative effects.

10 Silicone-backed elastic This elastic has either spots or strips of silicone along one side of the elastic and is commonly used in sportswear such as cycling tights or shorts at the waistline or leg cuff to grip the clothing to the wearer.

11 Drawstring elastic This elastic has a cord that runs the length of it and is ideal for waistbands that require both elastic and a draw cord.

12 Buttonhole elastic This is commonly used for waistbands in childrenswear and works in conjunction with buttons which are placed inside the waist edge to allow the garment to be loosened or tightened to adjust the fit and to allow for growth.

ELASTIC GATHERING ATTACHMENT OR FOOT

This attachment makes sewing elastic onto fabric much quicker and easier. The device holds the elastic and stretches it evenly as you attach it to your fabric (see 'Creating elasticated ruffles' on page 112). You may be able to use a variety of elastic widths with this accessory, or purchase attachments in different sizes. This attachment can also be used for applying tapes and ribbon to your projects – just release the tension on the device and it can be used as a taping guide (see page 92, 'Taping foot or guide').

Janome CoverPro (left); Janome 1200D (right).

SHIRRING ELASTIC

This is the narrowest of the elastics and is sometimes referred to as elastic thread. This type of cord elastic is slightly thicker than topstitching thread, comes on a spool and can be used in the bobbin of a sewing machine, in the upper looper of your overlocker or in the chain looper of your coverstitch machine. Shirring works best on light-weight fabrics that can be easily gathered. This technique can take some practice and results will vary depending on your machine, type of fabric, and the quality and thickness of the elastic. Chain stitch is used to apply shirring elastic, but the stitching on the wrong side of your project may or may not resemble a chain, depending on the brand and model of machine. Don't compare the look of your shop-bought, ready-to-wear shirring top to the results on your domestic coverstitch machine – in industry, a specific chain-stitch machine for elastic is used for mass-produced clothing (see other examples of this on page 59 ('Ideas to try: chain stitch') and page 107 ('Ideas to try: cuffs').

1 Set your machine to chain stitch with a stitch length of 3–4. Make sure the machine is stitching a perfectly balanced chain stitch before swapping the looper thread with the shirring elastic (see tips on page 30 for threading your machine with bulky threads).

2 Run a few tests on scrap fabric before working on your project. Set the foot pressure to medium/high. Make sure the elastic is in tension and being stretched slightly as it is applied – this will make the fabric bunch as you sew. For additional bunching, tighten the tension on the elastic and/or increase the differential feed.

3 Once you are ready to sew onto your project, begin stitching. If working in the round, continue in a spiral until you have completed the section to be shirred, using the edge of the presser foot or other marker as a guide to keep lines evenly spaced.

4 For rows of stitching, each line can be marked in advance or just mark the first line and stitch along the line, pivot at the end, take a few stitches along the width of the fabric and then pivot again to come back along the length of the fabric. Align the next row of stitching with the edge of the foot or other marker to keep stitching lines evenly spaced. You may need to set your differential feed to 1 or N to make the turning stitches.

Tips for shirring

- Use a thread net for elastic, snap-on thread guide (see page 14 'Must-have tools for coverstitch machines'), or keep an eye on how it is unravelling so it doesn't become tangled. Remove any threads not in use from the spool pins so these are not tangled in the elastic.

- If working in rows, make a continuous line of stitch, turning after each row. Alternatively, stitch onto water-soluble fabric at the end of each line of stitching to avoid the elastic being cut too short and pinging back into the machine.

- Bypass some of the thread guides if the looper is too tight.

- Loosening the tension on the needles and increasing the stitch length helps accentuate the gathering effect.

- Apply steam from the iron after you've finished, to encourage the fabric to bunch up further.

LINGERIE ELASTIC

Applying picot-edged elastic to lingerie projects can be completed much more quickly and professionally with the use of a coverstitch machine since you have the option to apply the elastic with just one line of sewing, rather than two. Elastic can be attached first with a regular sewing machine or overlocker, turned to the inside and then sewn again using the coverstitch machine or simply applied only with the coverstitch machine. The quickest method is to apply the elastic using a flat technique which uses only one line of stitching. Use regular threads in the needles and woolly nylon/polyester in the looper for a softer finish next to the skin.

Method 1: Two lines of stitching

Apply the elastic in the round for this technique (see 'Joining elastic in the round' on page 120).

1 Quarter the elastic and fabric edge and then match the straight edge of the elastic to the raw edge of the fabric, right sides together. If the elastic has a plush side this will be on the wrong side so it sits next to the skin once stitching is complete. Pin or hold the elastic with clips.

2 Overlock the elastic in place or use a narrow zigzag stitch on a sewing machine and stitch close to the picot edge. Stretch the elastic to fit as you stitch but don't stretch the fabric.

3 Turn the elastic to the inside so the picot edge is just showing from the right side of the fabric. Stitch in place using a narrow or wide coverstitch, keeping the right needle close to the picot edge.

Method 2: One line of stitching

Apply the elastic in the round or flat for this technique. You may wish to overlock the raw edge of the fabric before applying the elastic to stop it from rolling. The elastic can be applied to the right or wrong side of the fabric, depending on preference, comfort, the type of elastic and the type of stitch used.

1 Match the wrong side of the elastic to the right side of the fabric so the picot edge extends just beyond the raw edge. Pin or clip in place. Alternatively, use an elastic attachment to hold the elastic in tension and avoid using pins.

2 Stitch in place from the right side of the fabric using a narrow, wide or triple coverstitch, keeping the right needle close to the picot edge. Stretch the elastic to fit as you stitch but don't stretch the fabric.

Tip

If your machine has a top coverstitch option, you may find it quicker and easier to apply the right side of the elastic to the wrong side of the fabric, placing pins on the right side. Stitch in place from the right side, keeping the right needle in line with or slightly straddling the raw edge of the fabric. This way you can apply the elastic and finish the raw edge of fabric at the same time. Use woolly nylon/polyester in both the top-cover spreader and looper for the best coverage and comfort.

Tip
Some elastic will grow a little when it is stretched so before cutting and applying any elastic, stretch it out.

USING FOLD-OVER ELASTIC (FOE)

This elastic is brilliant for binding the edges on projects made from stretch fabric and is used for the armhole edges and straps of the Buenavista beach wrap on page 150. This elastic can be used with knit fabrics to be functional or for woven fabrics as a decorative edge finish. If you're using this on a pattern that has a seam allowance around the edge that you'll be applying your elastic to, you'll need to remove the seam allowance first. Avoid cutting the elastic to size until you're sure you have applied it correctly.

1 Choose which side of the fold-over elastic (FOE) you want to see on the outside of your project. Match the centre fold line of the elastic with the raw edge of the fabric and wrap the elastic around the fabric edge.

2 As you pin the elastic in place, hold it in tension or stretch it to get the best results. For straight edges on woven fabrics hold the elastic in tension; for knit fabrics stretch the elastic slightly but not so much that the fabric gathers. For curved edges on both knit and woven fabrics stretch the elastic a little more so it will sit flat once finished. Pin in place.

3 If you're not sure you've stretched the elastic enough for a flat finish, tack in place with hand or machine stitching and check.

4 Use chain stitch or coverstitch to stitch the elastic in place.

Using fold-over elastic in the round

If you're working in the round, begin at a seamline and leave a tail end of elastic at the start. Stretch and pin the elastic in place, leaving a tail end of elastic at the end. Check you're happy with the finish of the elastic by tacking in place and making sure it sits flat. Join the ends of elastic using one of the methods shown on pages 120–121, 'Joining elastic in the round' and then stitch the FOE with a chain or coverstitch.

CREATING ELASTICATED RUFFLES

Narrow knitted elastic can be used instead of a high differential-feed setting to create ruffles. This is ideal for adding an attractive effect to stretch clothing such as childrenswear or swimwear.

Tip

Elastic can be applied to the right or wrong side of the fabric strip for different effects.

1 Cut a 4cm (1½in) wide strip of fabric at least twice as long as you want the finished ruffle to be. Use scissors or a rotary cutter with a waved- or scalloped-edged blade to give a decorative effect.

2 Set your machine to chain stitch and a long stitch length. Place your fabric under the presser foot so the needle is in the centre. Use the elastic gathering attachment, tape guide or taping foot to align the elastic to the centre of the fabric and run this under the presser foot so there is around 3–5cm (1⅛–2in) beyond the back of the foot. Lower the needle into the fabric and take the first two stitches with the handwheel.

3 Adjust the tension on the elastic attachment or, if you don't have this accessory, stretch the elastic as it is applied and stitch along the length of your fabric.

The finished elasticated ruffle.

USING SWIMWEAR ELASTIC

There are three types of elastic that can be applied to swimwear: clear, rubber and braided cotton swimwear elastic. These are best applied to the wrong side of the fabric and then wrapped or enclosed by folding the fabric over so the elastic won't be in direct contact with skin when worn. The elastic will need to be held taught or slightly stretched as it is applied. How much it is stretched will depend on the part of the garment it is being applied to and personal preference for fit. If you are new to using swimwear elastic, you may find it easiest to use a chain stitch to apply it as this can be quickly unravelled if you go wrong. Use woolly nylon in the looper for stretch and added comfort. See the bikini on page 174 for more images of how this elastic is used.

1 Align the elastic to the wrong side of the garment edge, in line with the raw edge if overlocking or slightly within the edge if using a zigzag or chain stitch, so that the elastic won't poke out after it is sewn.

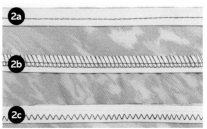

2 Use chain stitch (a); overlock the elastic in place, making sure not to cut the elastic as it is sewn (b); or use a narrow zigzag on a regular sewing machine, stitching close to the inner edge, as shown in image (c).

3 Fold the fabric edge to the wrong side of the garment, wrapping the elastic with the fabric, and using the inner edge of the elastic to guide the fold. Pin, clip or hold in place with your fingers.

4 Stitch from the right side of the garment and use a narrow or wide coverstitch to hold the elastic in place.

Tips

- Create cut-outs in your swimwear or other stretch garments using the technique opposite. Simply cut out the section of fabric, apply the swimwear elastic to the wrong side of the opening, overlapping ends slightly. Turn the elastic under and coverstitch in place.
- Elastic can also be applied while binding a garment edge, (see more details on page 126, 'Binding with elastic' or when making straps (see 'Making belt loops' on page 134).

Example of a cut-out.

ADJUSTING THE MACHINE SETTINGS FOR SWIMWEAR AND OTHER SEW-THROUGH ELASTICS

- As the elastic will add bulk to your project you may need to adjust the presser-foot pressure to accommodate this. For some models an increased presser-foot pressure will help to keep the fabric feeding through the machine.
- Use size 90/14 SUK needles so your machine can stitch through the layers of fabric and elastic.
- Increase the tension on the needles and looper if necessary, to accommodate the extra thickness of fabrics.
- Consider the position of the needles and aim to keep the feed-dog teeth and foot in contact with as much fabric as possible.
- There is a balance to be made with the settings for stitch length and differential feed when applying elastic. A long stitch length and high differential feed will give the least stretch with the possibility of looking gathered, conversely a short stitch length and low differential feed will give the most stretch with the possibility of stretching out of shape and appearing wavy.
- Experiment with scraps of fabric until you find the best settings for your machine.

SEWING-MACHINE AND OVERLOCKER STITCH SETTINGS FOR ELASTICS

When using a zigzag on the sewing machine, use a stitch length and width of 2.5. If using an overlocker, use a four-thread stitch with a stitch length of 3 to 4 and increase the differential feed slightly, if necessary, to 1.3. If you are concerned about cutting into the elastic, disengage the knife.

MAKING STRAPS WITH SWIMWEAR ELASTIC

If you're making swimwear (such as the bikini on page 174) or sportswear, include elastic in the straps to make them stronger and more supportive. There are a number of approaches to this including those which use specific attachments for your machine.

Method 1

This method allows you to produce separate straps that can be attached to a garment and creates a neat finish without visible stitching on the right side. However, it can be more difficult and time consuming to use this technique to turn long straps through to the right side. Make sure that the strips are cut accurately to size so the elastic is tightly enclosed within the strap. The finished strap will be the width of the elastic.

1 Cut a strip of fabric the length required for your strap and a width twice that of the elastic, plus two seam allowances, e.g. for 1cm (⅜in) of elastic and 6mm (¼in) seam allowances, cut the fabric strip 3.2cm (1¼in) wide. Fold the strip in half lengthways, right sides together. Pin or clip in place.

2 Overlock the edge or use a narrow zigzag.

3 Match the elastic to the overlocked edge and overlock or zigzag the elastic in place.

4 Use a loop turner or other device and turn the strip right sides out.

Tips

- You can use a length of overlocker chain to aid the turning process – before starting method 1, run off a chain of thread at least as long as your strap then without cutting it, lay the thread chain along the length of your strap and enclose this in step 1. Begin step 2, making sure that as you overlock the fabric you don't catch the thread chain. Once the elastic is attached to the fabric, pull on the thread chain to turn the strap to the right side.

- To speed up construction, the fabric strip can be folded and elastic applied as one step, instead of two as shown here.

Method 2

This technique works well for individual straps or when creating a bound edge which runs off into a strap, like those found on bralettes, sports tops and swimwear (see 'Single-layer binding with elastic' on page 126). It requires two lines of sewing and if done correctly will give a tightly wrapped elastic strap. Less accuracy is required for cutting the fabric strips, but it can be time consuming to wrap the elastic and trim away excess fabric.

The finished strap.

1 Cut a strip of fabric the length required for your strap and width at least three times as wide as your elastic, so for elastic that measures 1cm (⅜in), cut the fabric strip at least 3cm (1⅛in) wide.

2 Match the elastic to the wrong side of the fabric, along one of the long edges. Pin or clip in place.

3 Overlock, zigzag or use chain stitch to hold the elastic in place.

4 Wrap the fabric around the elastic so it is tightly enclosed. Pin or clip in place.

5 Set your machine to wide or narrow coverstitch, depending on the width of elastic. With the excess fabric underneath, coverstitch through all layers, keeping the stitching centred along the length of the strap.

6 Trim away any excess fabric.

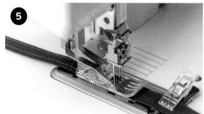

Method 3

This method is quick and easy, but requires a belt-loop foot or attachment for your machine. It is important that the elastic matches exactly to the width of the narrow end of the belt-loop attachment to avoid a baggy looking strap.

Follow the instructions for using the belt-loop attachment/foot on page 135.

The finished strap.

1 Once the fabric strip has been drawn through the machine and begins to fold, feed elastic into the device, pass this underneath the fabric strip so it is wrapped by the fabric. Pull the fabric through the device so the elastic is drawn through at the same time.

2 Attach the device to the machine if you haven't already. Place the folded fabric with elastic under the presser foot and begin stitching.

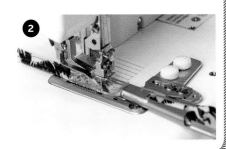

Method 4

Use a double-fold bias-binder attachment to fold the fabric and enclose elastic within the strap at the same time. Like method 2, this technique also works well when creating a bound edge which runs off into a strap. As with method 3, the elastic must match the width of the finished binding exactly or you end up with a baggy strap (see details on page 131 for binder attachments).

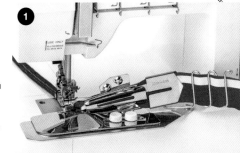

1 Align the top and bottom fold guides at the narrow end of the binder attachment so they sit directly above and below each other.

Once the fabric strip has been drawn through the machine and begins to fold, feed elastic into the device – pass this on top of the fabric strip so it will be wrapped by the fabric. Pull the fabric through the device so the elastic is drawn through at the same time. Position the elastic inside the top fold of fabric and keep the elastic positioned towards the top of the binder.

2 Align the binder correctly with the needles so the fold guides sit 2–3mm (1/16–1/8in) to the left of the left needle. Place the folded fabric with elastic under the presser foot and begin stitching.

The finished strap (front).

The finished strap (back).

> **Tip**
> This double-fold method can also be achieved without using a binder attachment, see page 126, 'Double-layer binding with elastic'.

ELASTICATED WAISTBANDS AND CASINGS: DIRECT-APPLICATION TECHNIQUES

There are a number of ways in which to attach elastic to create a waistband using a coverstitch machine, including the use of lingerie elastic as shown on page 110. Elastic may be directly applied to the garment or inserted into a casing. Techniques will vary depending on the type of elastic and the garment that is being made. For methods on joining elastic, see the options on page 120.

For the following methods, use regular polyester thread in the needles and choose regular polyester thread or a textured thread such as woolly nylon or woolly polyester in the looper. Textured thread will give a softer finish on the inside of the garment.

Lapped elastic method 1

This method requires just one line of machine stitching and leaves the elastic visible on the right side of the garment. It works perfectly for applying wide knitted elastic to sports bras, underpants or boxer shorts as it gives a smooth and non-bulky finish. It can also be used to apply stretch lace to lingerie or at the hems of cycling shorts to attach silicone gripper elastic.

The elastic is applied directly to the top of the garment and simply coverstitched in place. If you have a top-coverstitch option, this stitch could be used instead or you could reverse coverstitch from the wrong side of the garment. Use a soft, wide knitted elastic such as the 3.8cm (1½in) waistband elastic shown below.

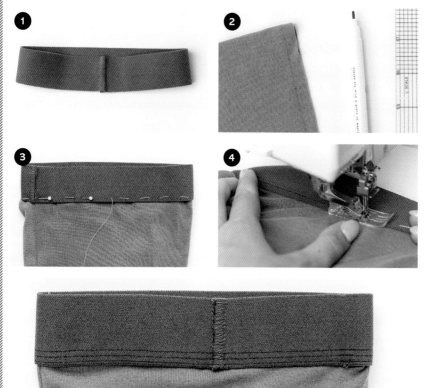

1 Join the elastic into a circle using an abutted seam or a flatlock method to give the flattest finish (see 'Joining elastic in the round' on page 120).

2 Draw a line on the right side of the fabric on the waist edge 7 or 8mm (¼ or ⁵⁄₁₆in) in from the edge (width depends on the maximum width of your wide coverstitch setting). Alternatively, overlock the waist edge using a four-thread wide stitch. This will provide an elastic placement line and also stop the edge of the fabric from rolling as the elastic is attached. Overlocking the edge is also required if you wish to use reverse coverstitching.

3 Quarter the elastic and quarter the waistline of the garment. With the join of the elastic at the centre back, match the quarter markings and align the inner edge of the elastic so it just covers the marked line on the right side of the fabric. Use pins or wash-away double-sided tape to hold the elastic in place. Use water-soluble thread to tack elastic in place if preferred.

4 Set your machine to triple coverstitch. Stitch the elastic in place from the right side of the garment, using the method for stitching in the round on page 79. (Or work from the wrong side and use reverse coverstitching.) Stretch the elastic to match the fabric but don't stretch the fabric and keep the left needle just inside the inner edge of the elastic.

The finished elastic.

Lapped elastic method 2

This alternative method can be used on light-weight fabrics. Include an additional 6mm (¼in) seam allowance on the top or waist edge of the fabric. Follow step 1 of 'Lapped elastic method 1' opposite.

1 Quarter the elastic and quarter the waistline of the garment. With the join of the elastic at the centre back, match the quarter markings and place wrong sides together, keeping the edge of the elastic aligned with the raw edge of the fabric. Pin in place and use chain stitch or zigzag to attach it.

2 Pull the elastic away from the garment edge, then follow steps 4 and 5 of 'Lapped elastic method 1' opposite to complete, keeping the right needle in line with the seam line.

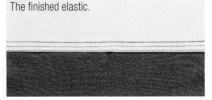
The finished elastic.

Enclosed method

This technique works well for a range of garments including bandeau tops, strapless dresses, leggings, skirts, running trousers and shorts. The elastic is stitched to the top of the garment, enclosed within a fold of fabric, then coverstitched in place. Use knitted or woven elastic in a width of your choice. The example below uses 2cm (¾in) wide knitted elastic.

1 Join the elastic into a circle using an abutted seam or a flatlock method (see pages 120–121). Quarter the elastic and quarter the waistline of the garment. With the elastic join at the centre back, match the quarter markings and align the outer edge of the elastic 1–2mm (⅛–¹⁄₁₆in) from the raw edge on the wrong side of the fabric. Use pins to hold the elastic in place.

2 Overlock the elastic in place, stretching it to match the fabric but not stretching the fabric. Allow the blade to trim off the 2mm (¹⁄₁₆in) protruding fabric, but don't cut the elastic. Turn the garment right side out.

3 Fold the top edge of the garment to the inside, using the inner edge of the elastic as a guide so the elastic is tightly wrapped. Pin in place, placing pins on the right side of the garment or clip in place.

4 Set your machine to a wide coverstitch and use a longer stitch length. You may also need to increase the differential feed, presser-foot pressure and tension dials. Stitch the elastic in place from the right side of the garment, using the method for stitching in the round on page 79. Keep the left needle just inside the inner edge of the elastic so both needles stitch through the elastic and fabric. Stretch the elastic as you stitch so the fabric becomes flat, but don't stretch the fabric.

The finished elastic.

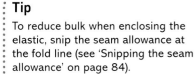
Tip
To reduce bulk when enclosing the elastic, snip the seam allowance at the fold line (see 'Snipping the seam allowance' on page 84).

For close-fitting garments the enclosed method can be used without completing the coverstitching in step 4. Once the elastic has been enclosed by the fabric simply hold this in place at the side seams with some hand stitching (see the image on the right).

ELASTICATED WAISTBANDS AND CASINGS: CASING TECHNIQUES

In the following methods a channel is created through which the elastic can be inserted. This channel, or casing, can be formed from a separate strip of fabric or by folding the waistline edge of the garment to the inside. A separate casing is a good way to incorporate contrasting fabric. For this method, cut the fabric for the casing the length of the measurement of the waistline edge plus seam allowance by twice the depth of the elastic plus seam allowance and 3mm (⅛in). For the fold-over casing, the casing depth should be the width of the elastic plus the width of the stitch required to hold it in place plus 3mm (⅛in). There is no need to include a seam or hem allowance since the coverstitch machine will be used to hold the casing in place and edge finish the raw edge of fabric at the same time. Use a knitted elastic for light- to medium-weight fabrics or a woven elastic for medium to heavy fabrics. Once the elastic is inserted into the channel, additional stitching can be added using chain stitch or regular machine stitch to ensure the elastic stays in position.

Separate casing

This technique works well if you want to have a contrasting waistline fabric or have included hip pockets. (For hip pockets, see pages 164–165.)

1 Cut the casing to the required measurements. In this example 3.8cm (1½in) wide elastic has been used so the casing is cut 10cm (4in) wide (twice the width of the elastic plus two seam allowances of 1cm (⅜in) each) plus a little more (4mm/³⁄₁₆in) to give extra room for the elastic, turn of fabric and allowances for inaccuracies in stitching.

2 With right sides together, stitch the short ends of the casing, leaving a gap on one side in the upper section of the seam through which to feed the elastic (see step 4 photo).

3 With wrong sides together, fold the casing in half lengthways and match the raw edges. Machine tack within the seam allowance to hold the long edges together.

4 Match the casing right sides together with the top edge of the garment, so the gap in the casing seam is on the outside. Overlock or machine stitch the casing in place.

5 Fold out the casing, pressing the seam allowance towards the garment. Topstitching can be added to the waistline using regular or reverse coverstitch at this stage if required.

6 Feed the elastic through the casing using a safety pin or elastic threader. Overlap the end of the elastic and join using one of the techniques described on pages 120–121.

7 Push the elastic back into the casing and close up the hole using slip stitch or another invisible hand-stitch technique.

Simple casing for narrow elastic

This technique can be used through a single layer of fabric to create a simple casing for the waistline of a dress, or as part of a hemming technique for cuffs in light-weight fabrics. Use a narrow 5mm (¼in) knitted elastic. When constructing, leave a side seam open until the elastic casing is complete.

1 For a cuff, turn up the hem and use a wide coverstitch with a long stitch length to hold in place. For a waistline casing, decide on the position of the casing and stitch all the way around the garment.

2 Feed narrow elastic through the 'casing' and pull up to the desired measurement then pin to hold in place.

3 Stitch the side seam, stitching through the elastic ends at the same time.

Fold-over casing with drawstring

This method is an ideal alternative to the 'Enclosed method' on page 117. Narrow 2cm (¾in) drawstring elastic is used in this example and buttonholes formed at the centre front of the garment to allow for the drawstring. If regular elastic is used, a drawstring can be made from ribbon, cord or fabric and inserted on top of the elastic. You could even make your drawstring with matching fabric using the belt-loop or binder attachment. (See 'Hove skirt' on page 160 for more details on these techniques.) Alternatively, omit the drawstring. Using the drawstring elastic works best where there is a centre-front seam to enable easier access through a gap in that seam to the cord and buttonholes.

1 Press a crease along the fold line for the casing. Create a gap in the centre-front seam between the fold line for the casing and the raw edge. This will make it easier to complete the casing and insert the elastic, particularly when using drawstring elastic. For regular elastic and when there is no centre-front seam, the gap can be made in the side seam.

2 To create the opening for the drawstring on the outside of the garment, at the centre front, open out the folded fabric. Measure down from the fold line half the width of the elastic and place a pin.

3 Mark a small horizontal buttonhole 1cm (⅜in) either side of the centre front through a single layer of fabric, in line with your pin. To place the drawstring opening on the inside of the garment, mark the buttonholes between the fold line and the raw edge. You can also use eyelets instead of buttonholes.

4 Use interfacing on the wrong side of the fabric to reinforce the buttonhole or eyelet. Make the buttonholes or insert eyelets. For fabrics that don't easily fray, cut a hole into the fabric without the need for reinforcement buttonhole stitching.

5 Fold over the casing and pin in place. Set your machine for narrow or wide coverstitch and stitch the casing in place.

6 Feed the elastic through the casing using a safety pin or elastic threader. Before joining the elastic, pull the cord out of the drawstring channel, approx. 2.5cm (1in) from either end. Overlap the ends of the elastic and join with a zigzag as shown on page 120 without stitching over the drawstring.

7 Make sure the drawstring side of the elastic is facing the outside of the casing. Push the elastic back into the casing and pull each end of the drawstring through each of the buttonholes at the centre front.

8 Close up the hole in the seam using slip stitch or another invisible hand stitch.

9 Tie knots in the ends of the drawcord to prevent fraying.

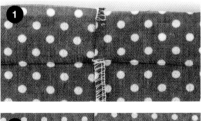

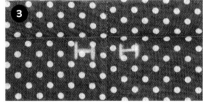

How long should the elastic be?

This really depends on the type of elastic, the fabric you're working with and the project, although there are some general rules that can be applied.

If you're cutting elastic for a waistband and using a woven or firm elastic it can be cut the same measurement or just fractionally shorter than the waist measurement. Firm elastics won't reduce in width when stretched and have plenty of grip so you don't need to cut them shorter to compensate for their stretch.

For lingerie elastics these can be cut 5–10% shorter than the fabric they are being applied to, depending on preference for fit.

For those elastics with high amounts of stretch which are easily expanded, cut the elastic at least 15% smaller than the opening it will be applied to.

For swimwear elastics around armholes and necklines, cut the elastic the same measurement or for low necklines cut the elastic 2–7cm (¾–2¾in) shorter to ensure a snug fit. On leg openings cut the elastic 2–5cm (¾–2in) shorter.

If you're making something for yourself, simply place the elastic around the part of the body where it will be worn and stretch just enough so that it feels comfortable and will stay in place.

Tip for stitching simple casings

The stitching for a simple casing (see page 119) can be done from the right or wrong side. Use a woolly nylon or other decorative thread to make a feature of the casing when using reverse coverstitch. You can also create multiple channels for elastic using this method.

Joining elastic in the round

For most of the elastic applications shown, the elastic needs to be joined in the round. There are a number of ways to join elastic using a regular sewing machine, overlocker or coverstitch machine.

Straight stitch This technique works well for thinner elastic such as lingerie elastic or fold-over elastic where there is less bulk.

1 Place the two ends of elastic together and use straight stitch on the sewing machine, overlock together or use chain stitch on the coverstitch machine. Press the seam allowance open or to one side.

Zigzag This is the easiest and most common way to join elastic to achieve a flat finish. The resulting stitching is usually covered by fabric so don't worry if it doesn't look too pretty.

1 Overlap the ends of the elastic, making sure it's not twisted, and zigzag back and forth until the elastic is held.

Abutted seam with zigzag This is a great way to get a completely flat finish but you need to make sure the elastic is held with your stitching.

1 Line the ends of elastic up to each other and use a wide zigzag stitch to sew back and forth until the elastic is held. For extra security place a thin layer of fabric under the join and stitch through this too.

Fold-over elastic (FOE).

Narrow braided elastic.

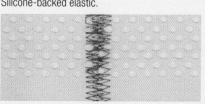

Silicone-backed elastic.

Ideas to try: elastic

A Neckline and armholes finished with contrasting fold-over elastic and topstitched with narrow coverstitch. The elastic is stretched a little as it is applied to ensure it sits flat once stitched.

B Decorative picot edged lingerie elastic is applied to the leg and waistline openings of a pair of knickers. The elastic is matched to the right side of the fabric and then coverstitched in place using woolly nylon in the looper for a soft finish. A decorative trim and reverse coverstitching is used to embellish the front piece.

C Knitted waistband elastic applied to boxer shorts using a lapped technique and stitched in place using triple reverse coverstitch with contrasting thread in the looper. Decorative reverse coverstitching is used to add detail to the seams.

D A separate casing is used to apply elastic to a waistband, this is topstitched using chain stitch to form three channels and a drawstring inserted through the centre channel, on top of the elastic.

E Silicone gripper elastic used in the inside of the leg opening of cycling shorts, applied initially using a lapped technique and then turned to the inside and sewn again with a narrow coverstitch.

F The enclosed method (page 117) on a pair of leggings. Knitted elastic is overlocked to the wrong side of the waistline and then enclosed by folding over the waistband and stitched in place using narrow coverstitch.

Overlocked flatlock This technique is slightly stronger than the abutted method.

1 Set your overlocker to a wide three-thread stitch. Shorten the stitch length to 2.5–3. Turn the tension up to 7 on the lower looper and turn the needle tension to 0.

2 Place the ends of elastic together and stitch across. Pull the seam open so it sits flat. Run a yarn needle or similar flat tool inside the stitch to encourage the seam to lie flat. Thread the chain ends into the seam.

Knitted waistband elastic.

Coverstitched flatlock Follow the instructions for the abutted seam but use a wide or triple coverstitch instead of a zigzag. Set the stitch length to between 2 and 3. For extra security, you can flip the elastic over and coverstitch again from the other side.

Knitted waistband elastic.

Combined overlocked and coverstitched flatlock Follow the instructions for the overlocked flatlock and then once the seam has been pulled flat, stitch over the top using a wide or triple coverstitch for extra strength.

Knitted waistband elastic.

Using binding

One reason that many people purchase a coverstitch machine is their ability to apply binding to garment edges with a professional finish. Binding can be used for a whole range of projects in woven and knit fabrics including the finishing of necklines, armholes, pocket openings, cut-out sections of garments, covering seam allowances on the inside of garments and for creating straps or ties. A variety of methods can be used to bind an edge, including the use of a binder attachment which can speed up the process when working on multiple items. The choice of method will depend on the type and thickness of the fabric, and personal preference.

WHAT IS BINDING?

There is often confusion between binding and a band, they are both used to finish edges but they are not the same thing. Binding covers and encloses the raw edge of an opening. A band is a strip of fabric which is usually folded in half and then sewn to the seam allowance at an opening, often adding extra depth at this point. The seam allowance will still be visible on the wrong side of the garment. The different processes of attaching a band and examples of these are covered on pages 98–107.

TYPES OF BINDING

The choice of binding will depend on the project and fabric type that you are working with. If you're working with a knit fabric, choose a knit binding as this will stretch more, like the fabric it will be applied to. If you're working with woven fabric, then woven or knit binding can be used. Take care when combining different types of fabrics as puckering may occur if the binding is more stable than the neckline and one fabric wants to stretch more than the other.

Purchased binding is sold in a range of colours as flat or unfolded, single binding, single-fold binding or double-fold binding (shown top to bottom in image below). Woven binding is generally always purchased as bias cut and may be referred to as bias tape.

Flat or unfolded binding ideal for use with a binder attachment as the device will fold the fabric for you.

Single binding just folded once in the centre.

Single-fold binding pre-folded with the raw edges meeting in the centre, this is the most common way to purchase bias binding.

Double-fold binding pre-folded with the raw edges meeting in the centre and then folded again in half.

Tip

You can turn your double-fold binding into single fold, single or flat binding by ironing it!

Tips

- Increase the presser-foot pressure and/or thread tension on the needles to help manage the multiple layers of fabric.
- Lower the differential feed and/or use a slightly lower stitch length to make sure that the opening retains an amount of stretch.
- One way to perfect the single-layer technique is to cut the binding wider than needed, then trim off the excess fabric once you've finished. This way, you can achieve a tightly bound edge and make sure that the needles are stitching through all the layers of fabric, without worrying that you'll miss the inside edge of the binding as you stitch.

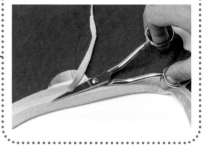

APPLICATIONS OF BINDING

The terminology used for binding techniques is a little confusing as these can also be referred to as single fold or double fold but this doesn't necessarily relate to the type of binding of the same name. For example, single-fold binding isn't used with a single-fold binder to give a single-fold bound edge. To simplify this, the techniques over the next few pages will be referred to as 'single-layer' and 'double-layer' binding. The methods shown over the next few pages will focus on the use of home-cut knit binding, although this can be substituted for purchased binding or woven binding as necessary.

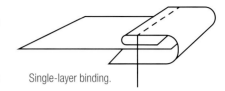

Single-layer binding.

Single-layer binding

Single-fold or single-layer binding is where the raw edge of the binding is turned over only on the outside of the project and a single layer of fabric wraps the raw edge and sits on the inside. This effect can be achieved with or without a single-fold binder attachment. The binding is usually stitched in place from the right side using chain stitch or coverstitch. This finish is less bulky and can be used on a variety of fabrics, particularly heavier fabrics.

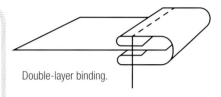

Double-layer binding.

Method 1: In the round

Although binding is often attached flat, a neater finish can be achieved by working in the round.

1 Cut a strip of fabric the length required for the garment opening (see 'Tips for cutting binding the correct size' on page 129) plus seam allowance with a width three and a half times as wide as the desired binding plus 2–5mm (1/16–1/4in) for turn of cloth, depending on the thickness of fabric.

2 Join the short ends of the fabric with chain stitch and press the seam allowances open or overlock and press to one side.

3 Quarter the binding and opening. With right sides together, align the binding seam to the shoulder seam, match quarter markings and keep raw edges even. Pin or clip binding in place, then overlock or use chain stitch to hold, keeping the seam allowance correct.

4 If you intend to complete the final topstitching with chain stitch, overlock the unstitched long edge of the binding.

5 Press the seam allowance towards the binding and use the raw edges of the opening as a guide to turn the binding to the inside. Pin or clip in place.

6 Use chain stitch or coverstitch to sew along the binding from the right side or reverse coverstitch from the inside. Begin on the back, just before the shoulder seam. To cover the binding perfectly on the inside, straddle the seam line of the binding with a narrow coverstitch, as shown here.

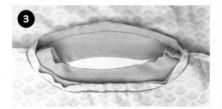

The finished binding.

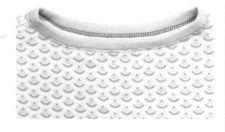

Method 2: Working flat

A quick way to attach binding is to work flat and sew the seam after the binding has been attached. A flat approach would also be used for pocket openings where the ends of binding are taken into a waistline or side seam. If using this approach on a neckline (as shown below), sew together one of the shoulder seams first.

1 Follow steps 1 and 4 of method 1.

The finished binding.

2 With right sides together and raw edges even, pin or clip the binding in place, stretching the binding a little as you go. Overlock or use chain stitch to hold in place.

3 Follow steps 5 and 6 for method 1. Stitch the remaining seam if required. (See page 78 on 'Overlocking a seam after hemming flat'.)

Method 3: Using piping

This method can be completed in the round or flat (as described on page 123) and includes a decorative strip of piping which is sewn alongside the binding. The piped section can be filled with cord or left empty.

Cut the piping strip the length required for the garment opening plus seam allowances with a width twice as wide as the desired piping plus two seam allowances.

1 With wrong sides together, fold the piping strip in half lengthwise and match to the right side of the fabric with raw edges aligned. Stretch the piping strip slightly to fit around curves. Pin or clip in place.

2 Tack the piping in place using a chain stitch, keeping within the seam allowance, close to the raw edge.

3 Continue, following the instructions on page 123 for 'Method 2: Working flat'. The binding will be applied on top of the piping and stitched so the piped edge is visible once the binding is turned to the underside.

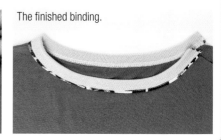

The finished binding.

WORKING FLAT OR IN THE ROUND?

A flat approach is used where there isn't the need for a joined seam, for example on pocket openings where the ends of binding are taken into a waistline or side seam. This is also the method used when working with a binder attachment.

Working flat is usually a quicker way to attach binding as less precision is required for cutting fabric binding strips to the right length and it can be stretched and sewn in place at the same time. Any excess binding can be cut off at the end and remaining seams can be sewn once the binding is in place. This method doesn't always give the neatest finish, particularly on a neckline, cuff or armhole as the final seam through the binding can appear bulky.

Working in the round will produce a smoother, flatter end result but it will take a little longer to prepare the binding accurately to the correct length, stitch the short ends, quarter the opening and binding, and stretch in place correctly.

Tips for reducing bulky bindings

- Excess bulk can often occur when overlocking is used to form seams and apply binding, particularly when working in the round. When attaching the binding in the round, press seam allowances for the binding and the project seams in opposite directions.
- Bulk can also be reduced when folding the binding by snipping into the overlocked seam allowance at the fold line and pressing the seam in opposite directions above and below the snip, similar to the technique used for hemming on page 84 for managing bulky seams.

WHICH STITCH SHOULD I USE?

Use chain stitch to attach the binding for the first line of stitching: this will be less bulky than overlocking and can be easily undone if anything goes wrong. Using this stitch also gives you more control over the width of the seam allowance. Alternatively, you can use a long machine stitch on your sewing machine.

If you are overlocking seams on the binding or overlocking the binding edge, use a three- or four-thread stitch with stitch length of 3 to 4. You may need to increase the differential feed slightly to avoid a wavy edge. For overlocked seams in knit fabrics a four-thread stitch should be used since this is stronger and will withstand stretch and stress.

If you are using a zigzag stitch on your sewing machine to apply elastics or to make seams, use a width and length of 2.5–3.

For openings that need a lot of stretch use coverstitch instead of chain stitch for topstitching.

When topstitching narrow binding, use the left needle to chain stitch or left and centre needles to coverstitch so there is more surface area of fabric in contact with the feed-dog teeth and the presser foot to enable smoother feeding through the machine. On some machines, better results may be produced for narrow coverstitch with the centre and right needles.

Double-layer binding

Double-fold or double-layer binding is folded under on both the outside and underside of the fabric so can create additional bulk for heavier fabrics. The binding is attached to the wrong side of the fabric, folded over to the right side and then stitched in place with chain stitch or coverstitch. This technique can be achieved with a double-fold binder and is more suited to light- or medium-weight fabrics. Choose a light-weight knit fabric for the binding for the flattest finish.

Method 1: In the round

This technique works well to cover armhole edges and form straps on tops, including those in woven fabrics. This method can add additional bulk to the fabric edges so a flatter finish can be achieved by working in the round.

Cut a strip of fabric the length required for the garment opening plus seam allowances with a width four-and-a-half times as wide as the desired binding plus 5mm (¼in) for turn of cloth and narrowing of the fabric as it is stretched.

1 With right sides together, stitch the short ends of the binding using chain or overlock stitches. Press the seam open or to one side. Quarter the binding and opening. Place the right side of the binding to the wrong side of the opening. Match seams, quarter markings and keep raw edges even. Pin or clip the binding in place, then overlock or use chain stitch to hold, stitching along at the depth required for the binding.

2 Press the seam allowance towards the binding, turn under the unstitched edge of the binding so the raw edges meet in the centre and fold over again so the first line of stitching is just covered by the folded edge of the binding. Pin or clip in place. Hand tack if desired.

3 Use chain stitch or coverstitch to sew along binding from the right side.

The finished binding.

Method 2: Working flat

Cut the fabric strip as noted in method 1.

1 Place the right side of the binding to the wrong side of the opening. Keeping raw edges even, pin or clip the binding in place and stretch the binding to fit around the curve as necessary. Overlock or use chain stitch to hold.

2 Follow steps 2 and 3 for method 1 to complete the binding.

3 Stitch the remaining seam if required. (See notes on page 78 on 'Overlocking a seam after hemming flat'.)

Tip for applying binding in the round

If you are unsure about the length of fabric required for working in the round, after cutting the fabric strip don't sew the ends of binding yet. Use chain stitch to apply the binding, stretching as you sew. Leave excess binding at each end, then make the seam once the binding has been sewn to most of the opening. This prevents you cutting the fabric too short.

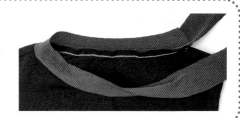

BINDING WITH ELASTIC

Elastic can be applied at the same time as the binding. This is particularly useful when making swimwear, sports tops or bralettes to provide extra stretch and support. Both single- and double-layer binding finishes can be produced, including using the binder attachment. (See page 115 for tips on setting up the binder attachment with elastic.)

If you want to replace the regular swimwear elastic method shown on page 112, with an elasticated binding, remove the depth of the elastic from the garment edge first.

Single-layer binding with elastic

Follow the instructions for single-layer binding on page 123 to cut the binding to the correct dimensions. Use elastic with a width to match the depth of the finished binding and cut to the required length. The method is explained as a flat technique, but could also be used in the round for leg openings and armholes.

The finished binding.

1 Apply the elastic to the wrong side of the binding using zigzag, chain or overlock stitch. Keep the elastic in line with one of the raw edges of the binding.

2 With right sides together, apply the binding to the opening, matching the elastic and binding to the raw edge. Pin in place. Stretch the binding to fit as required and use a zigzag, chain or overlock stitch to hold in place.

3 Keep the elastic on the right side of the opening and wrap the binding over the elastic to the inside of the garment, so any previous lines of stitching are hidden.

4 Stitch in place using a narrow or wide coverstitch.

This technique can be used to **bind armhole edges and form straps**. To do this, combine the method for single-layer binding with elastic with method 2 of 'Making straps with swimwear elastic' on page 114. If elasticated bound edges will cross, remove the elastic from the section that overlaps to reduce bulk.

Double-layer binding with elastic

Use method 2 for 'Double layer binding' on page 125 but with the following adaptations.

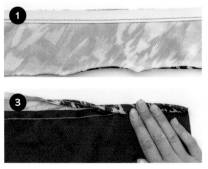

1 Attach the elastic to one long edge of the binding before you begin.

2 When attaching the binding to the garment opening, attach the long edge without the elastic to the wrong side of the garment.

3 Once the binding is attached, pull the binding away from the garment and fold each of the edges towards each other using the edge of the elastic as a guide to fold along. Fold the strip in half so raw edges are enclosed.

4 Coverstitch in place.

USING BINDING AS A FACING

This technique is often shown on sewing patterns to bind the neckline and armhole edges of both knits and woven garments. The binding is attached to the right side of the opening and the binding and seam allowance are both turned to the inside of the garment so they are no longer visible. The binding is then topstitched in place. This technique is usually completed in the round, as explained below.

Cut a strip of fabric the length required for the garment opening plus seam allowances with a width four times as wide as the desired facing plus 5mm (¼in) for turn of cloth.

1 Join the short ends of the binding with a chain stitch and press seams open or overlock and press to one side. With wrong sides together, fold the binding in half lengthways. Press flat. Quarter the binding and opening. With right sides together match seams, quarter markings and keep raw edges even. Pin or clip the binding in place.

2 Use chain stitch to hold the binding in place, stitching just to the right of the centre of the strip to ensure the raw edge will be covered in step 4.

3 Press the folded edge of the binding to meet the raw edge and then fold under again so it sits on the wrong side of the fabric.

4 Stitch in place from the right or wrong side of the fabric using chain stitch or coverstitch.

A less bulky finish can be achieved by cutting the fabric strip twice as wide as the desired binding and applying as described above but without folding the binding in half first. Overlock the raw edge of the binding and chain stitch in place or use coverstitch and sew from the right side to finish.

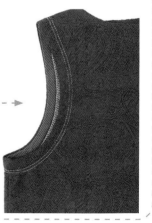

CUTTING BINDING STRIPS

Unless you only want to bind straight edges, woven binding should be cut on the bias (at 45° to the straight grain), this will allow it to bend around the curves of armholes and necklines.

As knit fabric stretches, knit binding can be cut crosswise from selvedge to selvedge, or lengthwise, parallel to the selvedge, in the direction of greatest stretch. It may be preferable to cut four-way stretch fabrics parallel to the selvedge to avoid the fabric rolling at the edges.

The best and most accurate way to cut even strips is to use a cutting mat, rotary cutter and a pattern drafter's or quilter's ruler, cutting separate strips for small pieces of binding or using a continuous-strip method for larger projects, as explained below.

JOINING STRIPS

Both woven and knit binding strips can be joined as follows. Although it's possible to join knit fabrics without creating an angled seam, this method is less noticeable and creates less bulk, particularly when using a binder attachment.

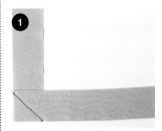

1 Place short ends right sides together at a right angle, forming an L shape. Stitch across the strips from bottom right to top left using chain stitch or straight stitch on your sewing machine.

2 Trim and press open the seam allowances.

MAKING CONTINUOUS BINDING STRIPS
Woven fabrics

If you have a lot of binding to do it's much quicker to create a long continuous strip, rather than joining separate strips of fabric.

The starting point for creating a continuous strip from woven fabric is a parallelogram-shaped piece of fabric, where the two opposite long edges of the parallelogram are cut on the bias. It sounds confusing, but there is an easy method.

1 Cut a square of fabric on the straight grain (make your square at least 30 x 30cm (12 x 12in) and cut it in half from the top left to bottom right corner to create two triangles.

2 Bring the left edge of the square to the right edge of the square to form a parallelogram.

3 With right sides together, pin the two edges together, so the pointed ends overlap slightly and stitch along this edge using a 6mm (¼in) seam allowance on a sewing machine. Press the seam open.

4 Mark lines onto the fabric, across the longest edge (this is the bias) at the width you require for your binding.

5 With right sides together, bring the row ends together so these overhang by the width of one strip and stitch again with a 6mm (¼in) seam allowance. Press the seam open.

6 Using scissors, cut along the strips, cutting a continuous line through your fabric until you have cut out your strip of continuous binding.

Knitted fabrics

This method works best on tubular knits so you can avoid the seam line throughout the binding. To begin, you need to remove a triangle of fabric from the raw edge as follows:

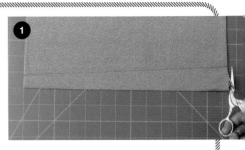

1 Make sure the edge of the fabric is straight, or use a rotary cutter to trim and level. On the right folded edge, measure up from the raw edge to the depth of your binding and mark a point. Mark a point on the opposite fold which is half the width of the binding from the raw edge. Join the two points with chalk or other marker to create a slanting line. Using scissors, cut up the right fold to the marked point.

2 Place a cutting mat inside the tube of fabric and use a rotary cutter to cut along the slanting line, cutting only through the top layer of fabric.

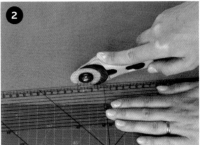

3 Pull the cut slither of fabric to the left. Take the cutting mat out of the fabric tube and place it under the fabric tube.

4 Draw a line from the lower right corner of the folded edge to the mark on the left folded edge. Cut along the marked line.

5 Turn the fabric over so the cut-out section is to the left and place the cutting mat back inside the tube. Now you can begin cutting the continuous strip, moving the ruler and mat as you go, until you have cut the amount of binding required.

6 Wind the binding into a roll. Wind around your fingers to get this started or use an empty tube to help the process.

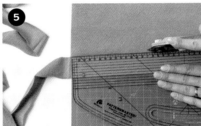

The resulting strip is cut ever so slightly off grain but this isn't very noticeable when sewing. For knit binding that is cut perfectly on the straight grain, cut and stitch strips together as shown on page 128, or purchase pre-cut strips.

Tips for cutting binding the correct size

- When cutting fabric strips yourself, see the instructions for single- and double-layer methods for the specific dimensions required.
- When using a binder attachment, use the measurement specified for the binder.
- For thick or very stretchy fabrics cut the binding slightly wider than specified as it will narrow as it is stretched into place.
- For advice on length of binding for stretch fabrics, see page 100 for 'How big should the band be?' and follow the same recommendations.
- When measuring binding strips, the blade and ruler edge may add a fractional extra to the width or length so cut slightly narrower that specified to allow for this.

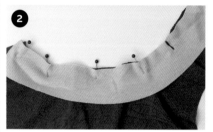

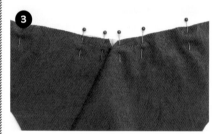

BINDING A V-NECK

This example shows a flat construction method for single-layer binding so begin by joining the right shoulder seam only. Refer also to the instructions for 'Single-layer binding, method 2, Working flat' on page 123 to measure the length of the binding and 'Finishing a v-neck' on page 101.

1 For woven fabrics, staystitch the neckline just inside the seamline, 2.5cm (1in) either side of the V, and then snip into the V up to the staystitching. For knit fabrics that don't fray, miss out the staystitching and just snip into the V. On the wrong side of the fabric mark a short line straight down from the V to indicate the centre front of the fabric.

2 Measure the back neckline and calculate 75% of this. Mark this measurement onto the binding strip. With right sides together and raw edges even, match the binding to the back neckline, placing the mark on the binding strip to the right shoulder seam. Stretch the binding to fit the back neckline and pin in place, positioning pins on the wrong side of the garment.

3 Find the centre point of the remaining binding and place this at the V. Straighten the fabric out at the V and continue matching the binding to the front neckline without stretching. Pin in place.

4 Attach the binding to the neckline using chain stitch.

5 Wrap the binding over the raw edge and to the inside so the chain stitching is enclosed. Clip in place or pin, placing pins on the right side of the garment.

6 Stitch from the right side using a narrow coverstitch, keeping the edge flat along the V section.

7 Mitre the corner of the V as follows: fold the garment at the V with right sides together, along the line you marked in step 1. Use a straight stitch on a sewing machine to sew along the binding in line with the centre-front fold. To get the neatest finish, stitch only up to where the coverstitching ends and not all the way across the binding. You may find that a compensation plate and wash-away or tear-away stabilizer can help with this step.

8 Stitch remaining shoulder seam. (See page 78 on 'Overlocking a seam after hemming flat'.) If the binding at the V is bulky, trim the excess fabric and press open the binding at the V.

The back (left) and front (right).

BINDER ATTACHMENTS

These devices can speed up the process of attaching binding as they will fold, wrap and allow you to stitch all in one go. They can take a bit of practice to achieve the desired result but if you make a lot of things which require binding then they are really worth having.

An adjustable bias-binding foot or attachment is available for some models of machine and works with single binding, single-fold binding with widths from 1–4cm (⅜–1½in) or with fold-over elastic. The pre-folded binding is fed into the foot which folds it in half and encases the fabric edge. The device can be adjusted to correctly line up with the needle position. Other accessories are available with a set width to create a single-layer or double-layer bound finish.

The binder attachments most commonly used with coverstitch machines are those which work with unfolded binding strips as the device will fold and hold the strip ready to be attached to a fabric edge. Binder attachments for domestic machines generally fall into two categories: 'A style' which produces a single-layer binding and 'B style' which produces a double-layer binding. Binder attachments may come with or without a guide rake which holds the fabric in tension and guides it towards the part of the device that folds the strip. The binders with the rake are better for attaching knit binding.

A binder attachment will work with a specific size or width of binding strip and may require a mounting plate or an accessory adapter to hold the device at the correct height on the machine. Some machines also require a specific binding foot, shorter than the standard presser foot, to work with the binder attachment.

Each binder will usually have engraved measurements to denote the width to cut the binding strip and the width of the finished binding once it is folded and stitched in place.

For really stretchy fabrics and ribbing that will be under tension as it is fed, cut the strip slightly wider to compensate for the narrowing of the strip as it is stretched. This only works for certain knits and having a strip too wide can create issues for less stretchy fabrics. For very heavy fabrics cut these fractionally narrower to compensate for the bulk.

It is not possible to work in the round with a binder attachment, so you may need to plan your project to stitch seams in the right order.

Adjustable bias-binder foot, Janome 1200D.

'A style' without a rake, baby lock.

Mounting plate, Janome CoverPro (top); accessory adapter, baby lock (bottom).

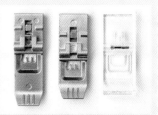

Standard presser foot (left); binder foot (middle); clear binder foot (right), all for use with Janome CoverPro models.

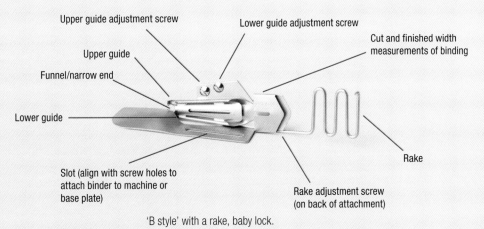

Upper guide adjustment screw
Lower guide adjustment screw
Upper guide
Funnel/narrow end
Cut and finished width measurements of binding
Lower guide
Rake
Slot (align with screw holes to attach binder to machine or base plate)
Rake adjustment screw (on back of attachment)

'B style' with a rake, baby lock.

Setting up a binder attachment

Before inserting fabric or attaching the binder to your machine, check the position of the upper and lower guides. These can be adjusted depending on the result that you want to achieve or the item that you are stitching, as shown in the diagram on the right.

A shows the upper and lower guides level with each other. This positioning may be preferable when using chain stitch to bind an edge, or when creating swimwear straps as shown in method 4 on page 115.

B shows the lower guide positioned to the right of the upper guide. This arrangement will work perfectly for most types of binding that use two or three needles. With the guides in this position, the very edge of the binding will be stitched on the underside. Position the lower guide approximately 2–3mm (¹⁄₁₆–⅛in) to the right of the upper guide.

C shows the lower guide positioned to the left of the upper guide. This is suitable for coverstitching that straddles the binding, i.e. one line of stitching through the fabric only, the other line(s) of stitching through the binding.

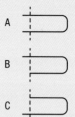

A

B

C

= left needle alignment

Using a binder attachment

Some instructions suggest that the fabric strip should be fed into the device first before attaching it to the machine and others suggest the device is attached first so test out both approaches to find the one that suits you best. The attachment may come with the rake folded flat against the binder so you'll need to open it out in order to use it. Loosen the rake adjustment screw on the back of the binder attachment if the rake does not easily move. Make sure you have plenty of extra binding as you'll need to do a few tests to make sure you're happy with the result before binding the edges of your project.

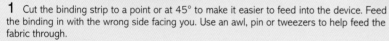

The finished binding.

1 Cut the binding strip to a point or at 45° to make it easier to feed into the device. Feed the binding in with the wrong side facing you. Use an awl, pin or tweezers to help feed the fabric through.

2 Pull the fabric through the device and make sure it is folding correctly at the narrow end. Keep pulling until there is enough fabric to reach under the foot plus 2cm (¾in) extra to hold onto. Now wind the binding fabric around the prongs of the rake and use these to adjust the tension on the fabric.

3 With the project fabric right side up, line up the raw edge to be bound with the binding, sliding this between the two folded edges of the binding.

4 Adjust the position of the binding to line up correctly with the needles so 2–3mm (¹⁄₁₆–⅛in) of binding fabric is to the left of the left needle. Begin stitching, sewing first through the binding only and then through the binding and project fabric.

5 Once you reach the end of the project fabric, keep going and stitch through the binding only until you can cut the binding away from the machine.

6 Trim the ends of the binding flush with the ends of the project fabric and close any remaining seams. See notes on page 78 on 'Overlocking a seam after hemming flat'.

Tips for using a binder attachment

- Don't pull on the binding once it's set up and stitching, just let it feed.
- Using a clear presser foot makes it easier to see where the binding is being stitched.
- Once you have the exact position for your binder, use masking tape or pen to mark the position of the binder on the machine casing so

Creating a binding holder

If you are binding long edges or working on multiple items and using a roll of binding, you'll need to use a binding holder or tape stand to help the roll of binding unravel as it is fed into the machine. These can be purchased as specific devices, as shown in the images here, but it is quite easy to create your own using household items such as a kitchen-roll holder, large spool cone or adhesive putty and an old CD or DVD. The important thing is to make sure that the roll of binding is positioned so it is in line with the rake of the binder.

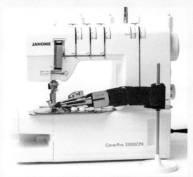

Janome tape stand and tape binder.

If you're using elastic with the binder, this could be included on an additional roll positioned above the binding.

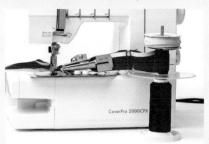

Ideas to try: binding

A Camisole top in cotton jersey with stretch-lace panel applied using lapped coverstitch seam. Armhole edges and straps formed with narrow double-layer binding and finished with narrow coverstitch.

B Baby sleepsuit envelope neckline opening with single-layer binding and narrow coverstitch.

C Swimwear binding with elastic around neckline using single-layer technique and narrow coverstitch.

D Pocket edge bound using single-layer technique and piping.

E Lower edge of shorts finished with double-layer binding and narrow reverse coverstitch.

F Edges of bib and ties formed using double-layer technique and narrow coverstitch.

that next time you use it, you'll know where to line it up.

- Use an adjustable seam guide or other device to keep the binding in position as it comes out of the binder. A toy block or pad of sticky notes placed to the right of the presser foot works well.

- Adjust the differential feed or hold the project fabric in tension to allow it to feed evenly and avoid gathering the edge as it is bound.

- Use the left needle for chain stitch and choose between left and centre or right and centre to produce a narrow coverstitch.

- Ensure the binding is feeding evenly into the machine with just the right amount of tension. Use the prongs or alter the angle of the rake to apply more or less tension on the binding strip, winding around more prongs or increasing the angle of the rake to increase the tension.

- For flimsy or slippery binding, you may wish to use fusible interfacing or wash-away stabilizer to help control the fabric strips through the binder attachment.

Making belt loops

Making belt loops is easy on a coverstitch machine. Simply feed single-fold bias binding into your machine and stitch, or with the use of the belt-loop attachment you can fold and stitch fabric strips in one go, ready to apply to a range of projects. Belt loops can be used for many more purposes than the name suggests, such as straps, bag handles, drawstrings and decorative tape.

Britannia belt-loop folder.

BELT-LOOP FOLDER

This attachment has a wide funnel section at one end, into which fabric strips are inserted. As the fabric is pushed through the device, the long raw edges are folded towards each other to the underside of the fabric, forming single-fold binding (see 'Types of binding' on page 122). The device for some machines comes as part of a special foot but the majority of belt-loop folders are sold as separate accessories which can be purchased for specific machines or as generic attachments to work with a number of different models. These come in a variety of sizes to create belt loops of differing widths. A long length of folded and stitched strip can be made and cut into smaller sections for belt loops or other purposes.

Janome 1200D foot with folder.

CUTTING FABRIC STRIPS

Each attachment will specify the width to cut the fabric strips and this is usually engraved onto the device. The measurement shown will usually be the cutting width and this will result in a stitched strip of roughly half this measurement, but check the instructions that come with the device to make sure. Measure and cut accurately to ensure the resulting folded belt loop is an even width. If there are no measurements supplied with your device, experiment by using strips double the width of the narrow end of the device, adjusting the measurement until you perfect the result.

Brother belt-loop folder.

Tips for cutting fabric strips

- Use a cutting mat, ruler and rotary cutter for the most accuracy.
- Cut the fabric strip longer than required as it may take a while to perfect the positioning of the stitch line and then you can cut around any section that isn't perfectly sewn.

- Cut woven fabric on the straight grain for the strongest belt loop or strap.
- Use bias-cut strips to produce a diagonal effect when working with striped fabric. Insert ribbon or twill tape to give a more stable and secure strap. (Use the same technique for including elastic shown on page 115 'Making straps with swimwear elastic, method 3.')

- Cut stretch fabrics on the straight grain and use to make straps.
- Insert elastic when using stretch fabrics to give more stability and better support, particularly for lingerie, sportswear or swimwear (see page 115 'Making straps with swimwear elastic, method 3').

How to use the belt-loop folder

Before you begin, set your machine for wide coverstitch or triple coverstitch for a more decorative finish. Set the stitch length to 3–4.

1 Attach the device to the machine using the white attachment screws provided with your machine or with the accessory. Screw in place loosely so further adjustments can be made.

2 Cut the fabric strip at 45° or to a point and with the right side up, push the strip into the device. Use an awl, pin or tweezers to guide the fabric through the device and pull the folded fabric out at the other end.

3 Pull through enough folded fabric to run it under the presser foot with 2.5cm (1in) extending beyond the presser foot.

4 Adjust the position of the device so the small opening is close to the presser foot and the needles are centred on the folded strip. You may need to use a screwdriver to loosen the metal screws on the device to improve the alignment. Tighten all white and metal screws before beginning to sew. Lower the presser foot, take two or three stitches with the handwheel and then continue using the foot pedal. You may need to fine-tune the position of the belt-loop folder to produce a perfectly centred stitching line. Continue stitching until you have sewn the whole strip. Secure stitching using one of the methods shown on pages 33–37.

> **Tip**
> You may find it easier to insert the fabric strip before attaching the device to the machine.

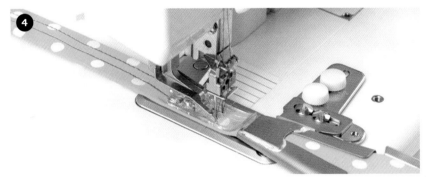

MAKING BELT LOOPS WITHOUT THE ATTACHMENT

If you don't have the belt-loop attachment you can still make belt loops but it might not be as quick or simple. For some of the methods shown below you'll need to press the fabric strip to create single-fold bias tape first, before stitching the folds in place on the coverstitch machine. For this reason, these methods are best used for fabrics which press well and can take the heat of the iron.

With a bias tape maker

Like the belt-loop folder, this accessory comes in a variety of sizes to produce different widths of single-fold bias binding. Use this in the same way as the belt-loop attachment by placing the device upside down on your machine and attaching with adhesive tape or putty. Feed the fabric through the device before attaching it to your machine.

Using a long pin

Mark two dots on your ironing board that are as far apart as the width of the belt loop you wish to make, e.g. 1.5cm (⅝in). Use a long pin and enter the fabric close to the first dot and come out into the first dot, then enter the fabric again at the second dot. Start off the folds on your fabric strip, then feed the strip into this pin guide, pulling the folded strip out from the pin and pressing in place as you go.

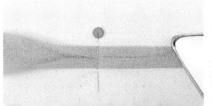

Folding and pressing

With wrong sides together, fold your fabric strip in half lengthways and press. Open out the fold, then fold each of the raw edges into the centre. Take care not to burn your fingers on the iron!

Using four pins

Mark dots on your ironing board as described for 'Using a long pin' on page 135 then repeat 2cm (¾in) to the right. Place pins in each of the dots, the lower two sloping forwards and the back two sloping backwards. Use this pin guide in the same way as the 'long pin' method.

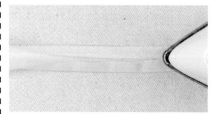

Ideas to try: belt loops

A The belt-loop folder is used to create a long piece of folded and stitched fabric. This is cut into sections and plaited to form a belt with matching belt loops.

B Drawstring for bag created using a belt-loop folder and variegated thread.

C Triple coverstitch in contrasting thread is used to create strips of stitched faux suede. This is cut into pieces and woven to form a decorative panel on an evening bag. Another strip is used to form a matching strap.

D A wide bias tape maker is used to create bag handles. Twill tape is inserted into each strap for additional strength (as explained in 'Tips' section on page 134).

E A summer top with interlinked straps is formed using a belt-loop folder and contrasting thread.

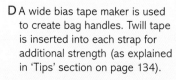

Inserting zips

This may sound like a bizarre or scary thing to do, but zips can be attached to a range of projects using a coverstitch machine. Narrow, wide or triple coverstitch will add perfectly parallel topstitching to the front of a project, or, if stitched from the underside, show off the decorative reverse side of the stitch. It can take a little practice to align the zip correctly and maintain a straight stitch, particularly when using reverse coverstitch, but by using the tips below combined with a few trial runs you'll be able to insert zips beautifully with your machine.

PRESSER FEET

It is possible to insert a zip with the standard foot, and this is easiest when making bags, purses or cushions since a longer zip can be used for this type of application and you can avoid issues with dealing with space and bulkiness around the head or end of the zip.

Unlike a sewing machine, there aren't specific feet for the coverstitch machine to insert zips but there are some feet available that can aid the process to allow close stitching to the zipper teeth and help to keep your stitching straight. A compensating foot, available only on specific brands of machine will allow you to stitch along uneven surfaces so you can stitch close to the zip teeth with one side of the foot riding along the zip coil. A clear presser foot is available for most machine models and allows you the best view for the most accurate stitching. For some models it is possible to purchase a narrower chain-stitch foot which means you can stitch closer to the zip teeth.

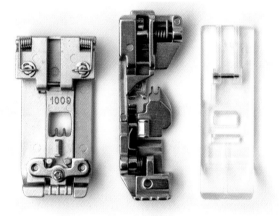

Juki compensating foot (left); Juki chain-stitch foot (middle); Janome 1200D clear chain-stitch foot (right).

INSERTING A FULL-LENGTH EXPOSED ZIP

This type of zip application runs the full length of the project with the teeth slightly exposed in the centre. There are two general approaches to applying the zip, either taking one line of stitching or two to attach each side of the zip. The zip can be stitched first with chain stitch or narrow coverstitch and then topstitched, or simply positioned in place and topstitched. The technique chosen will depend on the type of zip, fabric, desired result and personal preference.

For each of the following methods, use a zip that is at least 8cm (3⅛in) longer than the opening it will be applied to. This will make it easier to work around the bulky ends of the zip. The samples on the next pages show the use of continuous zip tape, commonly used for upholstery projects. It can be cut to any desired length and a zip pull attached. See 'Ideas to try: zips' on page 141 for how these different techniques can be used.

A simple method for inserting a zip in a lined bag using double-sided tape is also given on page 167.

TWO-PASS WIDE TECHNIQUE

This is the easiest method and eliminates the issues of bulk from the zip head and lower end of the zip. Use a chunky zip with a wide tape (often referred to as type number 5) so you have plenty of space on which to stitch. Use 6mm (¼in) wide double-sided wash-away tape to make this process even easier. This tape is particularly useful when working with stretch fabrics to avoid stretching out the fabric edge.

1 On the right side of the fabric, apply double-sided tape along the raw edge where the zip will go. With right sides together, place the zip face down onto the fabric, matching the outer edge of the zip to the raw edge of the fabric. (If not using tape, pin or clip in place.)

2 Set your machine to chain stitch using the left needle. Position the fabric, keeping the right needle marking on the presser foot in line with the raw edge of the fabric. Stitch the zip in place. Repeat with the other side of the zip.

3 Fold the zip over so the right side shows and finger press or iron on medium/low heat to create a crease in the fabric.

4 Set your machine to narrow, wide or triple coverstitch and sew down each side of the zip, from the right or wrong side of the fabric, aligning the right needle marking on the presser foot just inside the folded edge of fabric, or if reverse coverstitching, keep the right needle in line with the raw edge of the fabric.

TWO-PASS NARROW TECHNIQUE

This method shows you how to stitch closer to the zip teeth. This may not work on all machines since the presser foot (depending on its width) will need to ride along the zip teeth as you topstitch.

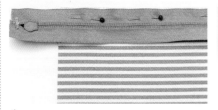

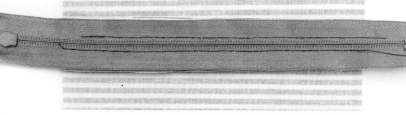

1 With right sides together, place the zip face down onto the fabric, matching the outer edge of the zip to the raw edge of the fabric. Pin or clip in place.

2 Stitch in place, with the presser foot riding along the zip tape to sew close to the teeth. Repeat for the other edge of the zip. Follow steps 3 and 4 above, topstitching as close as your machine will allow to the zip teeth.

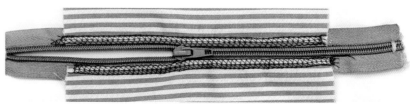

Finished zip (closed).

Finished zip (open).

ONE-PASS TECHNIQUE

1 Apply a strip of wash-away double-sided tape along the raw edge of the fabric, where the zip will be positioned. The sample shows the use of 8mm ($^5/_{16}$in) tape.

2 Lay the zip face down so the outer edge of the zip is in line with the raw edge of fabric and stick the zip in place. Repeat for the other edge of the zip. Follow steps 3 and 4 opposite.

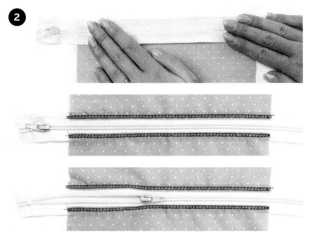

Finished zip, closed (top); finished zip, open (bottom).

PRESSED-EDGE TECHNIQUE

1 Press the seam allowance to the wrong side along the fabric edges where the zip will be positioned.

2 Align the folded edges to the centre of the zip tape or close to the zip teeth. Pin in place.

Follow step 4 opposite.

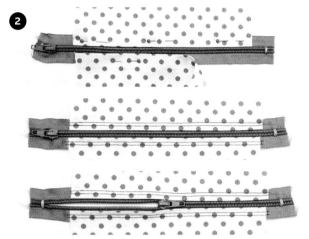

Finished zip, closed (top); finished zip, open (bottom).

BOUND-EDGE TECHNIQUE

1 Remove the seam allowance from the opening edges and follow the instructions for single- or double-layer binding using a flat technique without a binder attachment on pages 123 and 125, or using fold-over elastic on page 111 but omit the final line of topstitching.

2 Align the bound edges to the centre of the zip tape or close to the zip teeth and pin in place. Follow step 4 opposite.

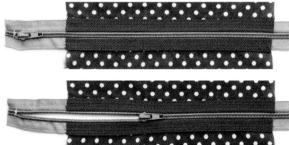

Finished zip, closed (top); finished zip, open (bottom).

OVERLOCKED-EDGE TECHNIQUE

1 Overlock the raw edges of the opening where the zip will be positioned. Remove the seam allowance with the cutting knife. Use a narrow stitch width, a short stitch length and decorative thread in the upper looper for a unique finish. The sample shows the use of a variegated cotton thread.

2 Align the overlocked edges to the centre of the zip tape or close to the zip teeth and pin in place. Follow step 4 opposite.

For fabrics which fray easily, follow step 1 of the 'Pressed-edge technique', then use a short stitch length to overlock the folded edge, without cutting into the fold, creating a decorative edge that looks like piping.

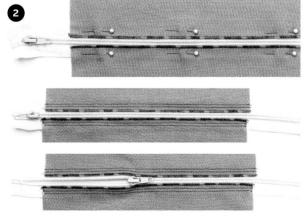

Finished zip, closed (top); finished zip, open (bottom).

INSERTING A QUARTER-LENGTH EXPOSED ZIP

This zip is often seen on clothing where the teeth are exposed and the zip only reaches part way down the centre front. The opening is formed using a placket which is sewn on a sewing machine. The placket is cut open, turned to the inside and the zip applied and topstitched. This method also works well for lace or other decorative exposed zips which can be applied to the right side of the garment.

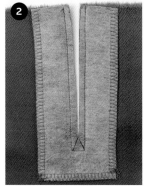

1 Apply interfacing to the placket and edge finish then place this right sides together with the front garment piece. Pin in place and stitch using a sewing machine, along the placket opening lines, pivoting at the corners.

2 Cut down the centre of the placket and diagonally into the corners.

3 Turn the placket to the inside and press in place.

4 For a regular zip, place the right side of the zip to the underside of the opening and pin in place. For a decorative zip, as shown in sample C of the 'Ideas to try', place and pin on the outside of the opening. The zip extends 4cm (1½in) beyond the opening.

5 Set your machine to narrow, wide or triple coverstitch and topstitch in place. Stitch in one go, using the cornering techniques on pages 87–88, or sew in three steps, sewing down each side and then across the bottom.

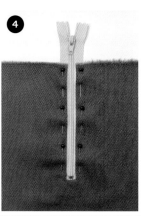

INSERTING A SHORT CENTRED ZIP INTO A SEAM

This zip is used at the bottom of trouser legs or sleeves of sportswear and runs along a seam line. The teeth of the zip are partially covered by fabric. The seam is sewn first using tacking stitches to help centre and position the zip.

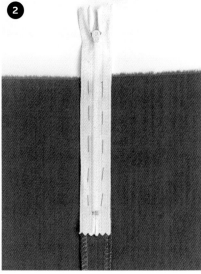

1 Sew the seam on a sewing machine, using machine tacking along the section where the zip will go and a regular length stitch for the rest of the seam. Press the seam open and edge finish the seam allowance.

2 Place the zip face down along the seam line with the zip pull at the end with the tacking stitches. The zip pull extends 4cm (1½in) beyond the opening. Pin and hand tack in place.

3 Set your machine to a narrow coverstitch. From the right side of the fabric, topstitch the zip in place, using the techniques on pages 87–88 to turn the corner at the end.

4 Remove the tacking stitches.

Tips for inserting zips

- Use a zip at least 8cm (3⅛in) longer than required to avoid issues with bulk when stitching close to the head or end of the zip.
- Use a long stitch length, increase tension and adjust the presser-foot pressure to help manage the additional layers.
- Use a wash-away double-sided tape or water-soluble glue to attach the zip to the fabric. This will keep it in place without pins.
- When working with stretch fabrics, stabilize the opening with interfacing and/or use a wash-away double-sided tape to stop the fabric from stretching out of shape as you apply the zip.

Ideas to try: zips

A Lapped zip application on shorts using a narrow coverstitch.

B Exposed centred zip applied with double layer binding to create a decorative edging (see binding techniques on page 125). A triple coverstitch is used for topstitching with the stitching straddling the binding.

C A decorative lace zip topstitched in place with matching thread so the zip is secure but the stitching hidden.

D Reverse coverstitching used for a zip on a washbag. (See Weekend in Whitby washbag project on page 166.)

E Single-layer binding with overlocked piping detail used on the fabric edges before stitching the zip in place.

F Reverse coverstitching used for a zip on a pocket.

G A centre zip technique used to insert a zip on the sleeve of a top.

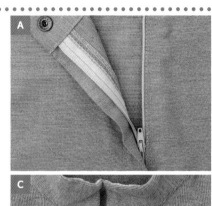

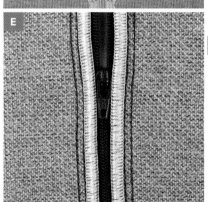

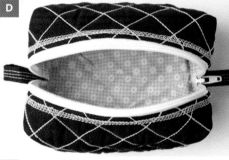

Projects

If you've read through the pages of this book then you know that there's a lot more to your coverstitch machine than just basic hemming. The projects that follow will enable you to practise and show off a range of skills and techniques while you test out your machine on different fabrics. The projects appear in order of difficulty, so if you are a beginner I would recommend starting with the gift bag, but if you are more confident then you can choose any project! Many of the projects will also require the use of a sewing machine and/or overlocker.

The projects in this book have been made using metric measurements, and the imperial equivalents provided have been calculated following standard conversion practices. The imperial measurements are often rounded to the nearest ⅛in for ease of use except in rare circumstances; however, if you need more exact measurements, there are a number of excellent online converters that you can use. Always use either metric or imperial measurements, not a combination of both.

For projects that include patterns, copies of these are available to download from www.bookmarkedhub.com.

Quick and easy gift bag

This project allows you to show off your reverse coverstitching skills with decorative threads. These small gift bags measure approximately 13 x 9cm (5 x 3½in) and are ideal for storing jewellery, wedding favours or Christmas-tree treats. The size of the bag can be altered to suit larger gifts or for storing household items. Additional embellishment can be added in decorative thread, strips of ribbon or lace and a faggoting technique. See image on page 94 for other embellishment ideas.

YOU WILL NEED

- 20 x 17cm (8 x 6¾in) light- to medium-weight fabric
- Four spools of polyester thread for seams and hem
- 90cm (1yd) narrow ribbon, no wider than 6mm (¼in)
- Large-eyed needle, loop turner or bodkin

Optional

- Decorative threads
- 1cm (⅜in) wide ribbon for faggoting
- Small beads to add to drawstring ribbon

Techniques required

- Coverstitch or top coverstitch for hemming (pages 60–65)
- Overlocked seams

Optional techniques

- Stitching with decorative threads (page 92)
- Ideas to try: stitch techniques (page 97)
- Lace effects (faggoting) (page 97)
- Lapped seam construction (page 70)

OPTIONAL FINISHES

- Add small beads to the ends of the drawstring ribbon before tying the ribbon in a knot.

- To add ribbon using a faggoting technique: follow instructions on page 97 'Lace effects' to create a panel of stitched ribbon, using 20cm (8in) lengths of 1cm (⅜in) wide ribbon.
  Next, measure the depth of the panel, add 2.5cm (1in) and remove this from the 17cm (6¾in) side of the main fabric piece.
  Attach the ribbon panel to the main fabric piece using the lapped seam technique from page 70. Stitch from the wrong side of the fabric so the looper thread appears on the right side of the bag.
  Construct the bag as explained opposite, threading the ribbon ties through the lapped seam stitching.

I am using the Britannia InStyle CS4000 coverstitch machine and Janome 9300DX overlocker for this project.

INSTRUCTIONS

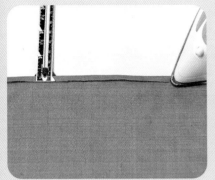

1 On one long edge of the fabric, turn under 6mm (¼in) to the wrong side and press. This will be the top opening of the bag.

2 Turn under again by 2.5cm (1in) and press. A sewing gauge helps keep the hem allowance accurate.

3 From the wrong side of the fabric, stitch along the inner folded edge using a wide coverstitch with a stitch length of 2–3.

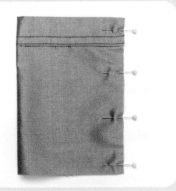

4 Fold the fabric right sides together, matching the two shorter sides. Pin or clip in place.

5 Use a four-thread overlock stitch to sew the side and lower edge of the fabric, with a 6mm (¼in) seam allowance. Use a large-eyed needle, loop turner or bodkin to draw overlocked ends through stitches to finish off.

6 To create box corners at the lower edge, first bring the side seam and lower seam together.

7 Draw a line onto the fabric 1.5cm (⅝in) from the corner and then stitch across this line as shown. Repeat for the other side and finish off the thread ends as in step 5. Turn the bag right side out.

8 Cut the narrow ribbon in half. Starting from the side seam, use a large-eyed needle to thread one length of ribbon through the stitching on the upper hem all the way round and back to the starting point.

9 Trim the ribbon ends if necessary and tie together in a knot. Repeat, using the other length of ribbon. Start and end at the opposite side.

Brighton skirt

This skirt can be made in under an hour and is the perfect, easy-to-wear garment for a range of occasions. No ease is added to the body measurement which gives the skirt its close fit.

Make this in medium- to heavy-weight fabric such as ponte roma or scuba for the cooler months, or a light-weight fabric such as jersey or interlock for summer temperatures. Add shaping at the side seams for a tapered look and choose whether to apply the elastic so it is visible or enclosed.

YOU WILL NEED

- 50–75cm (½–¾yd) stretch fabric for a short skirt, 1.5–2m (1¾–2¼yd) for a long skirt, depending on width
- Approx. 1m (1yd) knitted waistband elastic, 3.8cm (1½in) wide. Exact amount depends on waist measurement
- Four spools of polyester thread

Techniques required

- Seam techniques (page 68)
- Using elastic (page 108)
- Joining elastic (page 120)
- Hems (page 74)

VARIATIONS

Skirt A is made in ponte roma polyester fabric (double-knit jersey) with straight side seams and an enclosed waistband with topstitching.

Skirt B is made in scuba polyester fabric with tapered side seams. The elastic waistband is exposed. Side seams and the waistband are topstitched with narrow coverstitch to flatten the seam allowance.

Skirt C is made in a textured viscose polyester jersey fabric. The waistband is enclosed with hand stitching to hold it at the side seams, rather than topstitching. A slit from just below the knee is included in one side seam for ease of movement.

I am using the Pfaff Coverlock 4.0 combination overlocker and coverstitch machine for this project.

TAKING MEASUREMENTS

1 Measure the waist and divide this by four to give your quarter waist measurement.

2 Measure the hips and divide this by four to give your quarter hip measurement.

3 Measure the distance from waist to hips down the side of the body – approx. 20cm (8in) for an adult.

4 Decide on the skirt length from waist and note this down. Add 2cm (¾in) for a simple hem or 4cm (1½in) for a mock-band hem.

5 For tapered side seams, measure loosely around your legs at the point where the lower edge of the skirt will fall. Divide this measurement by four and use this as the lower-edge measurement.

The front and back pattern pieces will be the same. See the notes below for additional styles and adaptations to the basic pattern. Draw out the pattern onto paper or directly onto the fabric as follows.

Seam allowances of 6mm (¼in) are included in the above measurements.

Tips

• For a short skirt (around knee length) you can taper the side seams if required. Use the lower-edge measurement from step 5 of 'Taking measurements' and draw a line from the lower edge to meet the hip measurement line. I've drawn a straight line but you can curve this slightly if preferred.

• For a longer skirt you can continue to flare out the side seam as shown in the diagram, or include a slit in the side seams for ease of movement (see skirt C).

BASIC PATTERN

1 Fold fabric with right sides together in direction of greatest stretch.

2 Start at least 5cm (2in) from the top of the fabric and draw a horizontal line from the folded edge, equal to your quarter waist measurement. This is the waistline.

3 Measure from this line your waist-to-hip measurement down the folded edge of fabric. From this point, measure across the fabric, parallel to the line drawn in step 2, your quarter hip measurement. Add 2.5cm (1in) if you want to add ease and have a looser fit at the hip.

4 From the waistline, measure down the folded edge the length of skirt required. Draw a straight line across the fabric, parallel to the waistline for the lower edge.

5 Join the end of the waistline to the end of the hip line with a slight curve.

6 Draw a straight line from the end of the hip line, parallel to the folded edge, to join the line marked in step 4.

7 Decide on the waist finish. For an enclosed elastic, as in skirt A, add the width of the elastic to the top of the pattern, in this case 3.8cm (1½in). For exposed elastic, as in skirt B, add a 6mm (¼in) seam allowance.

8 Cut out the fabric and use this as a template to cut out another identical piece.

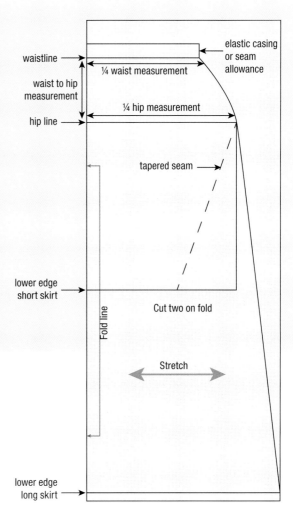

MAKING THE SKIRT

1 Place the two fabric pieces right sides together, pin, tack (if desired) and sew the side seams of the skirt using a four-thread overlock stitch. You may need to increase the differential feed to avoid wavy edges – test the stitch first on a long length of fabric before making the seams in the skirt.

If you have added a side slit for a longer skirt as shown on skirt C, you will need to stitch the seam up to the slit, then finish the slit as described under 'Adding side slits and hem shaping' for the Santorini summer dress on page 159.

2 Try on the skirt and check you are happy with the shape. Make any adjustments and overlock the seams again if necessary.

3 Press the seams towards the back and topstitch if desired, as shown on skirt B. (See 'Creating a welt seam' and 'Using reverse coverstitch to create a mock flatlock seam' on pages 72–73).

6 If you want the elastic to be visible with visible topstitching, apply it to the right side of the fabric and follow the instructions for the lapped method on pages 116–117 for the flattest application, or if you'd prefer a visible waistband with hidden stitches, as shown in skirt B, apply the elastic to the right side of the fabric and follow the instructions for the enclosed method on page 117 up to and including step 2. Fold elastic away from the garment and press seam allowance towards the garment. Add topstitching to the seam if desired.

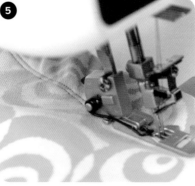

4 Cut a piece of elastic 2.5cm (1in) shorter than the waistline. Woven or firm elastics can be cut the same measurement or only fractionally shorter than the waistline. (See 'How long should the elastic be?') on page 120. Join the short ends using a suitable method (see page 120). These examples show the use of a three-thread wide flatlock stitch on an overlocker.

5 If you want the elastic to be enclosed, apply it to the wrong side of the fabric and follow the instructions for the enclosed method on page 117.

Tip
Pin elastic slightly within the edge of the fabric so that as this is attached, the overlocker blade can trim the very edge of the fabric but not the elastic.

8 To make a mock-band hem, turn under the raw edge to the wrong side by 4cm (1½in) and follow instructions on page 105 to complete.

7 To make a simple hem, turn under the raw edge to the wrong side by 2cm (¾in) and follow instructions for hemming in the round on page 79.

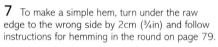

Buenavista beach wrap

This simple wrap dress is perfect for covering up on the beach or by the pool. It's an ideal quick project to test out your coverstitching skills and get started with using fold-over elastic. You can adapt the length of the dress to suit you and also change the style of the hem to create a straight, diagonal or curved edge.

YOU WILL NEED

- 1–2m (1–2yd) single jersey. Viscose is ideal to give drape
- 1.2m (1½yd) fold-over elastic, 2.5cm (1in) (or narrower if preferred)
- Three or four spools of polyester thread

Techniques required

- Coverstitch, triple coverstitch or top coverstitch (pages 60–65)
- Hemming a curved edge (page 90)
- Hemming corners (page 89)
- Joining elastic (page 120)
- Using fold-over elastic (page 111)
- Hemming in the round (page 79)

Elastic measurements
Small = 48cm (19in)
Medium = 52cm (20½in)
Large = 56cm (22in)

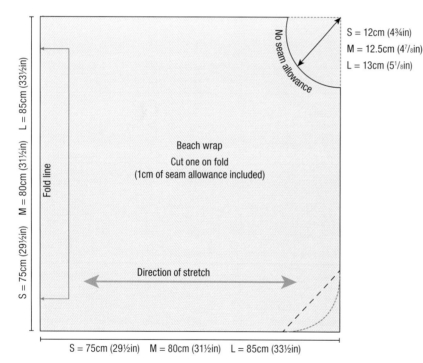

No seam allowance

S = 12cm (4¾in)
M = 12.5cm (4⁷/₈in)
L = 13cm (5¹/₈in)

Fold line

Beach wrap
Cut one on fold
(1cm of seam allowance included)

Direction of stretch

L = 85cm (33½in)
M = 80cm (31½in)
S = 75cm (29½in)

S = 75cm (29½in)   M = 80cm (31½in)   L = 85cm (33½in)

CUTTING OUT THE FABRIC

- Note that a smaller size may be needed for very stretchy fabrics.

- Fold the fabric right sides together (in the direction of greatest stretch, if possible) and draw out pattern as follows in size small/medium/large).

- Mark out from the folded edge, the other sides of a square measuring 75cm/80cm/85cm (29½in/31½in/33½in) – the folded edge is one of the sides of the square.

- From the top-right corner (not on the folded edge) draw in a curve of radius 12cm/12.5cm/13cm (4¾in/4⁷/₈in/5¹/₈in) to mark armhole edges.

- Choose a style for the lower-right corner: straight, diagonal or curved. A straight edge is the easiest to stitch.

- Cut out your fabric, then open out the folded edge. A 1cm (⅜in) hemming allowance is included on all sides except the armhole edge where this is not required.

- Cut two lengths of fold-over elastic each 48cm/52cm/56cm (19in/20½in/22in). 6mm (¼in) of seam allowance is included on the elastic.

To wear the beach wrap, hold the garment out behind you, with one strap in each hand and the wrong side of the fabric facing you. Place your left arm into the strap in your right hand and your right arm into the strap in your left hand.

I am using the Janome 1200D combination overlocker and coverstitch machine for this project.

INSTRUCTIONS

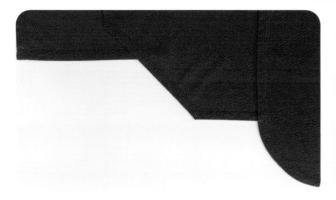

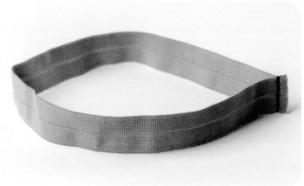

1 Open out the folded edge and make a 1cm (⅜in) hem on all edges except for the armhole curves. This can be done with coverstitch, reverse coverstitch or top coverstitch and your choice on number and position of needles. For techniques on hemming curves see page 90, and for corners see page 89.

2 Join the short ends of each of the elastic pieces using one of the methods shown in 'Joining elastic in the round' on pages 120–121. Here, the straight stitch method has been used, and the ends reinforced.

3 Trim the corners of the seam allowance on the elastic, if necessary and bury any thread ends on the wrong side of the elastic. Secure the thread ends and/or elastic ends with hand stitching if you wish. Finger press seam allowance open.

4 Fold the elastic in half along the crease line. Match the seam in the elastic to the finished side hem and pin in place. If one side of the folded elastic is wider than the other, match the wider edge to the wrong side of the beach wrap.

5 Continue to pin the elastic around the curve of the armhole. Align the raw edge of the fabric up to the crease line on the inside of the fold-over elastic. Stretch the elastic slightly as you go around the curve – this will allow it to sit flat along the curved edge of the fabric.

7 Use hand tacking to hold in place if you wish.

6 Fold and pin together the edges of the remaining elastic.

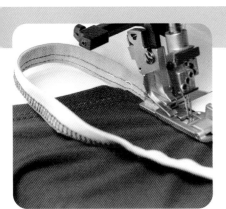

8 Start approx. 10cm (4in) from the seam and stitch the elastic using chain stitch or narrow coverstitch, stitching close to the inside edge of the elastic. For techniques on how to stitch in the round see page 79. Repeat steps 4–7 for the other armhole edge. Remove any tacking stitches.

The finished strap.

Light-weight viscose jersey in a bold print is used for this example.

Santorini summer dress

This project is a super-quick loose-fitting dress that can be made for any age, in any size. It's even suitable for stretch and non-stretch fabrics, depending on how close fitting you'd like it to be. The basic dress can be made in less than an hour and includes a narrow casing for elastic across the waist and simple turned and stitched hems for all garment openings. Keep the garment quick and easy or pick and choose from the optional extras to add pockets, waist ties, drawstring, belt, shirring, bound edges and hemline shaping.

I am using the Huskylock S21 combination overlocker and coverstitch machine for this project.

YOU WILL NEED

- 1–4m (1–4½yd) light- to medium-weight woven fabric such as lawn, challis or crepe, or 1–4m (1–4½yd) of light- to medium-weight knit fabric such as jersey or interlock. Exact amount depends on width of fabric and length/size of dress required
- 1–1.5m (1–1½yd) narrow clear elastic or stretch stay tape for stabilizing the shoulder seam
- 1–1.5m (1–1½yd) 5mm (¼in) knitted elastic for elastic casing at waistline
- Three or four spools of polyester thread

Optional

- Spool of shirring elastic for shirring at waistline
- 1–2m (1–2yd) of 2cm (¾in) wide single-fold bias binding, or 4cm (1½in) wide flat/unfolded binding (for binding neckline and armhole edges). Add an extra 2m (2yd) if you wish to bind the hem and pocket opening
- 10–25cm (4–10in) contrasting fabric to make a belt. Exact amount depends on width of belt
- 1–2m (1–2yd) of 3cm (1⅛in) wide single-fold bias binding, or 3cm (1⅛in) wide strip of fabric (to create casing for drawstring)
- 10cm (4in) contrasting fabric to make drawstring
- Two eyelets for drawstring, 6mm (¼in)
- Small piece of interfacing for eyelets or buttonholes
- Two large beads or cord ends for drawstring

Techniques required

- Coverstitch, triple coverstitch or top coverstitch (pages 60–65)
- Simple casing for narrow elastic (page 119)
- Joining elastic (pages 120–121)
- Hemming in the round (page 79)
- Overlocked seams

Optional techniques

- Shirring (using elastic thread in the looper) (page 109)
- Attaching pockets (page 91)
- Single-layer in-seam pockets (page 158)
- Binding opening edges (page 157)
- Making belt loops (page 134)
- Creating a drawstring and casing (page 159)
- Hemming a curved edge (page 90)

CREATING THE PATTERN

1 Measure the hips, divide by two and add 5–30cm (2–12in), depending on how loose-fitting you want the dress to be and how long you want the sleeves (see 'Variations' below). This is measurement 1.

2 Decide on the dress length from the shoulder and note this down as measurement 2.

3 Measure loosely around your neck and divide this by four to give your quarter neck measurement. It will be approx. 5cm (2in) for a small child and 10cm (4in) for an adult. This is measurement 3.

4 Measure shoulder to mid chest (child) or shoulder to bust point (adult) to work out size of armhole. This will be approx. 12.5cm (5in) for a small child and 25cm (10in) for an adult. This is measurement 4.

PREPARING FOR CONSTRUCTION

Decide if you want to include any additional design features and read the notes on these before beginning construction (see pages 157–159).

> **Tip**
> Shorten the pattern to create a top or add less ease to the hip measurement for a closer-fitting garment in stretch fabric.

VARIATIONS

- Dress A is the basic version in viscose stretch jersey with 30cm (12in) of ease added for measurement 1. A narrow casing with 5mm (¼in) elastic is used at the waistline with turned and stitched hems for the neckline, sleeves and lower hem.

- Dress B is embroidered medium-weight cotton fabric with 10cm (4in) of ease added to measurement 1, shirring elastic at the waist, single layer in-seam pockets and turned and stitched hems. The lower hem utilizes the embellished scalloped edge of the fabric.

- Dress C is viscose jersey with 10cm (4in) ease added to measurement 1. A drawstring casing and eyelets are added at the waistline. Single-layer in-seam pockets are added with a binding used on the opening. The neckline and sleeves are bound and the dress hem is turned and stitched.

CUTTING OUT THE FABRIC

The front and back pattern pieces are the same. Draw out and cut directly onto the fabric as follows:

- Measure and cut out two rectangles where the width (from selvedge to selvedge) is measurement 1 and the length (parallel to selvedge) is measurement 2 plus 2.5cm (1in) for hemming and seam allowance.

- A 6mm (¼in) seam allowance is included.

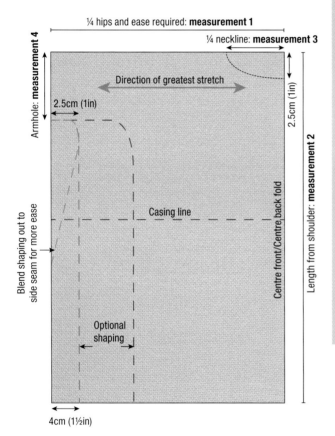

¼ hips and ease required: **measurement 1**

¼ neckline: **measurement 3**

Armhole: **measurement 4**

2.5cm (1in)

Direction of greatest stretch

2.5cm (1in)

Centre front/Centre back fold

Length from shoulder: **measurement 2**

Blend shaping out to side seam for more ease

Casing line

Optional shaping

4cm (1½in)

Tip for cutting the neckline

The front and back necklines don't have to be the same. You can make it deeper at the front for a more flattering fit. You can also make a wide neck opening if you prefer or copy the neckline of a favourite garment.

MAKING THE BASIC DRESS

1 Start by creating shaping for the neckline. Take one rectangle and fold it right sides together, matching the long edges. Take the quarter neck size from measurement 3 and measure and mark this along the top edge from the centre-front fold. Measure down the centre-front fold 2.5cm (1in) and place a mark. Join the two points with a curve as shown in the diagram. Repeat for the other rectangle.

2 Take the armhole size from measurement 4, measure and mark this down the long edge of the rectangles.

3 Cut out the neck opening, pin the shoulder seams together and place over your head. Check the neckline is suitable or adjust as necessary to create a lower neckline. Check the armhole measurement is correct, adjust as required and place marker.

4 Create shaping for armhole: from each armhole marker, measure in 2.5cm (1in) and mark with chalk or other fabric marker. Starting at the lower edge, draw a line parallel to the side seam, 4cm (1½in) from the edge on both sides; stop 2.5cm (1in) away from the armhole marker. Join to the line from the armhole marker with a curve as shown in the diagram on the left. Cut away excess fabric. You can blend the armhole shaping line back out to the side of the rectangle for more ease (shown as a blue dashed line), or form a more close-fitting garment by reducing the ease and making the sleeves longer (shown as a red dashed line). Add any in-seam pockets now (see page 158).

5 Decide on the position of the waistline casing and place a marker at the side seam. This will be approx. 40cm (16in) from the shoulder for an adult and 20cm (8in) for a small child.

6 To add the casing for narrow elastic, decide which way up to stitch (see page 119, 'Simple casing for narrow elastic') and mark a line across both the front and back fabric pieces, using the placement marker from the previous step. Stitch the casing using a wide coverstitch or top coverstitch. Additional lines of stitching can be added to create a series of narrow casings (see the image on page 120).

6

7 Feed narrow elastic through the casing, pull up to the desired amount and pin the ends in place.

8 Use a four-thread overlock stitch to sew shoulder seams together – include clear elastic or stay tape to stabilize seam as described on page 81.

9 With right sides together, pin or clip together side seams from armhole marker to lower edge. Match the elastic casings at the side seams. Sew side seams together using the same technique as for the shoulder seams.

10 To finish the neckline and armholes, turn under 1.5cm (⅝in) all the way round. Prepare and complete hem as described in 'Hemming in the round' on page 79.

11 Finish the hem on the lower edge by turning up 2cm (¾in) and completing as for the neckline.

OPTIONAL DESIGN FEATURES

Binding opening edges

Binding can be added to the neckline, armhole, single-layer in-seam pockets and lower hem as you construct the dress. Use binding in a contrasting colour to add interest to the opening edges.

If you wish to add binding to single-layer in-seam pockets, do this first and follow the instructions for the single-layer pocket overleaf. Instead of snipping and turning under the opening edge, cut away a curved section from the side seam and apply binding to this edge before continuing pocket construction at step 6 (page 158).

To add binding to the neckline edge, decide if you wish to stitch the binding flat or in the round. Follow steps 1–7 for the basic dress. To attach the binding flat, sew only one shoulder seam. To add the binding in the round, sew both shoulder seams.

To add binding at the armhole edge, complete the neckline edge first, then apply the binding flat before joining the side seams, or join the side seams first and then apply the binding in the round.

To add binding to the hem, complete this flat before sewing the side seams, or in the round after finishing the side seams.

See information and techniques on pages 122–133 for applying binding.

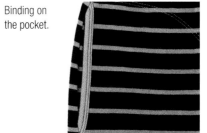

Binding on the pocket.

Binding on the neckline.

Single-layer in-seam pockets

Add these pockets before the casing and side seams are sewn. This project uses a single-layer technique which is stitched to the front of the garment resulting in visible stitching on the right side of the fabric.

Follow steps 1–4 of constructing the dress, then insert the pockets.

1 Decide on the position for the pocket and mark this with two dots on the wrong side of the fabric on each side of the front piece. Place dots 6mm (¼in) from raw edge. The opening for the pocket can be turned under and stitched in place as described below, or you can cut away a curved shape for the pocket opening, bind the edge using a method given on page 157, 'Binding opening edges' and then move to step 6.

2 Apply a 1.5cm (⅝in) strip of interfacing to the wrong side of the garment, along the pocket opening and extending 1.5cm (⅝in) at each end.

3 For wovens, staystitch along the seam line, the length of the pocket opening plus 1.5cm (⅝in) either end.

4 Snip into the seam allowance (6mm/¼in) up to the dots.

5 Fold the pocket opening to the wrong side, between the two snips. Press, pin and stitch in place, sewing close to the folded edge using a straight stitch, chain stitch or coverstitch.

6 Create a pattern piece for the pocket bag. Use an existing one from another pattern or create your own using the size of your hand for guidance. The piece may be curved or rectangular but must be at least 1cm (⅜in) wider than the pocket opening. Cut two pocket bags, one for each pocket.

7 Place each pocket bag with right side facing the wrong side of the garment, matching raw edges. Pin and stitch in place from the right or wrong side, depending on the desired finished look. For chain stitch or reverse coverstitch, edge finish the pocket bag first. If top coverstitch or coverstitch is to be used, use a tacking stitch and sew from the wrong side to mark the stitching line along the edge of the pocket as shown in the 'Appliqué' section on page 92.

Tip

Use the size of your hand as guidance for the size of the pocket opening.

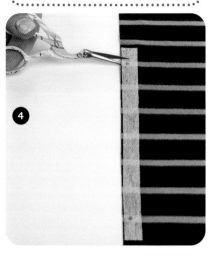

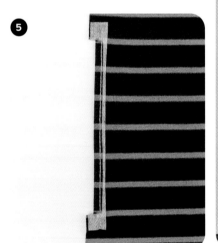

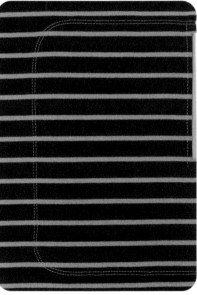

The finished pocket, on outside of garment.

Patch pockets

Add these at the start or once construction is complete. Decide on the size and shape you'd like, add a hemming allowance, then cut out your pattern pieces. Find inspiration and methods of attaching these using coverstitch or reverse coverstitch on page 91.

Shirred waistline

Follow the instructions for the basic dress above, up to and including step 4. Mark lines at the waistline across the rectangles as described in step 5. Decide on the number of lines of shirring and work in rows, starting from the line marked onto the fabric. Use a sewing machine to sew over the elastic ends within the seam allowance at the side seams. See tips on using shirring elastic on page 109. Continue following instructions for the basic dress from step 8 (page 157).

Drawstring

Use a length of ribbon, shoelace or cord for the drawstring or create your own as follows: cut a length of fabric twice the waist measurement x 2.4cm (1in) or the width required to fit your belt-loop folder. Follow the instructions on pages 134–136 'Making belt loops' to form one long folded and stitched strip.

To include a drawstring, you'll need to add buttonholes or eyelets at the centre front. Follow the instructions for the basic dress above, up to and including step 5.

Mark lines across the front and back pieces as described in step 6.

Work out the placement for the buttonholes or eyelets as follows: find the centre front, apply interfacing to a small section 1.5cm (⅝in) either side of the centre front, along the marked line for the casing for where the 1.2cm (½in) buttonholes or 6mm (¼in) eyelets will go.

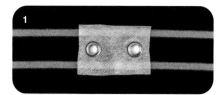

1 Make two horizontal buttonholes or insert eyelets, 1.5cm (⅝in) either side of the centre front on the marked line for the casing.

2 Follow steps 8–11 for the basic dress, matching the marked line for the casing at the side seams. Apply 3cm (1⅛in) single fold bias binding or a 3cm (1⅛in) strip of fabric to the wrong side of the fabric to form a casing, centring this along the marked line for the casing.

3 Start and end at the side seam and overlap the bias binding, turning under the raw edge of the top layer. Stitch the binding in place using chain stitch or coverstitch.

4 Use the buttonholes or eyelets to feed the drawstring through the casing and add beads or cord ends if desired.

Adding a belt

If you prefer, you can omit the casing method described above and just add a belt to draw in the fabric and create definition at the waist.

To create a 4cm (1½in) wide belt, cut a strip of fabric on the straight grain that measures twice the waist measurement with a depth of 10cm (4in). This will give a 4cm (1½in) wide belt and includes 1cm (⅜in) seam allowances. Cut the strip wider or narrower as desired.

1 Fold the fabric strip in half with right sides together and pin in place. Short ends can be cut at a 45° angle if desired.

2 Using a straight stitch on a sewing machine, or a four-thread overlock stitch, start from one end, stitch along the short end, pivot and stitch to the centre of the long edge. Secure stitches.

3 Leave a 5cm (2in) gap for turning and continue stitching the long edge; pivot at the end and stitch the short end.

4 If a straight stitch has been used, trim seam allowances at corners, then turn the belt to the right side.

5 Use a point turner to poke out the corners, and press seams flat.

6 Use hand stitching to close the gap in the seam neatly.

The belt can be worn without belt loops – simply tie it round your waist. To include belt loops, these can be made and added to the side seam as described in the 'Hove skirt' on page 165. Alternatively, thin belt loops can be made using a thread chain as shown in the 'Ideas to try: chain stitch' on page 59.

Adding side slits and hem shaping

If you want to add a side slit, do this before sewing the side seams. The shape of the side seam and lower hem can also be curved from the slit to the hem, if desired.

Follow steps 1–8 for the basic dress. Decide on the length of the side slit(s) and mark the end of each slit onto the wrong side of the fabric.

Draw on any side seam and hem shaping. Cut away excess fabric.

Complete steps 9 and 10 on page 157, sewing side seams up to the slit opening.

Finish the raw edges of the slits: turn under the raw edge by 6mm (¼in), press, pin or clip, and stitch in place using straight stitch, chain or coverstitch.

Complete the dress by hemming as described in step 11 on page 157. If the side seam and hem has been shaped, the slit and hem can be completed in one step.

Hove skirt

This project has plenty of optional design features so you can either keep things simple or try out a range of techniques including pockets, belt loops and decorative stitching. The original skirt is high waisted with a paper bag effect along the top edge; you can choose to add a belt or draw cord to add further detail to the waistline or simplify the style by making a smaller casing without the fluting. A separate casing for the elastic is used as this gives more flexibility in adapting the style of the skirt. Seam allowances of 1.5cm (⅝in) and a hemming allowance of 2cm (¾in) are included in the pattern. Information for the optional features and construction methods are given after the main instructions so make sure you read all the way through first, if you wish to include any of the additional details.

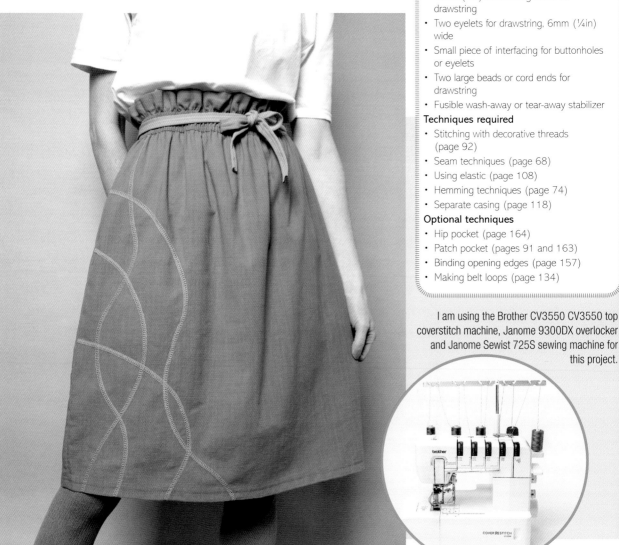

YOU WILL NEED

- 1.5m (1½yd) medium-weight cotton or other non-stretch woven dressmaking fabric. If a longer version is required, add an additional 50cm (20in)
- Approx. 1m (1yd) knitted waistband elastic, 3.8cm (1½in) wide. Exact amount depends on waist measurement
- Three or four spools of polyester thread, plus heavier thread for top coverstitch or looper, depending on type of machine and chosen stitch

Optional
- Thread palette for blending threads (see page 93)
- Approx. 50cm (20in) of single-fold bias binding. Exact amount depends on size of pocket opening
- 25cm (10in) contrasting fabric for belt
- 10cm (4in) contrasting fabric for drawstring
- Two eyelets for drawstring, 6mm (¼in) wide
- Small piece of interfacing for buttonholes or eyelets
- Two large beads or cord ends for drawstring
- Fusible wash-away or tear-away stabilizer

Techniques required
- Stitching with decorative threads (page 92)
- Seam techniques (page 68)
- Using elastic (page 108)
- Hemming techniques (page 74)
- Separate casing (page 118)

Optional techniques
- Hip pocket (page 164)
- Patch pocket (pages 91 and 163)
- Binding opening edges (page 157)
- Making belt loops (page 134)

I am using the Brother CV3550 CV3550 top coverstitch machine, Janome 9300DX overlocker and Janome Sewist 725S sewing machine for this project.

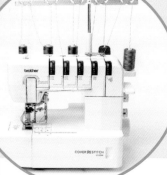

CREATING THE PATTERN

1 Measure the hips and waist. Take the larger of the two measurements and divide by two, then add 14cm (5½in) for ease and seam allowances. This is measurement 1.

2 Decide on the skirt length from waist, add 3.5cm (1⅜in) for seams and hem allowance. This is measurement 2.

CUTTING OUT THE FABRIC

- The front and back pattern pieces will be the same unless you are adding hip pockets (see notes below).

- Cut two rectangles of fabric for the front and back using measurement 1 for width and measurement 2 for length.

- Cut two rectangles for the casing pieces using the width of measurement 1 and a length of 16cm (6¼in) for the paper-bag skirt or 11cm (4⅜in) for a regular casing.

PREPARING FOR CONSTRUCTION

Decide if you want to include any additional features and read the notes on these before beginning construction.

EMBELLISHING YOUR FABRIC

- Decide if you want to plan and mark out the design, or freestyle: stitching and designing as you go.

- Decide on the stitch(es) you wish to use for your design. For inspiration, take a look at 'Ideas to try: embroidery and embellishment techniques' on page 93.

- Light- to medium-weight fabrics may work best with a stabilizer to keep the fabric and stitching flat.

- Mark your design onto the right or wrong side of the fabric (depending on which side you will sew, e.g. for chain stitch or reverse coverstitch, mark and sew from the wrong side).

- Consider the thread colour and type that you will use for your design and experiment on some scraps first before embellishing your fabric.

- Create your final design on the back and/or front skirt pieces.

MAKING THE BASIC SKIRT

1 Stitch the front to the back at the side seams using a sewing machine, overlocker or see 'Seams' on page 68.

2 Stitch the two short ends of the casing using a straight stitch on your sewing machine. Press the seam open.

3 With right sides together, place one long edge of the casing to the top of the skirt, matching side seams, pin and stitch with a straight stitch.

4 Layer the seam allowance by trimming the garment edge slightly.

5 Pull the casing away from the garment and press the seam allowances towards the casing.

6 Decide on the measurement for the elastic by placing the elastic around your waist (or the waist of whoever the skirt is for) and tightening just enough so that it is comfortable but will hold. This will be approx. 2.5cm (1in) shorter than the waist measurement. Allow a little extra for seam allowance to join elastic. (See 'How long should the elastic be?' on page 120.)

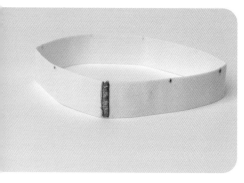

7 Join short ends of elastic using one of the methods on pages 120–121 'Joining elastic in the round'. Divide the elastic into eight sections by halving, halving and halving again. Mark the elastic at each section.

8 Split the top of the casing into eight sections and mark, so each can be matched to the marked sections of the elastic.

9 Match the elastic to the top edge of the wrong side of the casing, placing the join of the elastic to the centre back of the skirt. Pin in place, stretching to fit.

10 You may wish to use a temporary stitch to hold the elastic in place or just overlock this. Disengage the overlocker blade or take care to avoid cutting into the elastic as you stitch.

11 Fold the casing over and match the overlocked edge to the seam line of the casing and top of the skirt. Match side seams, centre front and centre back, stretch the elastic to fit and pin in place. Tack in place if desired.

12 Use a coverstitch or reverse coverstitch to hold the overlocked edge of elastic in place.

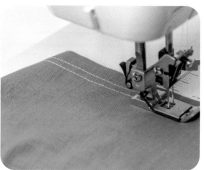

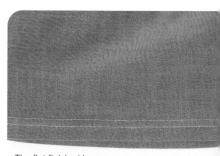

The flat finished hem.

13 Stitch again using the same stitch as in step 12, sewing along the other edge of the elastic, stretching the elastic to fit. This line of stitching will be approximately 3.5cm (1⅜in) from the fold line.

14 Turn up a 2cm (¾in) hem at the lower edge of the skirt and stitch in place using one of the techniques for 'Hemming in the round' on page 79.

OPTIONAL DESIGN FEATURES

Narrow casing

If you prefer to have a regular casing, without the paper-bag detail, simply cut the casing narrower. Instructions are given on page 161 for a casing of 11cm (4⅜in) deep which will work with elastic of width 3.8–4cm (1½in). Other widths of elastic can be used instead – just amend the measurement of the casing accordingly.

Follow step 1 of 'Making the basic skirt' and then the instructions on page 118 'Separate casing' on how to construct and attach this. Complete the skirt by hemming the lower edge, following step 11 of 'Making the basic skirt'.

Patch pockets

You can create and add these types of pockets easily before sewing the side seams, or after the project is finished. Decide on the size and shape you'd like, add a hemming allowance and then cut out your pattern pieces. Find inspiration and methods for attaching these using coverstitch or reverse coverstitch on page 91.

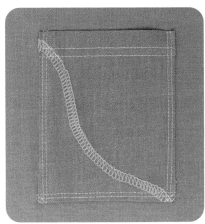

Embellished patch pocket sewn to garment using a narrow coverstitch and the 'overlapping corners technique' on page 87.

Drawstring

To include a drawstring, you'll need to add buttonholes or eyelets at the centre front of the casing. Make the buttonholes or eyelets before attaching the casing to the garment. In this example 1.2cm (½in) buttonholes are used to fit a 1.2cm (½in) wide drawstring. (See 'fold-over casing with drawstring on page 119 for buttonhole/eyelet placement.)

1 Work out the position of the buttonholes as follows: Add the seam allowance to half the depth of the elastic. In this case 1.5cm (⅝in) + 1.9cm (¾in) = 3.4cm (1⅜in).

2 Find the centre-front line of the casing. Apply interfacing to a small section where the buttonholes or eyelets will go, 1.5cm (⅝in) either side of the centre front and 3.4cm (1⅜in) from the raw edge.

3 Make two horizontal buttonholes or insert an eyelet, 3.4cm (1⅜in) from raw edge of the fabric and 1.5cm (⅝in) either side of the centre front of the casing.

4 Follow steps 1–11 of 'Making the basic skirt', attaching the long edge of the casing closest to the buttonholes/eyelets to the top of the skirt in step 3.

5 Use a length of ribbon, shoelace or cord for the drawstring or create your own as follows: cut a length of fabric twice the waist measurement x 2.4cm (1in) or the width required to fit your belt-loop folder. Follow the instructions on pages 134–136 'Making belt loops' to form one long folded and stitched strip.

6 An additional casing for the drawstring can be formed using chain stitch. Stitch 6mm (¼in) above and below the buttonholes all the way round the casing, stretching the elastic to fit as you sew.

7 Feed the drawstring through the casing and add beads or cord ends if desired.

CREATING THE PATTERN PIECES FOR HIP POCKETS

To include a hip pocket, you'll need to draw in the style line for your pocket, adapt the front pattern piece and also create a pattern for the pocket bag. The hip pocket is attached before you start following the basic skirt instructions. Instructions are given here for a simple curved opening but you could draw this straight or alter the size as necessary – just make sure you can fit your hand into it!

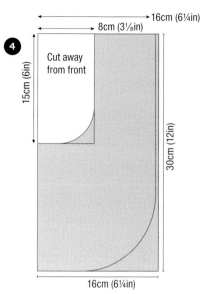

1 On paper, draw a rectangle 16 x 30cm (6¼ x 12in).

2 From the top-left corner measure and place a mark 8cm (3⅛in) across the top and another 15cm (6in) down the left side.

3 Draw a vertical line from the 8cm (3⅛in) mark and a horizontal line from the 15cm (6in) mark. Where the lines join, redraw this as a curve. (This is the style line for the pocket opening – you can alter the shape or size of this.)

4 Draw a curve in the lower right corner as shown in the diagram below. (This is the shape of the pocket bag – you can make this square or enlarge the size.)

5 Trace off the larger curved section. (Line shown in red on diagram.) This will become the pattern piece for the pocket bag.

6 Cut away the smaller curved section and use this as a template to remove the top left and right corners of the front skirt piece.

Pocket bag

Cut away

Cut away

Front

(with sections removed for hip pocket openings)

MAKING THE POCKET

Prepare the front skirt piece as in step 6 opposite and cut two pocket bags (see step 5 opposite).

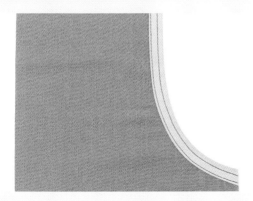

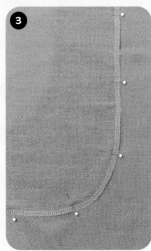

1 Bind the curved edges on the skirt front (for the pocket opening) using one of the single- or double-layer flat methods shown on pages 123 and 125 'Using binding'. Choose which stitch to use to attach the pocket bag to the skirt front (chain stitch, coverstitch, reverse coverstitch or top coverstitch).

2 If reverse coverstitch or chain stitch is to be used, overlock the curved edge of the pocket bag.

3 Lay the pocket bags with the right side facing the wrong side of the garment front. Align raw edges and pin in place.

4 Tack the waistline and side-seam edges of the pocket bag in place using hand or machine stitching.

5 Stitch the curved edge of the pocket in place using your choice of stitch. If top coverstitch or coverstitch is to be used, use a tacking stitch and sew from the wrong side to mark the stitching line along the edge of the pocket as shown in the appliqué section on page 92.

6 Continue, following the instructions for 'Making the basic skirt' on page 161.

The finished pocket (from the inside).

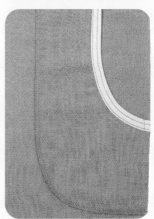

The finished pocket (from the outside), stitched with reverse coverstitch.

ADDING BELT LOOPS

Decide how many belt loops you'd like on your skirt – look at other skirts and trousers you have to help you decide. Two may be enough to hold a light-weight belt at the side seams or you may want to include one or two loops at the centre back and centre front.

Decide on the length of the belt loops: for the paper-bag style skirt allow 8cm (3⅛in) per belt loop – a length of 6cm (2⅜in) plus 2cm (¾in) of hem allowance. To create six belt loops, cut a length of fabric 60cm (23⅝in) x width required; this will allow for adjustment to needle alignments to be made when starting to stitch.

1 Make belt loops using instructions on pages 134–136 'Making belt loops'.

2 Cut the belt loops to the required length.

3 Turn under 1cm (⅜in) on each end of the belt loops and pin and attach to the skirt using a straight stitch or narrow zigzag on a sewing machine.

ADDING A BELT

See instructions on page 159 for adding a belt to the Santorini summer dress.

Weekend in Whitby washbag

Test out your zip-insertion skills with this next project. Choose a bright and colourful pattern or pick a solid colour and add your own embellishments using decorative threads and your choice of stitching lines. I have used a zebra-print scuba fabric, but any medium- to heavy-weight fabric is ideal. Depending on how rigid you want the bag to be, use interfacing to strengthen and stabilize your fabric. The zip is applied using reverse coverstitch to create a lacy stitch on the right side but you could use regular coverstitch, triple or top coverstitch for your project.

I am using the Juki MCS1800 coverstitch machine and Janome 9300DX overlocker for this project.

YOU WILL NEED

- 50cm (20in) medium- to heavy-weight fabric for outer layer – choose something without a directional print
- 50cm (20in) lining fabric
- 40cm (16in) zip – either open or closed end as the ends will be cut off. I have used number 5 open-ended zips for a chunky look and for ease of stitching around the zip tape
- 6mm (¼in) wide water-soluble double-sided tape (or pins)

Optional
- 50cm (20in) medium-weight interfacing
- 50cm (20in) quilting wadding (batting)
- 70cm (27½in) bias binding or fold-over elastic for seam binding, 2.5cm (1in) wide

Techniques required
- Reverse coverstitch (page 60)
- Inserting a zip – using water-soluble double-sided tape (explained opposite)
- Making belt loops (for the tabs) (pages 134–136)
- Seam techniques (page 68)

Optional techniques
- Decorative stitching (Ideas to try: embroidery and embellishment techniques, page 93)
- Binding fabric edges and seams with double-layer binding (page 125) or fold-over elastic (page 111)

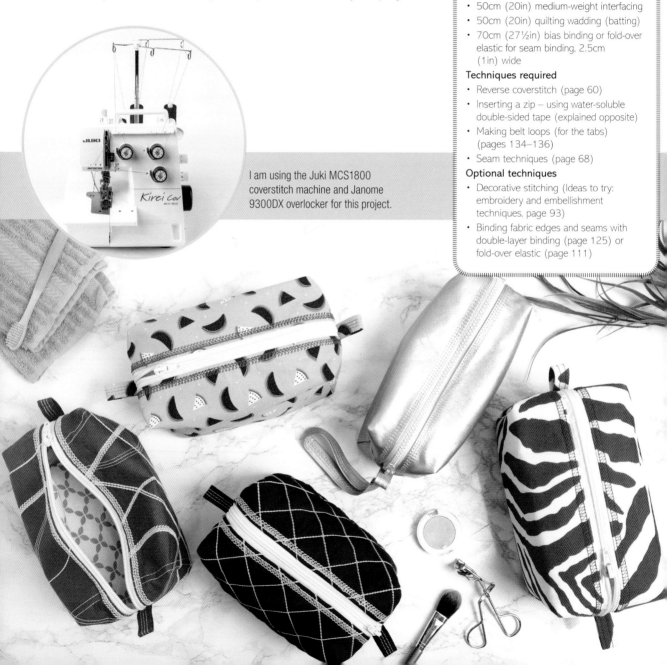

CUTTING OUT THE FABRIC

- Cut a rectangle 32 x 42cm (12⅝ x 16½in) from each of the main and lining fabrics.

- Cut a strip 25 x 4cm (10 x 1½in) for tabs or use a width suitable for your belt-loop folder or bias tape maker.

MAKING THE WASHBAG

If you wish to embellish your bag with decorative stitches, do this first and follow the suggestions on page 93 using the main fabric piece. For a quilted effect, use the larger main piece and wadding together. As you stitch through the wadding and main fabric, this piece will shrink slightly, so it's been cut slightly larger for this purpose. Cut the lining piece to match, once you've finished the decorative stitching.

OPTIONAL

- For extra strength, apply interfacing to the main fabric.

- For a quilted effect with decorative stitching, cut the main piece 34 x 44cm (13⅜ x 17¼in) and cut out an additional rectangle 36 x 46cm (14¼ x 18⅛in) in wadding.

- Make a longer hanging loop as shown on the gold version opposite. Cut an additional strip of fabric 30 x 4cm (12 x 1½in), form another belt loop, fold in half and attach to zip opening end on top of or instead of tab in step 10.

1 With the right side of the main fabric facing up, place water-soluble double-sided tape along each of the short edges.

2 Lay the zip face down, matching the edge of the zip to the raw edge of the fabric and stick it to the double-sided tape. There should be around 4cm (1½in) of zip overhanging each end.

3 Take the lining fabric and place it right sides together with the main fabric, matching the short edge to the short edge of main fabric, sandwiching the zip in between. Pin, clip or use another strip of water-soluble double-sided tape.

4 Set up your machine to chain stitch using the left needle. Position the fabric with the right needle marking on the presser foot in line with the raw edge of the fabric. Stitch through all three layers.

5 Open out the fabric layers to reveal the zip, then place wrong sides of fabric together. Pull the two layers of fabric away from the zip, press if necessary and then pin through all layers close to zip teeth, placing the pins on the lining side.

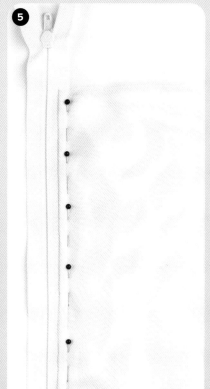

6 Set the machine to wide coverstitch. Position the fabric with the lining side up and the right needle just inside the folded edge of the fabric. Stitch to produce a reverse coverstitch effect, removing the pins as you go.

7 Repeat for the other side of the zip. You may find it easier to open the zip to sew.

8 With the right side of the fabric facing you, fold the bag in half so that the zip is at one end. Make a small snip through the lining and main fabric to mark the centre of the long edges.

MAKING THE TABS

9 Using the narrow strip of fabric you have cut, create belt loops using the wide coverstitch setting and one of the methods for forming belt loops on pages 135–136. Cut two strips each 10cm (4in) in length.

Right side (left); wrong side (right).

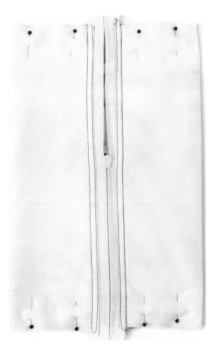

10 Fold each tab in half with wrong sides together, matching short ends. Pin a tab to each end of the zip. Hand tack in place if desired to make sure that the tab is centred correctly.

11 Turn the bag to the wrong side and place flat, centring the zip by matching the ends of the zip to the snip marks on each of the long raw edges of fabric. Open the zip slightly and pin the lining and main fabric together along raw edges.

12 In each of the four corners, mark a rectangle 5 x 4cm (2 x 1½in). The longest length of the rectangle runs parallel to the zip.

13 Cut the rectangles away from the fabric and leave the pins in.

14 Partly close up the zip so the zip head is in the centre of the bag. Trim off any excess zip tape and use a 1cm (⅜in) seam allowance to stitch across the zip ends of the bag.

15 Bind the seam allowance if desired for a neat finish. (See techniques on 'Double-layer binding' on page 125 or 'Using fold-over elastic' on page 111.)

16 Open out the cut-out corners and match the raw edges together to form a straight line. Pin in place.

17 Use a 1cm (⅜in) seam allowance and stitch across the ends. Bind seams if desired.

You may wish to stitch the remaining seams of your bag with your sewing machine, a three- or four-thread overlock stitch, or you can continue using the coverstitch machine and finish the seams with chain stitch. Additionally, seams can be bound with bias binding or fold-over elastic. On this example, fold-over elastic is used to cover the seam with the zip ends.

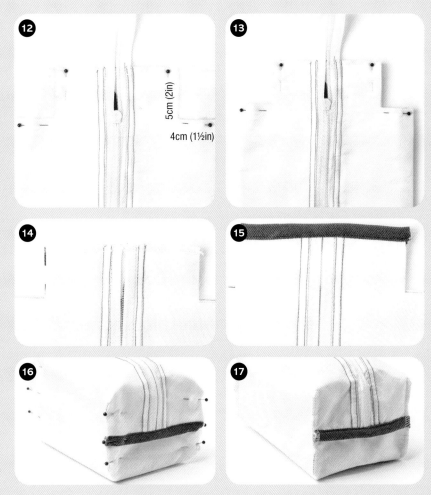

Show off your reverse coverstitch skills on this quick-to-make washbag.

Cambridge table runner

This project allows you to be creative and try out the decorative techniques shown on pages 92–97. Design your own table runner using the same or a variety of embroidery, embellishment or textured techniques on each panel to test what your machine can do. The finished project is made from a pack of eight plain cotton fat quarters in bright solid colours, but you could choose your own combination of patterned or plain quilting fabrics. It measures approx. 140 x 40cm (55 x 15¾in).

YOU WILL NEED

- Eight pieces of quilting cotton, approx. 50 x 50cm (20 x 20in), also known as fat quarters
- 1.5m (1½yd) cotton wadding (batting). Use heat-resistant wadding so the table runner is suitable for hot plates
- 4m (4½yd) single-fold binding, 2.5cm (1in) wide, or unfolded binding, 5cm (2in) wide
- Interfacing or stabilizer
- Variety of threads
- Thread palette (optional)

Techniques required

- Chain stitch, coverstitch and top coverstitch used decoratively (pages 56–65)
- Pintucks (page 95)
- Double-layer binding (page 125)
- Stitching corners and curves (pages 86–88)
- Stitching in circles (page 86)

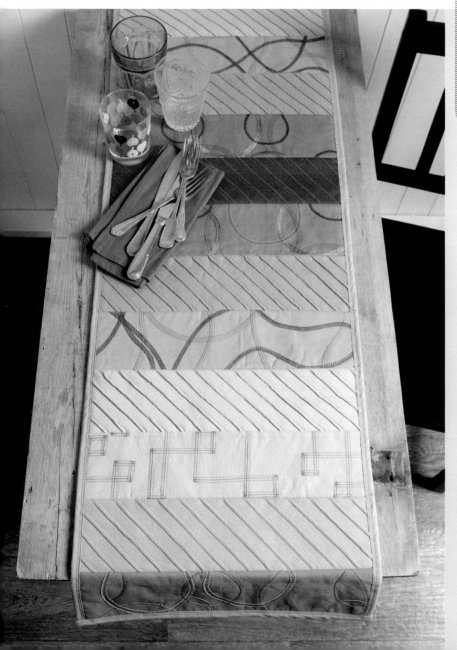

I am using the Janome CoverPro 2000CPX coverstitch machine and Janome 9300DX overlocker for this project.

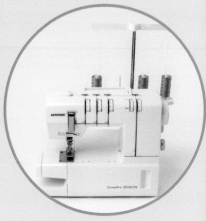

PREPARING THE FABRIC

- Add interfacing to the fabric or use a stabilizer to give more stability to the fabric before embellishing.

- Use the decorative stitch techniques shown in this book to create 15 embellished and/or textured panels and trim each to measure 10 x 40cm (4 x 15¾in). I cut each fat quarter into four pieces, each measuring approx. 12.5 x 50cm (5 x 20in).

- Practise each of the techniques on scrap fabrics before working on your project fabric.

- Some techniques, such as pintucks will require you to use pieces larger than 10 x 40cm (4 x 15¾in) to allow for the folds in fabric.

- Cut 15 pieces of backing fabric, each 10 x 40cm (4 x 15¾in).

- Cut 15 pieces of wadding, each 10 x 40cm (4 x 15¾in).

- If you are cutting your own binding, this can be cut on the straight grain since it will be applied only to straight edges. Use a contrasting fabric or piece together the leftover strips from the fat quarters to form a length 4m x 5cm (4½yd x 2in).

MAKING THE TABLE RUNNER

Embellish your fabric as described above and prepare the fabric panels ready for piecing together. You will need 15 embellished panels, 15 backing panels and 15 wadding panels. This project is pieced and overlocked together using a four-thread stitch. Use a stitch length of 3 to 4, differential feed of 1 or N and a lower foot pressure, if necessary, to accommodate the thickness of fabric.

The binding is attached with a double-layer method, using a chain stitch first before folding and topstitching with coverstitch. This could be applied using a single-layer technique or with a binder attachment if preferred.

Decide on the layout of the top panels and number these 1–15. Decide on the layout of the backing panels and letter these A–O.

When pressing the panels during construction, you may wish to use a pressing cloth to protect the embellished surface of the panels.

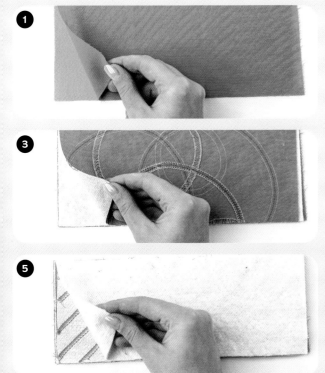

1 Lay piece B face up. Place piece A right sides together with piece B.
2 Place a strip of wadding on top.
3 Place piece 1, right side up on top of the wadding.
4 Place piece 2 on top, right side facing down.
5 Place another piece of wadding on top. Pin or clip layers together.

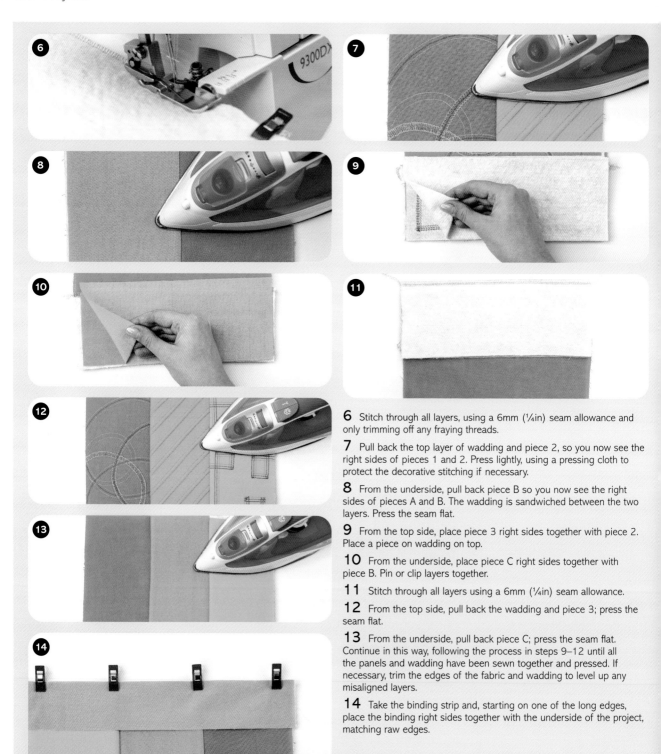

6 Stitch through all layers, using a 6mm (¼in) seam allowance and only trimming off any fraying threads.

7 Pull back the top layer of wadding and piece 2, so you now see the right sides of pieces 1 and 2. Press lightly, using a pressing cloth to protect the decorative stitching if necessary.

8 From the underside, pull back piece B so you now see the right sides of pieces A and B. The wadding is sandwiched between the two layers. Press the seam flat.

9 From the top side, place piece 3 right sides together with piece 2. Place a piece on wadding on top.

10 From the underside, place piece C right sides together with piece B. Pin or clip layers together.

11 Stitch through all layers using a 6mm (¼in) seam allowance.

12 From the top side, pull back the wadding and piece 3; press the seam flat.

13 From the underside, pull back piece C; press the seam flat. Continue in this way, following the process in steps 9–12 until all the panels and wadding have been sewn together and pressed. If necessary, trim the edges of the fabric and wadding to level up any misaligned layers.

14 Take the binding strip and, starting on one of the long edges, place the binding right sides together with the underside of the project, matching raw edges.

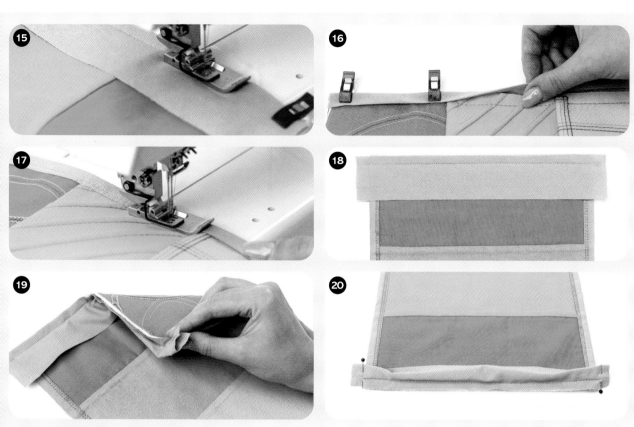

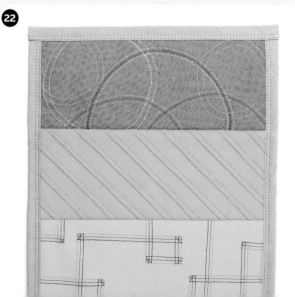

15 Stitch the binding in place with a 1cm (⅜in) seam allowance using chain stitch.

16 Fold the binding over to the right side of the project. Fold under the raw edge by 1cm (⅜in) and bring the folded edge over to just cover the stitching line from the previous step. Pin or clip in place.

17 Use chain stitch or coverstitch to stitch the binding in place from the right side. Repeat for the other long edge.

18 Follow steps 14–16 for the short edges but leave 1cm (⅜in) of binding overhanging at each end.

19 Place the right sides of the overhanging ends together as shown.

20 Pin overhanging ends together as shown.

21 Stitch in place, flush with the finished edge of the binding. Trim the seam allowance and turn the binding to the right side.

22 Fold and stitch in place as described in steps 16 and 17 to complete your project.

Belle Mare bikini

Get ready for summer! This bikini will test out your skills in working with swimwear fabrics and elastic. You can include additional details with padded cups, ruffles and decorative beads or cord ends. Since the top and bottom close with ties, the sizing is approximate.

YOU WILL NEED

- 50cm (20in) 4-way stretch swimwear fabric for main fabric
- 50cm (20in) 4-way stretch swimwear lining fabric – can be the same as the main fabric
- Approx 5m (5½yd) of 1cm (⅜in) wide swimwear elastic for ties (3m (3⅓yd) for top, 2m (2¼yd) for bottoms) plus an additional 3m (3½yd) swimwear elastic for stabilizing seams
- Three or four spools of polyester thread plus woolly nylon for looper, if desired

Optional

- One pair of swimwear cups, or cut your own using bra-making cut-and-sew foam
- Eight large beads or cord ends (four for the top, four for the bottoms)

Techniques required

- Chain stitch or overlocked seams (page 68)
- Using swimwear elastic (page 112)
- Making straps using swimwear elastic (page 114)

Note

This is an advanced project, so take it slowly and carefully.

I am using the baby lock BLCS2 coverstitch machine and Janome 9300DX overlocker for this project.

CREATING THE PATTERN

The pattern piece is symmetrical down the centre front, so the pattern that you draft will only be for one half. It is quicker and easier to cut pattern pieces out as a whole, so when drawing your pattern onto paper, fold the paper, draft one half as shown, add a 1cm (⅜in) seam allowance and then cut out the paper pattern as the whole piece. The 1cm (⅜in) seam allowance should be all the way around the pattern piece, except for the centre fold line.

PATTERN FOR BIKINI TOP

The pattern has instructions for three different cup sizes: A–B, C–D and E–F. Use the following measurements and the diagram to draft your pattern piece. Cup sizing refers to UK bra sizes.

Bikini top	Measurements (cm/in)		
Letter on diagram	To fit A–B cup	To fit C–D cup	To fit E–F cup
a	18.5cm (7¼in)	20cm (7⅞in)	21.5cm (8½in)
b	14cm (5½in)	15cm (5⅞in)	16cm (6¼in)
c	5.5cm (2⅛in)	6.25cm (2½in)	7cm (2¾in)
d	9cm (3½in)	9.75 (3⅞in)	10.5cm (4⅛in)
e	8.5cm (3⅜in)	9.5cm (3¾in)	10.5cm (4⅛in)

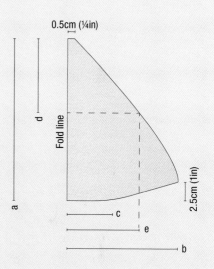

0.5cm (¼in)

Fold line

d

a

c

e

b

2.5cm (1in)

Bikini top

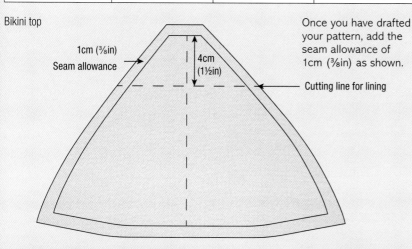

1cm (⅜in)
Seam allowance

4cm (1½in)

Once you have drafted your pattern, add the seam allowance of 1cm (⅜in) as shown.

Cutting line for lining

CUTTING OUT THE FABRIC

- Cut two of the pattern in main fabric.
- Cut two of the pattern in lining with 4cm (1½in) removed from top edge.
- Cut two neck ties 3.2cm (1¼in) wide: for cup A–B they should be 65cm (25½in) long; for cup C–D cut them 66cm (26in) long and for cup E–F cut them 67cm (26½in) long.
- Cut one chest tie 3.2cm (1¼in) x length of tie required for chest measurement (see the chart). Not all measurements are shown, so increase/decrease length of tie 4cm (1½in) for every 5cm (2in) change in chest measurement. To take the chest measurement, measure around the body *under* the bust.

Chest (underbust) measurement	Length of tie (cm/in)
76cm (30in)	116cm (45¾in)
81cm (32in)	120cm (47¼in)
86cm (34in)	124cm (48¾in)
91cm (36in)	128cm (50¼in)
96cm (38in)	132cm (52in)

MAKING THE BIKINI TOP

There are a number of ways to apply the elastic, so choose the method you feel most confident with.

Use a zigzag stitch on your sewing machine with a width and length of 2.5. Alternatively, a four-thread overlocking stitch can be used with a stitch length of 3, but the overlocking stitches may add additional bulk. You may need to increase the differential feed on your overlocker slightly to avoid wavy seams.

In these examples, I have used chain stitch to hold the elastic in place to maximize the use of chain stitches on the coverstitch machine. It's also quick and easy to remove chainstitching if you go wrong. Excess chain stitching can be removed at the end of the construction if preferred.

TIES

Make neck ties and chest tie using method 1 from page 114, 'Making straps with swimwear elastic' and 1cm (⅜in) wide elastic.

BIKINI TOP

Follow steps 1–8 to make up two matching front pieces.

1 Take the lining piece and turn 1cm (⅜in) to the wrong side along the top edge.

2 Zigzag or use a narrow coverstitch to hold in place.

3 Match the wrong side of the lining to the wrong side of the main fabric. Pin or clip along the three long edges, zigzag, overlock or use a chain stitch to hold in place.

4 Follow steps 1 and 2 on page 112 'Using swimwear elastic' to apply the elastic to the wrong side of the left and right edge but not the lower edge. Leave a 1.5cm (⅝in) gap at lower end to reduce bulk in further steps. Don't stretch the elastic as you attach it – it should just stabilize the edge and allow for stretch and security when worn.

5 Align raw edges and with right sides together, pin or clip a neck tie to the centre of the top edge. Machine stitch or zigzag in place.

6 Pull the tie away from garment and finger press the seam allowance towards the garment.

7 Follow steps 3 and 4 on page 112 'Using swimwear elastic' to finish applying the elastic to the two edges of the top.

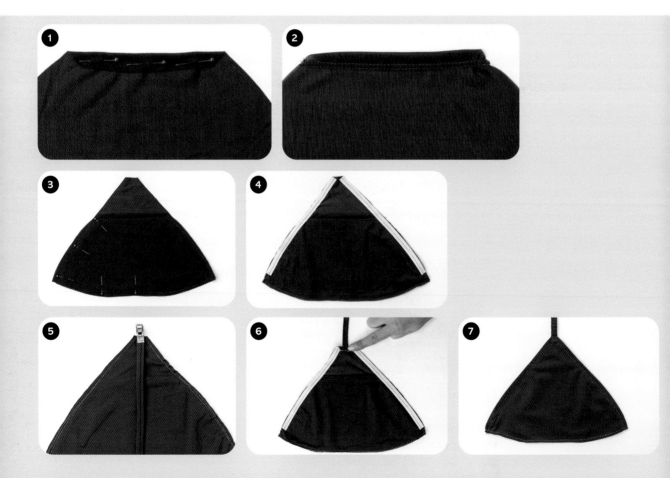

8 Turn up the lower edge to the wrong side by 1.5cm (⅝in) and clip or pin in place. Stitch in place with narrow coverstitch. Alternatively, use chain stitch, but overlock the raw edge first for a tidy finish. Place the stitching 1cm (⅜in) from the folded edge to leave a channel for the chest tie.

9 Feed the chest tie through the channel in each top piece.

10 Thread a large bead or cord end onto the end of each tie and tie a knot in the end to secure. If not using beads or cord ends, tie a knot in the ends.

11 Roll up and insert swimwear cups as required.

ADDING A RUFFLE

Ruffles can be added to the neck ties and chest tie of the bikini top or the side ties of the bikini bottoms before attaching the cord ends or tying knots. Since swimwear fabrics don't fray, the edges on the ruffle are left raw.

- For the neck ties cut two pieces, 8 x 50cm (3⅛ x 20in)

- For the chest tie cut two pieces, 8 x 50cm (3⅛ x 20in)

- For the side ties for bottoms, cut two pieces, 8 x 25cm (3⅛ x 10in)

If you want to add further detail, use a waved- or scalloped-edge rotary blade on the ruffle pieces (see page 112 'Creating elasticated ruffles' for an example). The width of the ruffle could be graded from wide to narrow if desired.

1 With wrong sides together, fold the strip in half, matching the long edges.

2 Use chain stitch, coverstitch or zigzag to stitch the casing in place, stitching 1cm (⅜in) from the folded edge to create a narrow channel.

3 Repeat for each strip.

4 Pass a tie through the channel and bunch up the ruffle fabric as required.

Neck tie.

PATTERN FOR BIKINI BOTTOMS

The pattern has instructions for four different sizes and relates to the following chart:

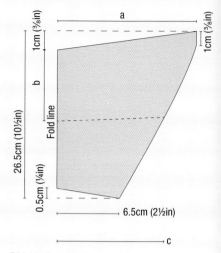

Size	8–10	12–14	16–18	20–22
Hips (cm/in)	92–96cm (36¼–37¾in)	100–104cm (39¼–41in)	108–112cm (42½–44in)	116–120cm (45½–47¼in)

Choose the size required, then use the following measurements and the diagrams on the right to draft your pattern piece.

Bikini bottoms back	Measurements (cm/in)			
Letter on diagram	Size 8–10	Size 12–14	Size 16–18	Size 20–22
a	17cm (6¾in)	19cm (7½in)	21cm (8¼in)	23cm (9in)
b	12cm (4¾in)	12.5cm (4⅞in)	13cm (5⅛in)	13.5cm (5¼in)
c	12.5cm (4⅞in)	13.5cm (5¼in)	14.5cm (5¾in)	15.5cm (6⅛in)
Bikini bottoms front				
d	26cm (10¼in)	28cm (11in)	30cm (11¾in)	32cm (12⅝in)
e	13cm (5⅛in)	15cm (5⅞in)	17cm (6¾in)	19cm (7½in)
f	8cm (3⅛in)	8.5cm (3⅜in)	9cm (3½in)	9.5cm (3¾in)
g	6cm (2⅜in)	7cm (2¾in)	8cm (3⅛in)	9cm (3½in)
h	8cm (3⅛in)	8.75cm (3½in)	9.5cm (3¾in)	10.25cm (4in)

Bikini bottoms back.

Using the diagrams, and referring to the chart above for the length of a, b, c, etc. draw up your pattern.

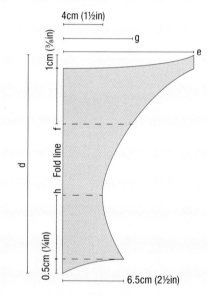

Bikini bottoms front.

CUTTING OUT THE FABRIC

• Cut one front in main fabric.

• Cut one front in lining.

• Cut one back in main fabric.

• Cut four side ties 3.2cm (1¼in) wide: for size 8–10 cut them 32cm (12¾in) long; for size 12–14 make them 34cm (13½in) long; for size 16–18 cut them 36cm (14¼in) long and for size 20–22 cut them 38cm (15in) long.

MAKING THE BIKINI BOTTOMS

Make four ties using method 1 from page 114 'Making straps with swimwear elastic' and 1cm (⅜in) wide elastic.

BIKINI BOTTOMS

1 With right sides together, pin or clip the front and back pieces along the lower edge to join the gusset.

2 Take the front lining and place right side of lining to wrong side of back piece; match along lower edge, re-pin or clip in place. The back piece will be sandwiched between the front and front lining pieces.

3 Stitch the seam using a zigzag or four-thread overlocking stitch.

4 Open out lining and place wrong side of front lining to wrong side of front. Pin or clip lining to main fabric on all edges.

5 Use chain stitch, zigzag or overlock in place.

6 Follow steps 1 and 2 on page 112 'Using swimwear elastic' to apply the elastic to the top of the front and the top of the back, leaving a 1cm (⅜in) gap at either end to reduce bulk in further steps. Don't stretch the elastic as you attach it – it should just stabilize the edge and allow for stretch when worn.

7 Repeat this process to apply elastic along the leg opening edges, starting from the front and continuing to the back. Leave a 1cm (⅜in) gap at either end again but in the back section, stretch the elastic slightly as it is attached to

make sure that your bottom will be held inside the garment when wearing.

8 Align raw edges and with right sides together pin or clip a tie to each end of the front and back edges. Machine stitch or zigzag in place.

9 Pull the tie away from garment and finger press the seam allowance towards the garment.

10 Follow steps 3 and 4 on page 112 'Using swimwear elastic' to finish applying the elastic to all edges. Stop and start at each of the ties.

11 Finish the cord ends as described and shown in step 10 of the bikini top (page 177).

Useful information

Buyer's guide

Deciding which machine to buy can be a daunting process. All coverstitch machines will have the same basic features, as described in the 'Anatomy of a coverstitch machine' on page 10, but some may require fine tuning to work with speciality fabrics or haberdashery. Many people like to stick with a brand they know and are familiar with and others may be limited by budget. Consider what it is you want to do with your machine, how often you will use it and how much space is available. Use the following buyer's guide to answer questions about your future machine and come to your own conclusion about what type of machine is best for you.

* **What type of sewing will you be doing?** If you just want to use the machine for hemming then a basic machine may be all you need, or a combination machine might be the best option. If you will use the machine more often or want to be more creative in using the machine for topstitching seams, working decoratively or with a broad range of fabrics, consider a high-end machine.

* **What stitch capability do you want?** Combination machines will have the most diverse range of stitches since they operate as both a coverstitch and overlocker. The most basic stand-alone machines will work with only two needles but the majority of machines work with three needles, enabling you to create narrow, wide and triple coverstitch. More advanced machines will produce a top coverstitch, which may be beneficial depending on the type of sewing you wish to do.

* **How much space do you have?** The size of machine varies considerably: some offer a large throat and machine bed space whereas other machines are small and compact. A combination machine may be best if your space and usage will be limited.

* **Is threading a concern?** Generally, coverstitch machines are easier to thread than overlockers and not much more difficult than threading a regular sewing machine. Every machine will come with clear colour-coded diagrams and threading pathways so it's just a case of practising. Some brands offer jet-air threading systems which make the job much easier, saving time and effort.

* **Are you concerned about altering tension settings?** Some combination machines will have automatic tension settings so you don't have to think too much about it – simply select the correct stitch programme and the tension is set for you. However, depending on the type of fabric you're using, there may be a need for fine tuning of the tensions, so it will be something you will have to experiment with.

* **How big a throat space do you need?** Are you planning on using the machine for decorative sewing and topstitching? Having a bigger throat space will definitely make this easier and you can also purchase an extension table for some models to create an even larger sewing space.

* **Would you benefit from a free arm?** Many coverstitch machines come with this option where part of the casing can be removed, making it easier to stitch tubular items such as sleeves and legs.

* **Are additional accessories and presser feet included?** Depending on the type of sewing that you intend to do, you may benefit from a variety of gadgets to make the job easier. Some brands offer a huge range of accessories for their machines whereas others offer few or none. Generic attachments can be purchased online but may not fit all models, or work as well as one which is specifically designed to work with your model.

* **What is your budget?** There is a huge difference in price between an entry-level coverstitch machine (indicated by '£' next to machines opposite) and a top-of-the-range machine (indicated by '££££' next to machine opposite). Consider the amount of usage you will get from your machine and spend as much as you can afford. More expensive machines are built to last so consider buying second hand if your budget is limited.

* **Can you try before you buy?** Where possible, visit a local sewing-machine shop to try out a range of coverstitch machines and ask lots of questions. Take samples of different fabrics that you want to be able to use so you can test out each machine's handling capabilities.

Large throat space: A, B, C, D, G, I
Top coverstitch: B, F
Combination machines: D, F, G, I
Air threading: H, I

Easier to thread: A, B, C, H
Large range of stitches: D, F, G, I
Free arm: A, B
Automatic tensions: D, F, G, I
Extension table: A, D, G, H, I

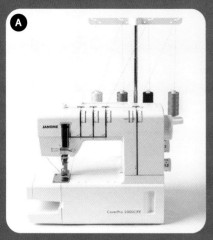

Janome CoverPro 2000CPX   £

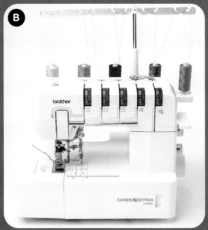

Brother CV3550   £

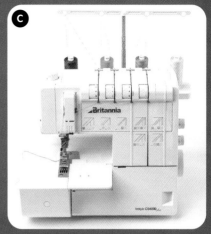

Britannia CS4000   £

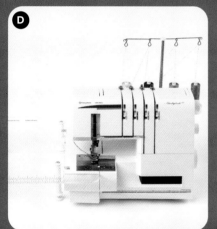

Huskylock S21   ££

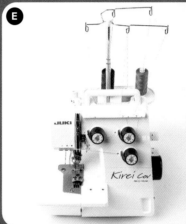

Juki MCS1800   ££

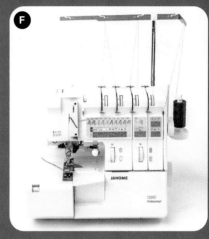

Janome 1200D   £££

Pfaff Coverlock 4.0   £££

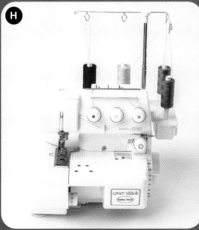

baby lock BLCS2   £££

baby lock Gloria   ££££

Troubleshooting

There will be times when you run into problems with your machine, particularly when you're just starting to get to know it. It can be frustrating if things don't work out first time but take each problem as a learning opportunity and you'll soon find that you've mastered your machine more quickly than expected. On most occasions it's not the machine that's at fault but the operator, with issues occurring due to incorrect threading or using bent, blunt or the wrong needles.

Nearly all problems can be solved by working your way through the following table. When making adjustments to the settings, try out one change at a time to see what the effect is before making further changes. Not all issues on all machines will be fixed with the same adjustments to settings so the advice provided here is general and broad. Consult the manual for your particular machine and see previous pages for more guidance and information.

PROBLEM-SOLVING CHECKLIST

For a machine or stitching issue, work through this checklist before trying any of the additional or more specific solutions opposite.

Problem	Solution	See page
Power connections	• Is the foot pedal connected firmly to the machine, machine plugged in and switched on? Check the connections and your own electricity supply if necessary.	–
Threading	• Is the machine threaded correctly or have you missed a threading guide? Check your manual or threading diagrams on the machine carefully and rethread in the specified order if necessary.	22–31
	• Is the thread guide bar in its highest position? Pull up the thread guide bar and lock in position as specified in your machine's manual.	22
	• Always thread your machine with the presser foot raised – on most machines this will release the tension discs so the thread will sit correctly between the discs as you pass the thread through the machine.	22
	• Are threads running through the tension discs with threads in tension? With the presser foot lowered, use a flossing motion either side of the tension dial to check that there is some resistance on the thread.	23
	• Is the thread being caught or not feeding evenly from the spool? Check for any snags or tangles and consider using spool mats, holders or nets.	14
Needles	• Are the correct size and type of needles being used? Check which needles are recommended for your machine and fabric.	19
	• Are the needles inserted correctly? Loosen the needle-clamp screw and check needles are pushed up as high as they will go before tightening securely.	49
	• Are the needles bent or blunt? Replace after every 8 to 10 hours of use, or if they are bent.	188
General settings	• Are your machine settings suitable for the type of fabric you are using? Check the recommended settings for your fabric type and adjust accordingly.	187
	• Are you pulling on the fabric as it feeds out of the machine? Let the machine do the work and just support the fabric as it travels through the machine.	–
	• Are you using a heavy fabric, is it sitting on your sewing table or hanging off the edge? Move your machine over to provide room for the fabric or use an additional platform to hold your fabric such as an extension table or chair to prevent drag.	–
Machine maintenance	• Is the machine clean, free of dust or lint, and oiled as specified in the manual? Use the cleaning brush provided with your machine and check your manual for specific advice on cleaning and oiling.	188
	• If your machine has a free arm, has this been replaced correctly? Check this is attached correctly and sitting flush with the rest of the machine casing.	–
	• If you have cleaned your machine, have you replaced the presser foot and needle plate correctly? Check the foot is attached securely and that the needle plate is correctly installed.	189

ADDITIONAL PROBLEMS, CAUSES AND SOLUTIONS

Problem	Solution	See page
Machine does not operate, runs slow, jams or makes a noise	Stop operating the machine and run through the above checklist and the following tips:	
	• Does your machine have a safety feature that stops it operating if the looper cover is open or the presser foot raised? Check the looper cover is properly closed and the presser foot lowered.	–
	• Is the chain looper engaged and pushed back into position after threading? Open the looper cover and check the looper is properly engaged for stitching.	23
	• For air-threading machines, is the machine-threading system unlocked and not set to 'threading'? Unlock the machine by moving the lock-button release lever to the right or move the threading lever to 'serging'.	27
	• For combination machines, has the machine been set correctly and all necessary adjustments made to change from overlocking to chain or coverstitch? Check your manual for specifics for your machine.	29
Fabric not feeding correctly	The balance of differential feed and stitch length should allow the fabric to move evenly through the machine but if it isn't then check through the following points:	
	• Is the presser foot lowered? Lower the presser foot.	–
	• Is the presser-foot pressure correct for the type or thickness of fabric layers being sewn? Consider increasing or decreasing the pressure.	53
	• Is the stitch length set correctly? Try a longer stitch length to get the fabric moving.	48
	• Is the differential feed set correctly? Set this to N or 1, then try increasing or decreasing to establish the correct amount of feed.	50–52
Fabric stuck in machine	• Is the presser foot raised? Raise the presser foot.	36 for tips on removing fabric from under presser foot
	• Check the position of the needles – are they in the highest position? Adjust the position of the handwheel and try again.	
	• Is the fabric still stuck and threads not feeding? Use the extra lift on the presser foot, if you have this function, to release any tension on the threads within the tension discs when pulling out the fabric.	
	• Does your machine have a tension release lever or device? Release the tension on the tension lever if your model has this.	
	• Are the threads still held in tension? Try setting the tension dials to 0.	
	• Are the fabric and threads still not moving? Turn the handwheel away from you (clockwise) to release the looper threads from the needle threads.	
	• Do you need a little extra thread to pull the fabric free? Pull slack on the needle threads, just above the needle eye.	
	• Are you using enough force? Try a quick tug of the threads to the back of the machine and then pull to the side.	
	• Are the threads stuck? Check that the threads are feeding evenly from the spool and are not caught on something or tangled.	
	• Is the fabric still not moving? Open the looper cover and release the looper by pushing or pulling the release knob, like you would do when threading. Don't forget to push it back to its original position before you start sewing again.	
Threads break	If threads are breaking, see 'Threading' opposite, and then ask the following questions:	
	• Are you using a good-quality thread? Swap the threads for a higher quality and use the same type of thread for each of the needles in use (looper may be a different thread type e.g. woolly nylon or decorative thread but make sure it's also of a high quality).	20–21
	• Is the stitch length set correctly? Check the suggested standard length for your machine and type of fabric being used.	48
	• Is the thread tension on the needles and/or looper set too high? Check the tension settings and adjust as necessary.	44–47

Problem	Solution	See page
Fabric or seams pucker	Puckered seams are often caused by incorrect settings, particularly on light-weight fabrics.	43
	• Is the tension on the needles too high? Check the tension settings and adjust as necessary.	44–47
	• Is the tension on the looper set too low? Check the tension and increase as necessary.	44–47
	• Is the stitch length set correctly or too long? Check the stitch length is correct for the type of fabric and adjust if necessary.	48
	• Is the differential feed set correctly or too high? Set the differential feed to N or 1 and then adjust further if necessary.	50–52
	• Is the presser-foot pressure set correctly? Check the suitable pressure setting for the type of fabric and consider loosening the pressure.	53
Skipped stitches	This is a common problem, usually caused by incorrect threading or needle issues. See 'Threading' and 'Needles' on page 182 and then try the following suggestions:	40
	• Do stitches skip when you start to sew? Begin with a scrap piece of fabric or start with the fabric under the needles and take the first few stitches using the handwheel. Hold on to the thread tails tightly to put these under tension and make sure they move away from the needles without tangling.	–
	• Is the machine feeding correctly? Increase the stitch length and/or differential feed.	48–52
	• Is the presser-foot pressure set correctly for the type of fabric or thickness of layers? Consider increasing the presser-foot pressure.	53
	• Are all needles entering the same thickness of fabric? Make sure all needles catch the same number of layers of fabric or adjust thread-tension settings accordingly.	–
	• Are you sewing over bulky seams? See page 84 'Managing bulky seams and hems' on how to remedy this.	84
	• For machines with a stitch or programme selector, is the correct type of stitch or programme number selected? Check and adjust programme settings as necessary.	–
	• Are you using the correct presser foot for the function being performed? Check the presser foot and swap to a standard or more suitable foot.	–
	• Are you using a slippery or light-weight fabric? Use a stabilizer or tissue paper under the fabric to help the fabric move more evenly through the machine.	82
	• Are there only one or two skipped stitches? If the majority of the stitching is perfect, use a hand sewing needle and thread and just catch the middle of the stitch in place. See page 38 'Fixing mistakes'.	38
Tunnelling	This is more likely to happen when working with light-weight knit or stretch fabrics. It can be avoided or eliminated by trying the following:	
	• Are all needles entering the same thickness of fabric? Make sure all needles catch the same number of layers of fabric, adjust the position of the fabric or adjust the thread-tension settings accordingly. A lower tension may be required for needles travelling through fewer layers.	–
	• Is the presser-foot pressure set correctly for your fabric type? Increasing the presser-foot pressure can help to reduce tunnelling, but may need to be adjusted along with other settings.	53
	• Is the tension on the looper set too high? Reduce the looper tension – in some cases you may need to miss out part of the threading pathway to reduce the looper tension further.	44–47
	• Are the tensions on the needles set too high? Reduce needle tension.	44–47
	• Is the differential feed set too high? Lower the differential feed slightly.	50–52
	• Have you lowered the differential feed? Increase your stitch length slightly to compensate.	48–52
	• Are you using slippery or light-weight fabric? Use a stabilizer under your fabric, between the presser foot and the bottom layer of fabric or between the layers of fabric. (See page 81 'Stabilizing fabrics'.)	81
	• Are you using a wide coverstitch setting? Try using a narrow setting instead.	48–49
	• Are you using woolly nylon or other textured thread in the looper? If you've tried everything else and can't stop the tunnelling, change to using regular overlocker thread.	20–21

Problem	Solution	See page
Roping	This is more common with stretch fabrics and on curved hems where one layer of fabric moves at a different rate to the other layer as it travels through the machine, causing draglines to appear or for the hem to look twisted. Roping can also cause hems to flip up and not sit flat. (see 'Managing hems that curl after stitching' on page 78)	52 78
	• Is the bottom layer of fabric moving faster than the upper layer of fabric? Lower the differential feed and/or loosen the presser-foot pressure.	50–53
	• Is the bottom layer of fabric moving slower than the top layer? increase the differential feed and/or increase the presser-foot pressure.	50–53
	• Does your hem appear twisted? Use a fabric glue, wash-away double-sided tape, stabilizer, hand tacking or machine tacking to hold the hem in place before stitching. (See page 81 'Stabilizing fabrics' and page 90 'Hemming a curved edge'.)	81 90
	• Is the twisting caused by pulling on the fabric in front of, or behind the presser foot? Allow the machine to do the work and try not to pull as the fabric travels through the machine.	–
	• After preparing your hem, is the fabric still slipping as you stitch? Try using tweezers or an awl to push the fabric towards the presser foot to encourage it to feed more evenly.	–

Guide to fabrics and machine settings

Your coverstitch machine will be set up at the factory to work with medium-weight, easy-to-handle fabrics. It is likely that you won't always be using this type of fabric and so you'll need to know what adjustments and fine-tuning are required on your machine in order to stitch perfectly on a range of different fabrics. Not all machines are the same and what works for one model may not work for another. It's really important to experiment with your machine to work out what will and won't work with different fabrics, so the following guide will provide advice for possible machine settings but should be used in conjunction with the manual for your machine and your own experiences. Always start with your machine set to the standard settings, test on scrap fabric and then make adjustments as directed below and in the troubleshooting section on page 182.

LIGHT-WEIGHT FABRICS

Light-weight fabrics are very thin and may be sheer. They vary in their drape and softness, making them more challenging to work with. Some light-weight fabrics may move around a lot as you work with them, making it more difficult to cut and sew them accurately.

A shorter stitch length and a thinner needle of size 80/12 may be preferable for light-weight fabrics. For really fine fabrics a needle of size 65/9, 70/10 or 75/11 can be used. Use the needle system compatible with your machine and use needles labelled SUK for knit fabrics.

Some light-weight fabrics will pucker when stitching. To eliminate this, loosen the needle tensions, lower the differential feed to below 1 and test the fabric in the machine again. The presser-foot pressure may also need to be loosened and you may require a slightly higher tension setting on the looper.

For some light-weight fabrics you may wish to use a stabilizer. This will give body to the fabric while you sew it but can be removed after stitching to allow the fabric to return to its original properties (see 'Stabilizing fabrics' on page 81). Using a stabilizer can also eliminate issues with tunnelling and roping (see 'Troubleshooting' page 182).

Consider the techniques to use with light-weight fabrics. Additional threads can add bulk and weight so make use of the chain stitch or narrow coverstitch in fine polyester threads and avoid triple stitches, top coverstitch or heavier and decorative threads.

MEDIUM-WEIGHT FABRICS

Your machine will be set up to work with medium-weight fabrics and will require little or no adjustments to create a balanced stitch. If the settings on your machine have been altered, check through the manual for what the standard settings are and make sure that the thread tensions, stitch length, and presser-foot pressure are all altered to the suggested settings. Differential feed should be set to 1 or N, unless you are working with stretch fabrics which may require a setting above 1 to avoid fluting or stretching of the fabric.

The presser-foot pressure should be set to a medium pressure for two to three layers of fabric or to a higher pressure if more than two layers of fabric are to be stitched.

Needle threads should all be set to the same tension, unless the needles are going through different thicknesses of material.

Use either an 80/12 needle or a 90/14, depending on the thickness of the fabric. Use a needle marked SUK for knits.

HEAVY-WEIGHT FABRICS

Some adjustments will need to be made when working with heavier fabrics and when sewing through many layers, for example, when binding or applying elastics.

A longer stitch length is usually preferable for heavier fabrics and due to the thickness of layers, a higher tension on the needle threads and/or a lower tension on the looper thread may be necessary.

The presser-foot pressure may also need to be increased to manage more layers.

Set the differential feed to 1 or N, unless using a knit fabric. If the fabric is stretched out of shape and becomes fluted, increase the differential feed to just above 1 or until the waviness is eliminated.

When sewing a bulk of stretch fabrics and elastic, or when topstitching ribbing, it may be necessary to use a lower differential feed to maintain the amount of stretch required in the garment.

Use a size 90/14 needle for heavy-weight fabrics and multiple layers.

WHICH THREADS SHOULD I USE ON DIFFERENT FABRICS?

It is possible to use a variety of thread types on most coverstitch machines but consider the weight of the fabric that you're using them with. For most types of sewing, a general-purpose polyester thread can be used for all fabrics. If you choose to use heavier or thicker threads, these work best on medium- to heavy-weight fabrics, or use these with a stabilizer on light- to medium-weight fabrics to provide more structure for the needles and thread to work through.

Type of fabric	Needle	Stitch length	Differential feed	Foot-presser pressure
Light-weight woven e.g. fine fabrics that tend to pucker such as voile, georgette, organza, crepe de chine, chiffon, lawn, mesh fabrics	65/9, 70/10, 75/11 or 80/12	2.5–3.5	0.7–1 0.7–N	Low/medium
Light-weight knit e.g. jersey, tricot, slinky knits	65/9 SUK or 70/10 SUK or 80/12 SUK	2.5–3.5	1–1.5 N–1.5	Low/medium
Medium-weight woven e.g. poplin, sateen, chambray	80/12 or 90/14	3–4	1 N	Medium
Medium-weight knit e.g. double knit, ponte roma, interlock twist yarn (ITY), ribbing, sweatshirting, scuba	80/12 SUK or 90/14 SUK	3–4	1–1.5 N–1.5	Medium
Heavy-weight woven e.g. denim, tweed, canvas, quilted fabrics, upholstery fabrics	90/14	3.5–4	1 N	Medium/high
Heavy-weight knit e.g. fleece, jacquards, sweater knit, pile knits	90/14 SUK	3.5–4	1–1.5 N–1.5	Medium/high

Maintenance

It is important to keep your machine maintained through cleaning, covering and careful storage when not in use. If you have a combination machine and use the overlocking function, fluff and lint inside the machine will build up very quickly and need regular attention. When your machine is not in use, cover it with the machine cover provided or a makeshift one, to avoid the build-up of dust. To ensure longevity of your machine, keep it out of direct sunlight, high humidity and away from any heat sources. Some machines also don't like cold temperatures and should be kept between 5–40°C (41–104°F). When performing any machine maintenance, as a safety precaution, always turn the machine off and unplug it. To maximize the life of your machine, have it regularly serviced.

REPLACING NEEDLES

At some point the needles will break or become blunt, causing irregular or skipped stitches. For the best stitch quality, change your needles every eight to ten hours and use the needles recommended for your machine. For guidance on how to remove and replace the needles, see page 49, which also includes information on how to use a needle holder to make this process easier. For the types of needle to use, check your manual and see further details on needles on pages 18–19.

CLEANING

Household dust and lint will build up on and in your machine, causing issues with performance and stitch formation. There are key areas on your machine to keep clean including the feed dogs, looper area and tension discs but you should also dust down the whole machine every so often and use the machine cover, a sheet or towel to protect the machine when it's not in use. If you spill or splash something onto your machine, use a damp, well rung cloth to wipe down the casing. Avoid using strong detergents or anything abrasive.

REPLACING LIGHT BULBS

On some machine models, particularly the older ones, you'll find a bulb similar to or the same as that on your sewing machine and/or overlocker. If this is the case, you will be able to replace the bulb with a matching type, using a similar process to replacing a sewing-machine bulb, but do check the specific instructions in your manual. Wait for the bulb to cool down before trying to remove it.

For many of the newer coverstitch models, the light bulb is an LED type instead of a regular incandescent sewing-machine bulb, which may not be easily removed and replaced. If there is no mention of how to replace the light bulb in your user manual then you can assume that you're not meant to touch it and you should take the machine to your local sewing-machine shop or get in touch directly with the manufacturer for advice on how to replace it.

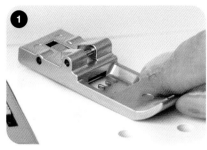

CLEANING THE FEED DOGS AND LOOPER AREA

Before proceeding, check your manual for specific instructions for your machine. If you're not sure about unscrewing and removing the following parts, visit your local sewing-machine shop for advice and a demonstration.

1 Remove the presser foot by pushing the button on the back of the foot.

2 Remove the needles (see tips on replacing needles on page 49). Use a piece of scrap fabric or a needle case to safely store them.

3 Remove the needle plate, following the instructions in your manual.

4 Use the lint brush provided with your machine, or other substitute (see page 14), to clean the feed dogs and around the needle bar.

5 Open the looper cover(s) and clean the inside of the machine thoroughly. Use a brush to clean away dust or build-up of threads and lint. If you have a combination machine and a lot of fabric fluff inside your machine, use a vacuum cleaner and brush the fluff towards the suction nozzle. If you are concerned about losing small parts from your machine, place a pair of thin socks or tights over the nozzle first. A mini vacuum cleaner is perfect for all the hard-to-reach places.

6 Close up the machine, replace the needle plate, needles and presser foot.

CLEANING THE TENSION DISCS

Tension discs attract dust and may also become clogged with tiny pieces of thread. Both of these can cause poor stitch performance and thread-tension issues. The tension devices are formed from two plates which hold the thread in place. You'll need to clean between these plates to remove any unwanted particles. Clean each of the tension discs in turn.

1 Raise the presser foot to release the tension from the tension discs – you should see the tension discs open up slightly as the foot is lifted. If your machine has a tension-release lever, you'll need to use this as you clean between the discs.

2 Remove the thread from the tension disc. (You don't need to unthread the machine – just lift the thread out of the tension disc.)

3 Remove any large pieces of thread or fluff with tweezers.

4 Use dental floss or heavy thread such as topstitching thread to clean back and forth in a flossing motion between the tension discs.

OILING

Very few machine manuals suggest the use of oil. The moving parts on the machine are usually well protected and don't need regular oiling. Only oil the machine if there are specific instructions to do this and high-grade sewing machine oil has been provided with the machine.

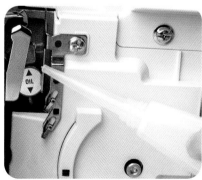

Glossary

Appliqué
A technique of layering fabrics to build up a picture or design. Fabric shapes are applied to a base layer of fabric, fused, pinned or tacked in place and then edge-stitched.

Back tack
The technique of reverse stitching on a sewing machine to sew over previous stitching. This is used at the beginning or end of a line of stitching to stop stitching from coming undone.

Balanced stitch
A correctly formed stitch where the needle threads sit correctly on the top of the fabric and the looper thread sits correctly on the underside.

Bias
The diagonal across the fabric – true bias is at a 45° angle to any straight edge when the grains are perpendicular.

Bias binding
Strips of fabric cut on the bias. It can be used to bind seams or hems by wrapping over fabric edges (see pages 122–133).

Bodkin
A needle with a large eye, sometimes sold as hand-embroidery needles for children, which may be plastic or metal with a blunt tip. Bodkins are great for finishing off the ends of overlocking threads and for feeding narrow ribbon or elastic through casings.

Chain off
A term used to mean stitching on the overlocker or coverstitch machine without fabric, creating a chained end which can then be cut using the thread cutter on the machine or scissors.

Chain stitch
A stitch formed with one looper and one needle. On the right side the stitch appears like a straight stitch and on the reverse of the fabric a chain is formed.

Coverstitch
Sometimes referred to as cover hem, a double or triple row of parallel straight stitching on the top side of the fabric with a grid pattern on the underside. It is most commonly used on knitted fabrics for hemming.

Differential feed
This works in conjunction with the feed-dog teeth and can be used to eliminate unwanted gathering, stretching or puckering on seams and hems. It can also be used to create gathers and stretch where required. The differential feed controls the speed at which the feed-dog teeth will move.

Ease stitching
Two lines of long machine or hand stitching are used to pull in the edges of a piece of fabric. This method is usually used when matching a larger piece to a smaller piece, such as a sleeve to an armhole. It can also be used to turn a hem on curved edges (see page 90).

Edge finishing
Finishing the raw edge of the fabric – this can be done with pinking shears, zigzag stitch on a conventional sewing machine or by overlocking the edge of the fabric.

Facing
A piece of fabric used to finish the unhemmed or unfinished edges of a garment. Facings are usually found on necklines, armholes, waistlines and shaped hems.

Faggoting
A technique where two pieces of fabric are joined together with stitches, leaving a gap in between (see page 97).

Feed-dog teeth
These teeth can be found below the presser foot. On an overlocker and a coverstitch machine there are two sets of teeth and these work with the differential feed. The teeth work independently of each other, one at the front guiding the fabric under the foot towards the needle and one at the rear of the machine taking the fabric from behind the needle.

Fell seam
A strong and stable seam finish often found on work wear or sportswear. The seam is stitched with the wrong sides of fabric together, layered and pressed, or simply pressed to one side and then sewn again to topstitch the seam flat. The first line of stitching may be done with an overlocking stitch and the second line with a chain or coverstitch.

French seam
A type of self-enclosed seam where the seam allowances are all enclosed within the stitching. As the seam is sewn twice it gives added strength to the stitching, making it more hard-wearing. Stitch first with wrong sides together, press the seam to one side and then fold right sides together and stitch again, enclosing the seam allowances.

Handwheel
Sometimes referred to as the flywheel. This can be turned by hand to move the position of the needles and looper when operating the machine. On a coverstitch machine, as a general rule, always turn the handwheel towards you. When the handwheel is turned away from you (clockwise), the looper thread disengages from the needle and can cause skipped stitches.

Interfacing
A layer of fabric which supports, shapes and stabilizes many areas of a garment. It is usually found in collars, cuffs, plackets, around buttonholes, waistbands and facings. It may be fusible (iron-on) or non-fusible (sew-in), woven or non-woven, and comes in different weights in either black, grey or white.

Layering
Where one seam allowance is trimmed more than the other to reduce bulk along a seam line, helping seams to sit flat.

Lint
Fluff from fabrics and threads which build up inside the machine.

Loop turner
A tool used for turning narrow straps through to the right side. It can also be used to pull threads through the looper side of coverstitching or overlocking stitches to fasten off.

Looper
The coverstitch machine has one looper, sometimes referred to as the chain looper which works with the needle threads. An overlocker will operate with two loopers, an upper and a lower one which work together to carry threads from side to side to wrap the edge of the fabric.

Looper cover
A cover on the machine to encase the looper(s). On some machines there is a cover on the left and right side of the machine. Some machines have a safety device which stops the machine from stitching if the looper covers are open.

Mock-band hem
A hem which resembles a band stitched to the edge of the fabric. This technique can be used to form cuffs or to finish the lower edge of trousers, tops, skirts and dresses.

Needle plate
Found under the presser foot, this gives a smooth surface to pass the fabric under the foot of the machine. It will have a hole in for the needles and the feed-dog teeth.

Overlocker
Also known as a serger in some countries. A machine that cuts, stitches and edge finishes fabric in one go.

Pintucks
Narrow rows of tucks formed using a coverstitch or chain stitch setting.

Pivot
A term used to describe the method of turning a corner when sewing by leaving the needle in the fabric, raising the presser foot, moving (or pivoting) the fabric, lowering the presser foot and continuing to stitch.

Press
Generally, this term is used to mean iron.

Presser foot
This holds the fabric flat as it is fed through the machine. A standard presser foot is provided with every machine – most types of stitching can be done with this foot. The pressure the foot places on the fabric can be adjusted to suit different weights or layers of fabric.

Reverse coverstitch
A method of stitching where a coverstitch is sewn from the underside or wrong side of the fabric, producing the overlock-style grid pattern on the right side of the fabric and leaving the rows of straight stitching on the wrong side of the fabric.

Roping
A term used to describe a twisted hem, where one layer of fabric moves at a different rate than the other layer as it travels through the machine. It is more common on stretch fabrics and curved hems.

Seam allowance
The amount of fabric between the stitching or seam line and the edge of fabric. Usually 1.5cm (⅝in).

Seams
A stitched line joining two pieces of fabric.

Shirring
A way of gathering fabric using thin cord elastic stitched in rows (see page 109).

Slip stitch
A hand sewing stitch used to close a seam or stitch a hem where the stitching is invisible from the right side.

Spool
A cylinder onto which thread is wound.

Stabilizer
Backing fabric used to add strength to a seam or fabric edge which is removed after sewing. Stabilizers can be torn away, washed away, heated away or cut away.

Staystitching
A line of straight stitching through a single layer of fabric. A regular stitch length of 2–3 should be used. Staystitching is sewn within the seam allowance, close to the stitching line and helps to stop the fabric from stretching out of shape during construction (see page 81).

Tacking
Temporary stitching by hand or machine using long stitches, also known as basting.

Tension
The control of how tightly or loosely the thread is held and pulled through the machine.

Thread guide bar
This keeps the threads untangled as they travel from the spool to the machine. This bar can be extended and should be raised up to its highest position to allow the threads to travel smoothly.

Thread guides
These hold the thread in place as it goes from the spool to its location on the machine, either to a needle or to a looper.

Top coverstitch
A type of stitch which is only available on a few domestic coverstitch machines. The stitch resembles a double-sided coverstitch with parallel lines of stitches on the right side of the fabric and a grid pattern on both the top and the underside. The stitch is made with two or three needles, a top cover spreader and the chain looper.

Topstitching
Machine stitching sewn onto the right side of the fabric for decoration or strength.

Tunnelling
This is where a ridge forms between the needle threads when sewing coverstitch. Usually seen as a fault in stitching, this can be done on purpose to form decorative pintucks.

Twill tape
Tape used to strengthen a seam and prevent it from stretching, often used at a waistline and made of non-stretch fabric.

Understitching
Understitching is a line of stitching only visible from the wrong side of a garment. It is used to keep a facing or lining in place on the underside of a garment. Press any seam allowance towards the facing or lining, trim, layer and clip curves of the seam allowance if necessary and then stitch from the right side of the garment, sewing through the facing (or lining) and through the seam allowance. Press the lining or facing to the underside.

Welt seam
A strong seam, similar in appearance to the fell seam. Stitch first with right sides together, layer and press or simply press to one side and then topstitch in place with chain stitch or coverstitch.

Index